BELFAST

For Joan — who else?

BELFAST

A history by
W.A. Maguire

CARNEGIE

Town and city histories available from Carnegie:

Derek Beattie, *Blackburn* (2007);   Prof. David Hey, *A History of Sheffield* (2005);
Prof. John K. Walton, *Blackpool*;   Prof. Graham Davis and Dr Penny Bonsall, *A History of Bath: Image and Reality* (2006);   Peter Aughton, *Bristol: A People's History*;
Dr John A. Hargreaves, *Halifax*;   Dr Andrew White (ed.), *A History of Lancaster*;
Peter Aughton, *Liverpool: A People's History*
Prof. Alan Kidd, *Manchester* (2006);   Dr Jeffrey Hill, *Nelson*;
Malcolm Neesam, *Harrogate Great Chronicle, 1332–1841* (2005)
Dr Mark Freeman, *St Albans* (2008);   Peter Shakeshaft, *St Anne's-on-the-Sea* (2008)
Prof. Jeremy Black, *London* (2009);   Dr David Hunt, *Preston* (2009)

Forthcoming town and city histories:
Prof. Carl Chinn, *Birmingham*;   Dr John Doran, *Chester*
Michael Baumber, *A History of Haworth* (2009);   Dr John A. Hargreaves, *Huddersfield*
Dr Andrew White, *Kendal*;   Dr Trevor Rowley, *A History of Oxford*
Dr Evelyn Lord, *Cambridge*;   Anthea Jones, *Cheltenham* (2010)
Prof. Richard Rodger (ed.), *Leicester: A modern history*

Full details and secure online ordering at www.carnegiepublishing.com

The publishers gratefully acknowledge financial contributions received from
The Belfast Natural History and Philosophical Society
and The Esme Mitchell Trust
which helped to fund the photograph and colour reproduction costs in this volume

Belfast: A history

Copyright © W.A. Maguire, 2009

Published by Carnegie Publishing Ltd
by Carnegie Publishing Ltd
Carnegie House
Chatsworth Road, Lancaster LA1 4SL
www.carnegiepublishing.com

ISBN: 978-1-85936-189-4

British Library Cataloguing-in-Publication data
A catalogue record for this book is available from the British Library

Designed and typeset by Carnegie Book Production, Lancaster
Printed and bound in Malta by Gutenberg Press

Contents

Belfast might not owe its foundation directly to the sea loch that bears its name, but over succeeding centuries the importance of these deep, sheltered waters – at the head of which was a shallow, alluvial river estuary – became greater and greater. By the time this photograph was taken of RMS *Titanic* steaming gently down the channel of Belfast Lough in 2 April 1912, Belfast was a great ship-building centre, a major port, an industrial city of great vibrancy, and the second city of Ireland. In this remarkable story geography – river, sea and land – was to play a crucial role.

PREFACE AND ACKNOWLEDGEMENTS

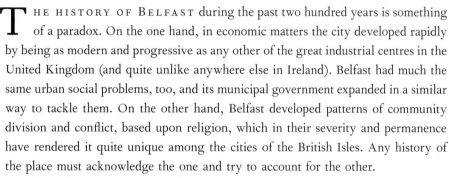

T HE HISTORY OF BELFAST during the past two hundred years is something of a paradox. On the one hand, in economic matters the city developed rapidly by being as modern and progressive as any other of the great industrial centres in the United Kingdom (and quite unlike anywhere else in Ireland). Belfast had much the same urban social problems, too, and its municipal government expanded in a similar way to tackle them. On the other hand, Belfast developed patterns of community division and conflict, based upon religion, which in their severity and permanence have rendered it quite unique among the cities of the British Isles. Any history of the place must acknowledge the one and try to account for the other.

Belfast's history is important because it plays such an essential role in defining identity and belonging. On either side of the 'peace lines' live communities that have long been segregated in religion, education, culture and tradition, each with their own quite different commentary on events in Belfast's past. These divergent narratives are made manifest in murals, memorials and statues to very different pantheons of martyrs, heroes and villains. Belfast can thus be seen to have had not one but two quite distinct sets of historical experience. The aspiring historian's task, therefore, might resemble that of Blondin, the famous French tightrope walker once used in a marketing stunt for the Belfast ropeworks.

Within the compass of this book fall events and people of great variety and interest: the great steel shell of RMS *Titanic* growing above her Queen's Island birthplace; the mighty Samson and Goliath cranes that for the past forty years have framed the harbour skyline so iconically; linen warehouses and tobacco factories; Orange lodges and streets of little terraced houses.

In the heyday of its industrial past Belfast was a great port, a powerhouse of ship-building and engineering, and a dominant force in the northern Irish economy. Now largely de-industrialised and scarred by the Troubles, its buildings and townscapes are enjoying a long-overdue period of redevelopment. With renewed peace has returned optimism for the future that was only partly dimmed by the recession of the late 2000s. Now is an excellent time to relate the story of Belfast.

This book is based upon a smaller, earlier volume of 1993. This new Carnegie edition is significantly different, larger in format, copiously illustrated and covering a much wider sweep of the history of the city. There are new chapters on the ancient and early modern periods, while, at the other end of the time-line, a good deal more has been included about the events of the past forty years. It aims to be a general, concise overview of a great city with a truly fascinating past.

ACKNOWLEDGEMENTS

There is no more agreeable task for any author than thanking people who have helped to bring a manuscript to book at last. First of all my thanks are due to the Belfast Natural History and Philosophical Society, and to the Esme Mitchell Trust for generous grants towards the cost of production. Second, I have to thank the Trustees, management and staff of the Public Record Office of Northern Ireland; the Linen Hall Library; Belfast Central Library; the Belfast Telegraph picture library and the Planning Department of Belfast City Council and its Director, Dr Marie-Therese McGivern.

The Ulster Museum on the Stranmillis Road is the source of many of the illustrations used in this book. I owe my former colleagues thanks for their help and expertise and the pleasure of long acquaintance. They are Trevor Parkhill, Dr Vivienne Pollock, Robert Heslip, Tom Wylie, Richard Warner, Winifred Glover, Cormac Bourke, Sinead McCartan, Deirdre Crone, Dr Eileen Black and Martyn Anglesea; for help with photographs and copyright matters, Pat McLean and Michael McKeown. I must, and do, thank Pauline Dickson for her usual good advice and a flying service second to none.

I must also mention also the staff of the Ulster Folk and Transport Museum at Cultra, especially T.K. Anderson, Clifford Harkness, Michael McCaughan, Roger Dixon and Lynda Ballard. Terence Reeves-Smyth of the Northern Ireland Environmental Agency and his colleagues were also most helpful. So, too, were Professor Alun Evans, Sir Peter Froggatt, Peter Francis, Dr W.H. Crawford, Roger Weatherup, Desmond Fitzgerald and Martin Moore.

The permission given by the late Sir Charles Brett to adapt the map of Belfast in 1985 from his book *Housing a Divided Community* has been kindly extended by his family. The cartoon entitled 'It Takes Two to Tango' is used with the permission of the artist. Deirdre Crone drew the O'Neill Chair. Raymond Gillespie's most recent work on the history of medieval and early modern Belfast, has provided a better understanding of the early Plantation town. The current issue of *The Ulster Journal of Archaeology* (editor Cormac Bourke) was by good fortune published just in time to include some of the recent findings in the archaeology of Belfast.

BELFAST'S FIRST HISTORIAN

George Benn (1801–82), antiquarian and first historian of Belfast.
PORTRAIT BY RICHARD HOOKE (1820–1908). © ULSTER MUSEUM, 2008

CHAPTER ONE

SITE FOR A CITY

BELFAST lies at the mouth of the river Lagan where it flows into Belfast Lough, overlooked from the County Antrim side by steep hills which form an escarpment in the Cave Hill and from the County Down side opposite by the gentler hills above Castlereagh and Holywood. Between the two is an alluvial site, across whose tidal flats the river made its way in meandering streams until comparatively modern times. The land around the river mouth and up the valley was thickly wooded.[1]

George Benn, Belfast's first historian worthy of the name, began his history of the town with the following words: 'Belfast, as a town, has no ancient history.' Benn was simply stating an obvious fact: Belfast lacked the attributes of an old town with a long history behind it, such as its small neighbour up the coast with its great medieval castle. Writing in the 1870s, he made it clear that he thought Belfast was woefully lacking in the sort of things that would 'deserve the notice of the antiquary … We have no musty charters or archives, no patron saint to reverence, no old buildings, civil or ecclesiastical, surrounded by historic associations, or glowing with the antique beauty of medieval days, no real archaeological lore, unless by connecting our locality with the Earls of Ulster, which would not be reasonable. All here is of modern design or modern fashion.'[2] It is clear Benn's ideal city was a medieval one, a dream of Camelot.

What Belfast did have of course was a particular geological history. Very briefly, what we learn is that successive ice ages carved out the shape of the which that was to be the site of the town. The broad valley that carried the river Lagan down to Belfast Lough followed a fault-line which lay deep under part of nearby Antrim. In the last phase of glacial activity a slow-moving sheet of ice shaped and rounded the mountain tops and widened the valley. For a long period the valley became a huge lake, dammed at both ends as the sea level rose. Later the waste land of rocks and sand that eventually emerged attracted first small cold-loving plants (basic alpines), then as the temperature began to rise, hardier plant life and shrubs. From about ten thousand years ago birch, holly, oak and elm trees covered the slopes above the

NORTHERN IRELAND

From the Act of Union in 1800 until 1921, the whole island of Ireland was part of the United Kingdom, but there were numerous outbreaks of discontent over the years. There was a demand for Home Rule for Ireland. A third Home Rule Bill (1912) was demanded by the Nationalist parties, but this was completely opposed by the northern Unionists. The outcome was the partition of the island in 1921. This map shows the six Unionist counties – Antrim, Armagh, Down, Fermanagh, Londonderry and Tyrone – which together formed the new state of Northern Ireland.

boggy river bottom and gave shelter to animal life – deer, wild boar, possibly wolves higher up, as well as to small mammals. The retreat of the ice at the end of the last ice age allowed the first human beings to explore the site that became Belfast.

The arrival of the first people made no visible difference to the scene, for they were Mesolithic (Middle Stone Age) hunter-gatherers. Evidence of their foraging activities in what is now part of Belfast, though literally fairly thin on the ground, was discovered many years ago, when some flint tools and weapons thought to be of appropriate kind and date were found at Ormeau and Sydenham. More recently, our knowledge of how these earliest of Ireland's inhabitants lived – the food they ate, the huts they built, how they adapted to their environment – has been increased enormously by scientific excavation, most notably of a site on the river Bann near Coleraine in County Antrim. Mount Sandel, as it is called, had long been of interest to antiquarians. Its true importance, however, was not discovered until

STONE AXE-HEADS

The earliest immigrants to settle in Ireland were hunter gatherers, living in small groups; their tools and weapons were made of stone. The best stone for shaping and chipping was flint, a hard material capable of resisting fractures and which could be ground and polished to a sharp edge. The most highly prized stone was porcellanite, which was mined from the basalt volcanic vent at Tievebulliagh, Co. Antrim, and Rathlin Island. The axes from the axe factory there formed the basis of an early export industry.

CROWN COPYRIGHT NIEA: BUILT HERITAGE

the 1970s, when Professor Woodman carried out a dig on behalf of the planning authorities in response to a building application. The material unearthed, supplemented subsequently by evidence from other sites in Ireland, has led scholars to divide the long Mesolithic into two periods – Early and Later.[3]

Many questions of course remain, and lead to new questions. Few can have received an answer so swift and satisfactory as that to a puzzle mentioned by the authors of a volume on the archaeology of Ulster published in 1991, namely that they did not have 'a single burial dating to the first three thousand years of human settlement of this island'. Within ten years, a dig in County Limerick had yielded up the cremated remains of an Early Mesolithic adult, along with objects supporting the estimated date. Mallory and McNeill do well to warn their readers against making unwarranted assumptions, commenting humanely:

We should emphasize that life during the Early Mesolithic did indeed involve seasonal movements of individual families or small bands of several families together, but we should also not imagine this as a life of unendurable hardship. Even today, where hunter-fisher-gathering societies often live in the most uninviting areas, they obtain their subsistence with less effort and greater free time than their supposedly civilized neighbours, including the professional archaeologists and anthropologists who are paid to study them. Moreover, we should also imagine that these Mesolithic societies were not solely concerned with obtaining their next meal but rather they possessed their own rituals, beliefs, ceremonies and art, all of which still lies beyond our limited ability to retrieve.[4]

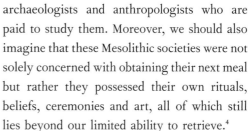

The successors of the hunter-gatherers were the people of the Neolithic period (New Stone Age), which in Ireland lasted from about 4000 BC to about 2500 BC. What was revolutionary about the New Stone Age and made it different from everything that had gone before was the practice of agriculture and the keeping of domestic animals. Tools and weapons continued to be made of stone, but were fashioned to meet different needs. True, in good seasons farming increased the range of food available, but blighted harvests and murrain among the livestock could wipe out a settlement just as effectively as the uncertainties of uncultivated nature.

Being settlers rather than nomads, the people of the Neolithic left behind them a great deal more evidence of their presence. In fact they began the process – which has gone on ever since – of altering the landscape they inhabited. The basic work

GIANT'S RING

Just outside the city limits at Ballynahatty, close to an early crossing place over the Lagan is a spectacular prehistoric monument, an enclosure over 200 metres in diameter surrounded by an earthwork bank 4 metres high. The earthwork circle was built about 2,700 BC, during the late Neolithic period. Similar monuments are found elsewhere in Britain and Ireland, but this is one of the finest. At the middle is a tomb (*above*) made up of five upright stones, a large capstone, the bare frame of what was originally a chambered grave, covered with a cairn of stones and earth.

of clearing virgin forest was done using polished stone axes. Experiments have proved that these tools were surprisingly effective: some years ago three Danish archaeologists cleared 500 square metres of birch forest in four hours.[5] Some of the finest examples discovered around Belfast, such as a large hoard found at Malone, and made from a rather rare stone called porcellanite, came from a considerable distance. The Malone axes, as it happens, were evidently of symbolic rather than practical use, for they are too large (20–38 cm long) and too heavy to be handled in the normal way. As Mallory and McNeill put it, it would 'have required the likes of Finn McCool to wield them'.[6]

The pottery the Neolithic settlers made, used and left behind them is a major source of knowledge (or speculation) about their culture and way of life. Many of the best-preserved examples have been found in association with the megalithic tombs and ritual monuments which are so numerous from this period of prehistory. One of the most impressive of these anywhere was constructed on a hill top just to the south of Belfast. Known as the Giant's Ring, this circular henge enclosure has a diameter of nearly 200 metres and its earthen bank (much reduced by time) is still nearly 4 metres high. At the centre of the ring is the remains of a small megalithic tomb, long ago plundered, which is believed to pre-date the great monument itself. Recent aerial photography has revealed traces of other, smaller circular enclosures nearby.[7] The function of the Ring is difficult to establish, but, given the communal effort its construction must have involved, a cautious judgment that it may have served as 'a major tribal centre for people occupying South Antrim and North Down at the end of the Neolithic' period may be as near as one can get to an answer.[8] Or, as Samuel Pepys remarked on seeing the great stones at Stonehenge in the summer of 1668, 'God knows what their use was'; their tale might be yet be told. At Belfast tombs on the tops of the hills to the west, above the tree line, were probably also erected by Neolithic people, but on a more domestic scale.

From about 2000 BC the knowledge of how to work metal spread throughout Ireland. Starting with copper, tools, weapons and other artefacts came to be fashioned in bronze, hence the name Bronze Age for the whole period 2000–600 BC. In terms of archaeology this era has been in some respects very productive. As with the Neolithic Age that preceded it, however, most of the evidence came from burials and told us little about the everyday life of the people. Some basic questions have proved hard to answer. Did this great change happen through the invasion and conquest of Ireland in a fairly short time or, rather, by piecemeal adoption of the new technology over a long period? For our present purpose we need only note that some fine specimens of the new metalwork have been found in the vicinity of what became Belfast – bronze axes nearly 4000 years old from the Cave Hill; bronze swords from the bed of the river Lagan; and occasionally ornaments made of gold. These last are seen as evidence of a new ruling class or, possibly, as examples of conspicuous consumption by members of an expanding elite.[9]

The process by which the Late Bronze Age was succeeded by the early Iron Age (300 BC–AD 400) is still more obscure; the label 'Dark Age' has been used.[10] The people who emerged and who are generally called the Celts brought with them a very early form of the Irish language which somehow came to be adopted as the common tongue of the whole island. Since there is little or no archaeological evidence of an unambiguous kind to suggest their presence in the Belfast area in the early Iron Age, linguistic evidence – which does exist – assumes particular importance. The main authority is the Greek geographer Ptolemy's map of Ireland, compiled by him in the library at Alexandria in Egypt sometime in the second century AD. Since he must have got his information in circuitous ways and from a wide variety of informants, the possibility of error or gross distortion must have been high. Ptolemy's map nevertheless shows a river 'Logia' flowing into the sea by way of an inlet closely resembling the present Belfast Lough. We know from medieval copies (none of Ptolemy's original manuscripts survived the great fire which destroyed the library in AD 642) that Belfast harbour was called, in later Irish, *Loch Loigh* ('the lough of the calf'). Farther north, a large offshore island called 'Ricini' (*Rechrann* in Irish) can scarcely be other than Rathlin.[11]

The Romans never attempted formally to conquer Ireland, but events in Ireland were certainly affected by their presence just across the sea and by occasional raiding expeditions. The conversion of the Irish to Christianity might have been begun by a Roman missionary called Palladius, though if that is true most of the credit was subsequently ascribed to Patrick, whose cult the Armagh clergy promoted very strongly.[12] By the late sixth century Ireland was to a considerable extent a Christian country. Monasteries were a strong feature of the early church, abbots often more influential than bishops. When a converted chieftain or other personage established a monastery in his territory, it was customary to endow it with land for its upkeep, but the benefactor expected that the abbots would be his own kinsmen. Far from being sheltered from real life, these institutions were embedded in local politics, and needed thorough reform by Patrick's successors.

left
NEOLITHIC FLINT FACTORY, BALLYMAGARRY

Flint had to be procured from the only certain source of supply, the chalk cliffs of Antrim, where the supply was inexhaustible. It was then collected and conveyed to the flintless regions of the south and west, mostly in the form of roughs. Ballymagarry is in north Antrim.

CROWN COPYRIGHT NIEA: BUILT HERITAGE

Some became famous nevertheless, because they had saintly abbots or because the work of their scribes and teaching were widely admired. In the north, for example, the great monastery of Bangor in County Down, founded at the end of the sixth century by St Comgall, attracted teachers and students from near and far and exported a stream of missionaries to evangelise the British Isles and Europe. When they sacked Bangor in 822, the Vikings are said to have murdered the abbot and nine hundred monks.[13] Though this figure may be a wild exaggeration, it is probably true that in the absence of towns the larger monasteries were the only urban centres in the country. Later scribes not only produced copies of the Gospels and other devotional works but also preserved the foundation myths of the Celtic Irish by writing down for the first time the oral tales of a race of superhuman warriors who lived in a golden period of the pre-Christian Iron Age. Later still, some monasteries also compiled annals of important historical events.[14] The last and most comprehensive of these – the Annals of the Four Masters – covered the whole country and drew on sources of many kinds; the earliest entry purported to record an event which happened forty days before the biblical Flood; the final one relates to the death of Hugh O'Neill, earl of Tyrone, in 1616.[15]

Direct evidence of early Christian worship in the area of Belfast can be found in the original name of the old church of Knock on the County Down side of the ford and a mile or two from it on the road from Bangor – Cnoc Cholm Cille ('Columcille's hill'). Columcille or Columba, founder of the abbey at Iona, died in 597. Another piece of evidence relates to the Antrim side of the ford, where the name Shankill (Irish *Seanchill*) meaning 'the old church' preserves the original name of the parish of Belfast. Some fragments of a ninth-century bronze crozier have been found there.[16]

The typical social and economic unit during the centuries between the settlement of the Irish and the arrival of the Normans was a family farm set in its own fields of arable and pasture, whose inhabitants – accompanied by their animals – withdrew at nightfall to the safety of a 'rath' or 'ring fort'. Though most of these once-common features of early farming have been destroyed by the growing city, a few on the outskirts have survived, such as those at Shaw's Bridge and Ballysillan. Some of the raths below the Cave Hill were found to have 'souterrains' in which the inhabitants could store provisions or possibly take refuge from slave raiders (Viking raids on coastal areas and inlets of Ireland began about AD 800), but although raids were frequent and destructive, in Ulster at any rate fiercely warlike kings, when not engaged in slaying each other, prevented the Norsemen from establishing permanent settlements to the extent they did elsewhere.[17]

The ford, at the lowest point where the Lagan could be crossed at low tide, was approached from the Antrim side along a sandbank which formed where two small tributary streams, the Farset and (slightly higher up) the Owenvarra or Blackstaff, flowed into the main current. The sandbank – in early Irish *Fearsaid* – was the

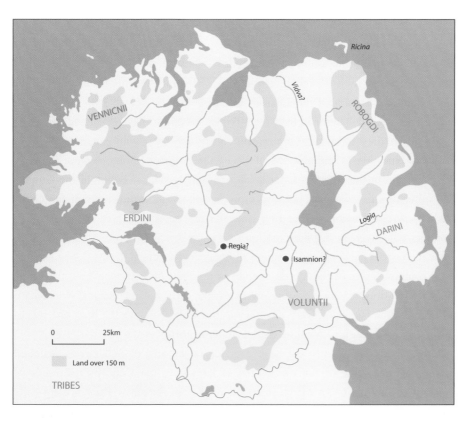

ANCIENT TRIBES OF NORTHERN IRELAND

Among other disciplines, Ptolemy (AD 90–168) studied the geography of the world during the Roman Empire. He derived his information from a variety of sources, and most of his informants of the world outside the Empire are thought to have been unreliable. In this particular case names in British languages have been translated to Latin and then subsequently into Ptolemy's native Greek. Nonetheless the information derived from his map of the Province of Ulster is the main source that we have for the Belfast area during the early Iron Age.

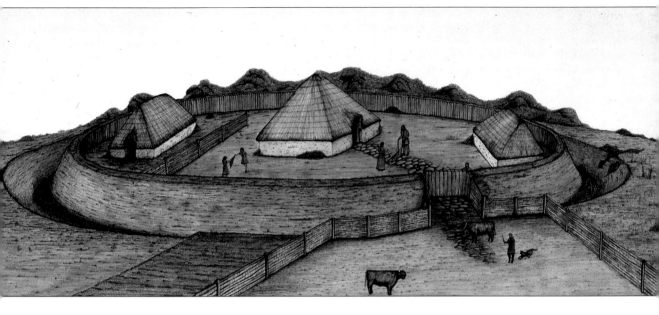

spot on which Belfast (*Beal Feirste*, meaning 'the approach to the sandbank') was later to be built; the name does not make its first appearance in the written record, however, until the 1470s. Other place-names commemorate long-forgotten notables. The Cave Hill is more correctly called, in its Irish form, Beann Mhadagain (mountain of Matudan). Matudan, son of Muiredach, was a ninth-century king of the group of tribes known as the Ulaidh (from which the name Ulster derives). On the promontory above the caves is an impressive ancient fortification, now known as MacArt's Fort but earlier still as Dun Mhadagain ('the fort of Matudan'); in the lake below the precipice are the remains of a crannog (an artificial island, easily defended) that might have been one of his residences.[18]

To sum up, by the twelfth century a new society, largely Christian, speaking one language, partly literate, and not entirely without some claim to be a land of 'saints and scholars' had emerged. The other side of this attractive state of affairs, however, was a political system which appeared almost to encourage a constant state of internecine warfare between kings and chieftains of all sorts. In fact Ulster, hitherto least affected by the Anglo-Norman régime in Dublin and The Pale, was about, one might say, to become a place fit for Normans to live in.

THE CASTLE AT THE FORD

The Normans came to Ireland almost exactly one hundred years after their conquest of England. They came at the invitation of an Irish king, to help him recover the kingdom he had lost to a rival. Having succeeded in their task, they stayed to carve out a future for themselves. In 1177 one John de Courcy, a little-known but highly capable and ambitious young soldier, got together a force of twenty horsemen supported by three hundred foot soldiers and archers, and, against the express wishes of King Henry II (his feudal lord) marched north and invaded Ulster. Defeating the local king of Ulidia near Downpatrick, these conquistadors rapidly overran most of the coastal areas of Down and Antrim and their immediate hinterland. Earthwork fortifications with wooden stockades (motte or motte-and-bailey castles), quickly erected, enabled the newcomers to consolidate their gains. As 'earl of Ulster' (self-proclaimed; he never got a royal patent for his conquest) de Courcy built castles of stone. From his two great strongholds on the coast, at Carrickfergus in County Antrim and Dundrum in County Down, he ruled his little kingdom virtually as an independent prince for the best part of three decades, despite royal disapproval, the hostility of the native clans and the jealously of rival Norman magnates.[19]

Unfortunately for his hopes of remaining independent, he and his wife (daughter of the Norse king of Man) had no children. King John, who had first visited Ireland twenty years earlier and had long been determined to bring both Irish kings and overmighty English lords to obedience, deprived de Courcy of his earldom and bestowed it on Hugh de Lacy. With the help of allies such as his father-in-law (who provided him with a fleet of warships) de Courcy for several years successfully resisted all attempts to displace him. In the end, unable to capture his own great fortress at Dundrum, where de Lacy had taken refuge, he was forced to submit. Surviving imprisonment, he was pardoned and even became one of the royal

DUNDRUM CASTLE

The great castle at Dundrum was probably started in the late twelfth century by John de Courcy, who fortified the upper part of the hill. The keep was added some time after his downfall in 1203, when the castle was in royal hands or after it had been granted to Hugh de Lacy. The cylindrical shape of the keep is rare in England, but many of the Normans who came to Ulster came from south Wales, where at Pembroke there is a very large cylindrical keep. Other improvements were made later, the last being a comfortable house inside the outer wall built by the Blundell family. By the eighteenth century the castle was in ruins, as this print of 1791 shows.

household, though his status was reduced to that of a mere knight. He died about 1220, possibly in France.[20]

Whoever was earl of Ulster, control of the ford at the mouth of the Lagan was vital to the survival of his fiefdom, which by the later thirteenth century (when it attained its maximum extent) stretched all the way from Carlingford Lough in the south to Lough Foyle in the north-west. In 1264 a branch of the de Burgo or de Burgh family replaced the de Lacys as earls. A castle of some sort had been erected at the ford at an early date, possibly by de Courcy, but almost nothing is known about it – not even its exact location, since no archaeological evidence about it has ever been uncovered. Under its protection a small settlement developed; a later map shows, in addition to the castle, a wayside chapel (presumably an offshoot of the monastic settlement at Shankill) and at 'Freerstown' to the south another ecclesiastical location with a few simple dwellings. The approaches to the ford were guarded by motte castles around the head of the lough, from Holywood, Dundonald and Knock to Belvoir; several of the mounds have survived, if somewhat precariously, in the outer suburbs of Belfast. Though in size, population, and trade the medieval proto-settlement at the Ford can never have been more than a small village, it was formally listed in medieval documents as a 'borough'. However, it apparently did not long survive the disasters that befell the earldom in the fourteenth century.

The first of these calamities was the invasion of Ireland in 1315 by Edward Bruce (King Robert's brother) with an army of six thousand mail-clad veterans of Bannockburn. Landing at Larne, the Scots defeated the Red Earl when he faced them at Connor. Many of the native Irish joined the Bruces in their triumphant but destructive campaigns in the south and midlands that followed, until the Scots were at last defeated (and Edward Bruce killed) near Dundalk in 1318. The castle at the ford had of course been easily taken; Carrickfergus had succumbed, too, though only after enduring a prolonged and gruesome siege.[21]

The earldom survived nevertheless, and the power of the English in the north even revived for a time. The next blow to it arose neither from Scottish invaders nor

IRELAND IN 1450

The O'Neills and the O'Donnells dominated early medieval Ulster. During the twelfth century the east of Ulster fell to the Normans, notably Hugh de Lacy (1176–1243), who founded the Earldom of Ulster. By the end of the fifteenth century the earldom had collapsed and Ulster became the only Irish province outside English control. This map shows the Norman decline, Anglo-Irish areas and the English-ruled Pale.

MacDonnells

O'Donnell

Donegal Bay

O'Neill

Earldom of Ulster

Magennis

Mayo

Burkes

O'Rourke

O'Reilly

Dundalk Bay

O'Connor

O'Farrell

O'Flaherty

Burkes

The Pale

Dempsey

Earldom of Kildare

Galway Bay

O'Brien

Earldom of Ormond

MacMurrough

Mouth of the Shannon

Wexford Lordship

Wexford Harbour

Dingle Bay

Earldom of Desmond

Mac Carthy Mor

Land held by native Irish

Land held by Anglo-Irish lords

Land held by English king

Bantry Bay

THE ANCIENT FORD

A detail from one of
J.W. Carey paintings in
the Ulster Hall. Carey
was a local illustrator
and painter. His best
known work is a series
of thirteen scenes from
Belfast history, which
were commissioned by
Belfast Corporation in
1903 for display in the
Ulster Hall. They have
recently been cleaned.
This is the first of six of
these romantic paintings
reproduced in this
volume.

BELFAST CITY COUNCIL

from incursions by the native Irish, but from bad blood between the earl of Ulster and some of his tenants and kinsfolk. Young William de Burgh, known as the Brown Earl, succeeded his grandfather in 1326. In 1333 members of the Mandeville family, led by one John Lagan, murdered him at the 'Ford of Carrickfergus'. The countess, with her infant daughter, fled to England, and the male line of the de Burgh earls came to an end. Later, the child was married to Lionel, duke of Clarence (second son of Edward III); through this union, the earldom became the property of the crown and gave theoretical title to successive English monarchs.[22]

The third catastrophe was the Black Death, which ravaged Irish society in 1348–49. Living, as they did, to a greater extent than the Irish at close quarters in towns, garrisons and fixed communities in general, the English settlers appear to have had a higher mortality rate than the Irish.[23] Combined, these three factors initiated a long period of comparative decline among the Anglo-Normans and their descendants, and of revival by the native families, which eventually reduced the earldom to little more than a small northern Pale, based on Carrickfergus. In east Ulster, a branch of the O'Neills resumed that great family's expansion from mid-Ulster into south Antrim and north Down and founded the kingdom of Clandeboye (from the Irish *Clann Aedha Buidhe* – 'the descendants of Aedh (Hugh) the Yellow-haired'). The castle at the Lagan ford was disputed between the English and the O'Neills and among the Irish themselves on many occasions. For the most part the Irish held it, however, for these chieftains had learned much from their opponents, not least the importance of stone fortresses in troubled times. They not only rebuilt the castle on the sandbank whenever it was taken and burned by the forces of the English lord

CARRICKFERGUS IN THE SIXTEENTH CENTURY

This is the earliest known plan of an Ulster town. The two most important early buildings are the great Norman castle, begun in 1178 by John de Courcy, and St Nicholas's church founded in 1180, also founded by de Courcy. The church of the friars (les freres) can be seen. (*top of plan*). This plan gives a clear impression of the town in the second half of the sixteenth century. The more important houses were small castles of the type Irish chiefs had begun to build after the coming of the Normans, and which were probably based on the design of the Norman keep; small towers were linked together by short terraces of lower buildings, the whole being welded into one composition. A considerable portion of the town within the enclosing rampart was unbuilt upon, if one is to disregard the temporary beehive huts which were constructed with a framework of wattle and covered with either thatch or green sedge on top of the clay. The stone buildings were also roofed with thatch and they had very small apertures for windows, so there was little light inside them.

BRITISH LIBRARY, COTTON AUGUSTUS, MS
I.II, FOL. 42

deputy's government in Dublin (or by the Carrickfergus garrison), but themselves built as their main residence a new 'grey castle' at Castlereagh, overlooking the ford, on the County Down side. Here for many years the O'Neill of Clandeboye was formally acclaimed and enthroned on a stone chair, which still survives.[24]

As it turned out, the victory of Henry Tudor over Richard III at Bosworth in 1485 ended the Wars of the Roses. During that long-drawn-out struggle some of the leading Old English families in Ireland were obliged to take sides. On the whole they tended to be Yorkists, and none more so than the greatest magnates of all – the Fitz-Geralds, earls of Kildare. Indeed, they continued to favour the Yorkist cause after 1485, recognising the pretenders Simnel and Warbeck when they appeared in Dublin, to Henry VII's great displeasure. However, the Kildares were so powerful in the lands they controlled, and in their connections with other great families, both English and Irish, that – however reluctantly – the Tudors continued to depend on them to rule Ireland in the name of the crown until the 1530s.[25] At a local level, on more than one occasion the Kildare of the time, in his capacity as lord deputy, intervened against the native rulers of Clandeboye in order to preserve what was left of the earldom of Ulster. The 'Great Earl' of Kildare demolished Belfast castle (held by a branch of the O'Neills) in 1500 and again in 1512; and his son in 1523 reported to Henry VIII similar chastisement for another O'Neill: 'I brake a castle of his, called Belfast, and burned 24 myle of his countrie …' [26]

From about 1530 onward, however, Henry's break with the papacy made him fear that unless Ireland were brought under closer control it might become a base for attempts by the Catholic powers of Europe to make trouble for him. This led to an important change of policy. From 1540 the leading gaelic chiefs, and also some Old English lords who held lands to which they could not produce titles valid in law, were offered royal confirmation of their estates if they first surrendered them to the crown and acknowledged Henry as King of Ireland (rather than 'Lord of Ireland', the title bestowed on Henry II and his successors by the pope nearly three centuries earlier). This policy of 'Surrender and Regrant' seemed at first to make little difference in practice to the power of the native chiefs, but it was to be the basis in English law of later confiscations and plantations. In the process, the power of the Kildares was broken. In the north, the leading Irish magnate, Conn Bacach O'Neill, accepted the title of earl of Tyrone and a little later Hugh O'Neill of Clandeboye also submitted, receiving from King Edward VI as part of the bargain a grant of the castle of Belfast.[27]

Such arrangements tended to be fragile, however, since at a local level neither party trusted the other. By 1567 the English had taken control of the castle at the ford again, for two officers wrote from Carrickfergus to report: 'We have fortified Belfast, and have placed there 15 horsemen, so that in this town we live as quietly as in Dublin.' [28] They were less well satisfied with the quality of the beer provided for the Belfast garrison. The following year, 1568, the lord deputy (Sir Henry Sidney) came north to Belfast to negotiate the transfer of the castle to Sir Brian MacPhelim O'Neill. Among other things O'Neill undertook to 'make or cause to be made, a good and sufficient bridge that man, horse, drag, cart, and wayne, with all manner of carriage, may safely pass and repass over and through the same in some convenient place over the Ford at Belfast, with causes [causeways] and [erche] end of the said bridge.' [29] O'Neill also agreed to supply wood to fuel brick-making at Carrickfergus. Clearly this particular Irish leader was more at ease with the modern world than many of his contemporaries; years later, James I's attorney-general in Ireland, Sir John Davies, could still remark that left to themselves the Irish 'would never (to the end of the world) build houses, make townships or villages'.

THE SITE OF CONN O'NEILL'S CASTLE

Conn O'Neill was the last known occupant of the castle at Castlereagh, which was then abandoned. The lands were much reduced by grants to neighbouring planters. In the mid-nineteenth century the steward of the property was instructed to plant a grove of trees. Some of the stones were used to build the wall which protected the planting. By the 1890s when this picturesque sketch was made, the history of the place had been largely forgotten.

It was to be more than a century before a bridge replaced the ford. Meanwhile, the pope's public excommunication of Elizabeth as a heretic in 1570, and his declaration releasing her Catholic subjects from their allegiance to her, led to increasing fears for her safety and increasing interest among her advisers in bringing Ulster – still largely untouched by English law, administration and culture – within the orbit of the government in Dublin. Permanent 'plantations' or settlements were the preferred method, on the lines of Virginia. Elizabeth, always anxious to keep expenditure as low as possible, encouraged private 'adventurers' to undertake this 'Enterprise of Ulster', as the plan of settlement was called. It was an attractive prospect for enterprising investors who hoped to acquire estates a lot closer to home than North America. The original forests in the immediate vicinity of Belfast had been cleared long ago for farming, but there were still great oak-woods all along the Lagan, plenty of fish in the rivers and virgin land to be developed.

One important proof of English interest in this domestic Virginia is the earliest detailed map of the Belfast area. Dateable to the early 1570s, the manuscript sketch names 'Sir Brian Macfelm' as the occupant of Castlereagh. 'Benmadiane' (Ben Madigan) is described as 'Hill with a Cave'. The castle of 'Bellfaste' is marked, unaccompanied by any other buildings, though a few dwellings are shown at 'Freerstone' (Friarstown or Friar's Bush).

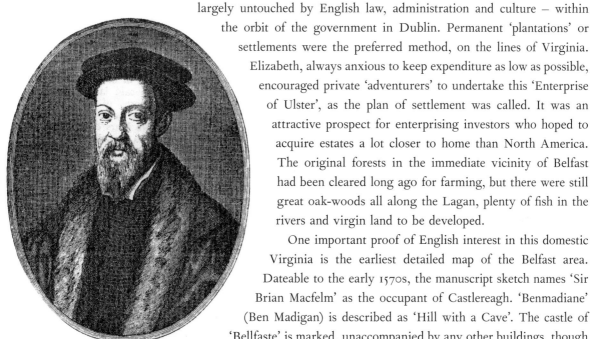

SIR THOMAS SMITH

Private secretary to Queen Elizabeth I, and thus well informed about the 'Enterprise of Ulster', Sir Thomas Smith was a distinguished lawyer and scholar. The elder Smith was vice-chancellor of Cambridge University and the author of an important book on the Anglo-Saxon constitution of England.

FACSIMILE OF THE PORTRAIT IN HIS 'LIFE', BY KIND PERMISSION OF THE LINEN HALL LIBRARY

At Cromac and along the Lagan ('Leganda') thick woods are shown, with this encouraging note to developers: 'Alonge this river by ye space of 26 miles groweth much woodes as well Okes for Tymber as hother woodde, which maie be brought in the baie of Cragfergus with bote or by dragge.' There is no matching note to warn unwary speculators that the lord of Castlereagh was likely to give them a hard time of it.

The first to try was Sir Thomas Smith, one of Elizabeth's secretaries, who in November 1571, in partnership with his natural son (also Thomas), was given a grant of the lands of the 'Ardes in Clandeboye, which lieth south to the castle called Belfast'. The territory he named 'belferst' was defined in Smith's grant as stretching 'from the river of ferst [Farset] mile and a half north, and from the same and the bay of Knockfergus west two miles, all of the same breadt'. O'Neill, who was on good terms with military officers and other well-informed people at Carrickfergus, had already heard about Smith's intentions. In fact the younger Smith, seeking investors, had composed and circulated alluring advertisements (or 'books' as they are called in the official correspondence) about the proposed enterprise.[30]

O'Neill's fears were confirmed in the spring of 1572, when he received a letter from Sir Thomas informing him that he himself would soon be coming to 'live near

him as a good neighbour' and trusting that they would be on friendly terms. Not surprisingly, the news that his possessions had been confiscated and reallocated to a stranger enraged the Irishman and drove him to revolt, just as the lord deputy in Dublin and Elizabeth's chief adviser in London, Lord Burleigh, had warned her it would. However, as Sir Thomas loftily remarked: 'MacPhelim is afraid, but shall not the Queen dispose of her own?'[31]

Smith sent over his son to make a reality of their grant. Young Smith was ludicrously ill-equipped for his mission to the Irish frontier. Apart from his evident lack of military experience and the absence of surprise, his little army was far too small. Writing to the Queen in September 1572, after reporting that Smith had 'now

SIXTEENTH-CENTURY
ULSTER

MS Cotton Augustus
I. ii. 19, showing the
province of Ulster, in
the second half of the
sixteenth century

BRITISH LIBRARY COTTON AUGUSTUS, MS
I.II, FOL. 19

at length come to the Ardes', the lord deputy remarked: 'I wish his number [such] as were able to help [us], and not such as shall need help; for if it be a full hundred it is not many more.' Smith must have hired some local mercenaries to swell the ranks. However many of them there were, they made little difference to the futility of a skirmishing campaign in north Down in 1573. Then, when his money ran out, so did most of his followers. In the end he was savagely murdered by some of his Irish retainers, who (it was said) threw him alive to their ravenous dogs.[32]

Even before the failure of the Smiths had become complete, a second, more extensive grant of the same land was made to Walter Devereux, earl of Essex. It included 'the dominions of Clandeboye … and all lands, tenements and hereditaments from Knockfergus Bay including the river of Belfast directly to the next part of the Lough'. As well as making good his patent, Essex had a wider, official brief – to establish the authority of the crown throughout Ulster. This task gave him much greater standing than Smith had enjoyed, as well as access to government resources. He lost no time in setting about it. Leaving Liverpool in mid-August 1573, he landed at Carrickfergus and moved south to Belfast, where he set up camp overlooking the ford. After some hesitation Brian O'Neill mustered his forces and, as an official account puts it, the English were 'stayed by the Rebels, who were gathered in great numbers upon the other side of the ford, to stop their passage'. The Irish were worsted on this occasion, however, and could not prevent the newcomers from marching into north Down as far as Comber and back again. Essex, who thought Carrickfergus unsuitable on several counts, wrote to the privy council from Belfast proposing to create a new settlement there:

> Belfaste is a place meet for a corporate towne, armed with all commodities, [such] as a principal haven, wood and good ground, standing also upon a border and a place of great importance for service [that is, of strategic importance]. I think it convenient that a fortification be made there at [in] the spring; the fortification for the circuit, and a storehouse for victuals to be at her Majesty's charges; all other buildings at mine, and such as may inhabit it.[33]

He also asked for the services of a military engineer to take charge of the construction of the defences and to build a bridge to replace the ford. The likely cost alarmed the privy council and Essex's dream never materialised, but he would never consider any other site. As he wrote later to the Queen:

> I resolve not to build but at one place; namelie, at Belfast, and that of little charge; a small towne there will keepe the passage, relieve Knockfergus with wood; and horsemen being laid there shall command the plains of Clandeboye; and may be victualled at pleasure by sea, without danger of Scot and pirate.[34]

The mention of hostile Scots refers to the MacDonnells and their followers from the west of Scotland who had been settling in north Antrim and the Glens since the early fifteenth century. By the 1560s, under James MacDonnell, they had become an important factor in the political and military affairs of Ulster – often at odds with the O'Neills to the east and south (who themselves were riven by divisions between rival claimants to the family's lands across the Bann and in Clandeboye) or with the English in Carrickfergus and Belfast.

CORONATION STONE

A rare, possibly unique survival of a gaelic chief's coronation stone. It is made from a single piece of whinstone, roughly shaped into a chair. It belonged to the o'Neills of Clandeboye, whose chieftain was proclaimed in the open air at Castlereagh.

DIERDRE CRONE

Though O'Neill prudently submitted to Elizabeth (he wrote a grovelling letter dated 8 May 1574 to tell her he renounced his title to Clandeboye, begging only that he might be the 'fermor' [leaseholder], as already agreed by Essex). In her reply, the Queen accepted his submission and confirmed whatever Essex had promised in her name.[35] During the latter part of 1574 Essex's forces were involved in an indecisive campaign against Turlough O'Neill and the Scots, in which O'Neill of Clandeboye appeared to be a friendly if not very cooperative ally of the English. When Essex's lack of success began to make Elizabeth impatient, he came to believe that the Irishman was secretly plotting against him. On the surface, however, relations between the two of them were so good that when they next met at Belfast in November a great banquet was arranged, to be held in the castle. It is not entirely clear from the records who played host, but it appears that Brian and his relations were occupying the castle when Essex, by his own account 'after consulting all his captains' gave orders to arrest O'Neill; the Irish, resisting, lost 'upwards of 100 men killed …' Other estimates vary between 115 and 200.

The *Annals of the Four Masters* gives a rather different, and much more vivid, account of what happened:

> Peace, sociability and friendship were established between Brian and the Earl of Essex; and a feast was afterwards prepared by Brian, to which the Lord Justice and the chiefs of his people were invited, and they passed three nights and days together pleasantly and cheerfully. At the expiration of this time, however, as they were agreeably drinking and making merry, Brian, his brother and his wife, were seized upon by the Earl, and all his people put unsparingly to the sword, men, women, youths and maidens, in Brian's own presence. Brian was afterwards sent to Dublin, together with his wife and brother, where they were cut in quarters as traitors.[36]

Essex later published a proclamation in which, among other things, he sought to mitigate this dreadful atrocity by saying that O'Neill had never had a safe-conduct. The outraged O'Neills rose in revolt and drove Essex out of the North. His great enterprise was cut back and then abandoned. When he died in Dublin in 1576, his long-held dream of a new town at Belfast appeared to have died with him.

CHAPTER TWO

FOUNDING FATHERS

WHERE Essex had failed in the 1570s, a later adventurer succeeded. In the interval, the balance of power in Ireland was transformed by the decisive victory of Elizabeth's armies over the Irish (and Anglo-Irish) lords who had so long defied her. Nowhere was the change greater than in Ulster, where the gaelic rulers had remained largely independent until Elizabeth was on her deathbed. The leading figure on the Irish side in this end-game of the Tudor conquest was Hugh O'Neill, second earl of Tyrone, whose military and diplomatic skills and commanding presence enabled him to persuade former rivals to accept his leadership and to recruit the assistance (though in the end not in sufficient strength) of the pope and the king of Spain – and to carry on, with some notable successes in the field, a war lasting nine years off and on. In the end, after Elizabeth's young favourite Robert Devereux, second earl of Essex, had failed as miserably as his father (more so indeed, for he lost his head as a consequence), the Irish were overcome by the superior abilities and ruthless scorched-earth tactics of Charles Blount, Lord Mountjoy and his equally ruthless right-hand man in the north, Arthur Chichester.

The crucial event in the defeat of the hitherto victorious Irish was the battle of Kinsale in December 1601. A Spanish force which had mistakenly landed there, far from the main centre of events, was besieged by Mountjoy's army, which was besieged in turn by O'Neill on his arrival from the north. Ambitious plans to destroy the English in a combined assault by the Spaniards and the Irish misfired, however. Forced to retreat back again to Ulster, O'Neill found his allies deserting him and was eventually forced to submit to Mountjoy at the end of March 1603, unaware that the Queen was already dead; had he known, he might have hoped to negotiate better terms from her successor, James VI and I.[1]

As it was, O'Neill and other leading rebels were treated with what at first glance looks like considerable leniency, in that large parts of their confiscated estates were restored to them, but – no longer their own masters – they had to admit English sheriffs and garrisons and use English law. Their lands 'before these last wars, like the kingdom of China, inaccessible to strangers', were thus laid open for exploitation.

left

**THE FOUNDER OF
MODERN BELFAST**

Sir Arthur Chichester, founder of Belfast, has his effigy in St Nicholas's church in Carrickfergus. Chichester was always closely concerned about Carrickfergus, and the house he built there for his retirement was a splendid one, Joymount, named after his patron, Mountjoy.

PHOTOGRAPH: CARNEGIE, 2009

The words quoted above were those of Arthur Chichester, the founding father of modern Belfast.[2]

Chichester was not the first of his family to seek his fortune in Ireland. An elder brother, John, who had served in the army there from 1595, had been appointed governor of Carrickfergus and was knighted for his services. In July 1597 he defeated the local allies of O'Neill, overcoming their thousand-strong force with his own much smaller contingent (250 foot and 30 horse). Belfast Castle, however, which had earlier 'cost some money in fortefying', had been taken by Shane McBrian O'Neill on 18 June 1597 (when the officer in command was drunk in Carrickfergus) and all the Englishmen in the garrison had been hanged and disembowelled. A short time later, Sir John Chichester recaptured the castle in a surprise attack from the sea. So complete was the surprise that there were no English casualties; and this time the Irish within were put to the sword. The official report to the authorities described Belfast at that time as 'a place which standeth 8 miles from Kerogfergus, and on the river, wher the sea ebbes and flowes, so that botes may be landed within a butte [crossbow] shotte of the said Castell'. Flushed by these easy successes, in November 1597 Chichester sallied forth from Carrickfergus to offer battle to a large and seasoned force of Scots from north Antrim who were menacing the town. The result was a complete disaster. The Scots, led by Sir James MacDonnell, caught the English in a well-laid ambush and not only inflicted heavy casualties on them but captured and killed the governor himself, afterwards beheading the corpse and sending the grisly trophy to Hugh O'Neill's camp, where it was reportedly kicked about like a football.[3]

When Arthur Chichester came to Ireland in 1599 he followed in his brother's footsteps, determined not only to make his own name and fortune but if possible to avenge the late governor (whom he succeeded in that post) by destroying MacDonnell and O'Neill. Before the Nine Years War ended in 1603 the Scot was dead, possibly assassinated on the orders of Chichester (or at any rate with his approval). O'Neill proved to be beyond his reach however, despite earlier hopes of 'soon beheading that wood-kerne Tyrone'.[4] Thereafter, O'Neill's decision in 1607 to leave Ireland, in the so-called Flight of the Earls, literally removed him from Chichester's sphere of influence. The departure of the great northern chiefs led to the confiscation of their property and the official plantation of Ulster.

In 1605 King James VI and I appointed Chichester lord deputy (chief governor) of Ireland and then kept him in the post for over ten years. Since the Plantation, the

Arthur Lord Chichester,
L.ᵈ Lieut. of Ireland A.° D. 1615.

ARTHUR CHICHESTER

A seventeenth-century engraving of Sir Arthur Chichester (1563–1625), founder of Belfast and Lord Deputy of Ireland for more than ten years.

© ULSTER MUSEUM, 2008

main Irish project of the reign, was planned and set in motion during those years, Chichester was well placed to add to the lands he had already acquired in Antrim; in the end, he was the greatest individual beneficiary of the Plantation. An enthusiastic coloniser, he declared that he 'would rather labour with his hands in the plantation of Ulster than dance or play in that of Virginia'. And once, in reflective mood, he remarked, 'We are now all of us become buylders and planters here, and not wasters and destroyers as in our younger yeares'.[5]

A NEW TOWN

The castle at Belfast was in ruins when Chichester got it in 1603, and the whole property so ravaged by the war that it yielded little in rent. At the time, he told the royal advisers that he would not expect to get more than five pounds for the freehold of the grant, including the governorship of Carrickfergus. No doubt he exaggerated his plight, but he was indeed in serious financial difficulty, which was made worse by a vexatious lawsuit challenging his title; until that was settled in his favour in 1608 there was little he was prepared to do by way of development. In the following year, however, he started investing in his new possessions. The commissioners appointed to report on the progress of the official plantation also visited Antrim and Down (which were not in the official scheme). They were favourably impressed by what they saw in Belfast, namely the nucleus of a planned settlement 'plotted out in a good forme, wherein are many famelyes of English, Scotch, and some Manksmen already inhabitinge, of which some are artificers who have buylte good tymber houses with chimneys after the fashion of the English palle [Pale], and one Inn with very good Lodginge which is a great comforte to the travellers in those partes'.[6]

The commissioners were particularly interested in the rebuilding of the castle, where workmen had 'taken down the ruins of the old castle almost to the valte above the Sellers, and had likewise layde the foundation of a bricke house 50 foote longe which is to be adjoyned to the sayd Castle …' The outer defences of the building were to consist of a bawn with four half-bulwarks encompassed by a deep moat. In the absence of reliable archaeological evidence no one is quite sure of the exact location of this building, but its approximate site was in an area bounded by Castle Place, Castle Lane and Donegall Place. The remarks of the commissioners remind us that in the absence of building stone in the vicinity, Belfast was always a brick town. Fortunately, there were large deposits of suitable clay nearby; Chichester fired thousands of them for use in the castle – enough, it was expected, to provide material for some other buildings too.[7]

It may be appropriate to mention at this point – however briefly – recent developments arising out of a programme of archaeological excavation. The two first examples are the original Anglo-Norman settlement and a probable small-scale one by the O'Neills of Clandeboye in the late medieval period. Thereafter the Plantation

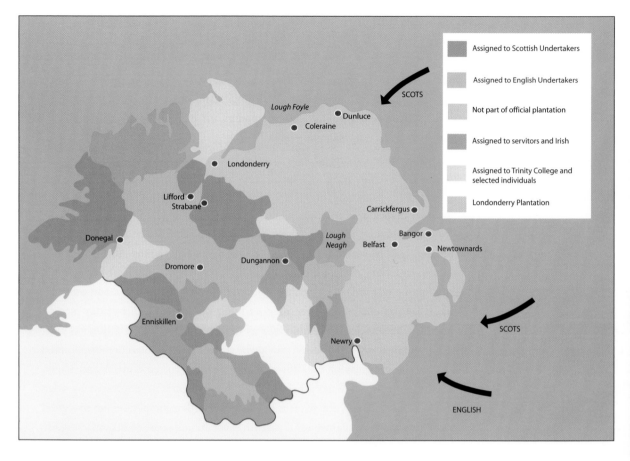

Assigned to Scottish Undertakers

Assigned to English Undertakers

Not part of official plantation

Assigned to servitors and Irish

Assigned to Trinity College and selected individuals

Londonderry Plantation

town planned by the first Arthur Chichester completely controlled the development of the town.

Until recently the conventional account was based on George Benn's analysis in his *History of Belfast*. Benn pointed out that the three things distinguishing the locality in early times were the castle, the church and the ford. Most early references to the castle and the ford were to be found in the Irish Annals, though the entries were usually very brief or cryptic and were used for headline events and so did not necessarily give much information. What kind of Anglo-Norman castle was built to guard the ford was not known. No trace of it has survived, no date is known for certain. Frequent battles and skirmishes testify however to the importance of the ford as far back as the great battle between the Ulaid and the Cruithin in AD 668.

Archaeologists have become increasingly concerned about the damage done to the historic centre of Belfast by German bombs in the Blitz, then by IRA bombs in the Troubles and more recently by careless or indifferent schemes of redevelopment. The Environment and Heritage Service has promoted and carried out an extensive programme of excavations. The first dig was in 1983; between that date and 2005 fifty-one excavations have been completed. Only summary reports have

THE PLANTATIONS OF ULSTER

Following the Irish defeat at the battle of Kinsale (1601), Elizabeth I's English forces subjugated Ireland, including Ulster. The Gaelic leaders of Ulster, the O'Neills and O'Donnells, fled *en masse* in 1607 to Europe, particularly to Spain and Italy. This 'Flight of the Earls' allowed the English Crown to colonise Ulster with more loyal English and Scottish 'planters', a process that began in earnest in 1610: King James I's plantation of Ulster.

BELFAST, C.1685

Plan of Belfast, after the
map of the fortifications
by Thomas Phillips.
Note 'the Belfast River'
(the Farset), flowing
down the middle of
High Street and into
the Lagan just below
the ford; the castle,
surrounded by gardens;
the tower of the
Market House nearby;
and the parish church.
All of this is within the
rampart built in 1641
(the 'old works').

BRITISH LIBRARY, MAPS K. TOP. 51. 37

been issued as yet for most of these but enough has been discovered to suggest that there is probably a good deal more to be found if the chance can be seized before it is too late.[8]

But to return to our main theme: two years later, in 1613, the little town was made into a corporate borough by royal charter, and its founder was created Baron Chichester of Belfast. For the next two centuries and more the fortunes of the town were to be closely bound up with those of the Chichester family, lords of Belfast, earls (from 1647) and marquesses (from 1791) of Donegall.

The reasons for the grant of the charter were entirely political. King James was about to summon a parliament in Dublin, and to make sure that its House of Commons would have a Protestant majority he created no fewer than forty new boroughs, each electing two members. So, as critics protested at the time, boroughs

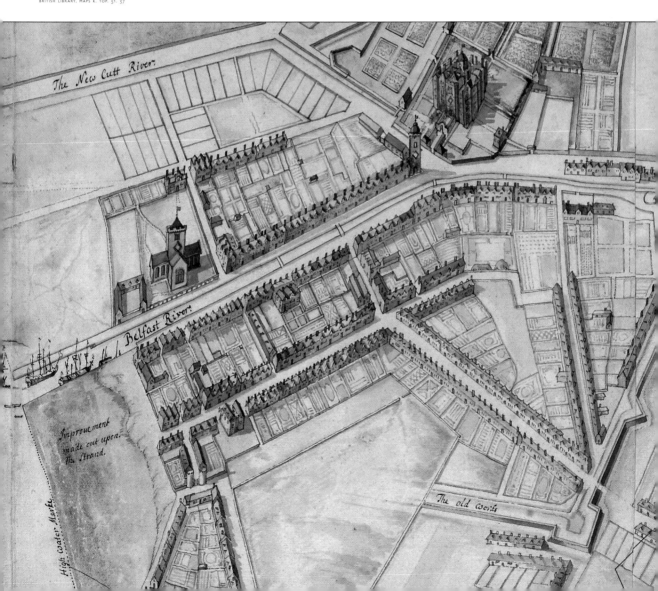

were created 'in places that can scantly pass the rank of the poorest villages in the poorest country of Christendom'. The terms of Belfast's charter gave the Chichesters exceptional control over the town, in addition to the wide powers enjoyed by them as sole owners (under the crown) of the ground on which it stood.[9] The corporation was made up of the lord of the castle, his deputy the constable, a sovereign (mayor) elected each year at the Feast of the Nativity of St John the Baptist (24 June), and twelve free burgesses appointed for life. Any vacancies that occurred were filled by the sovereign and remaining burgesses; the corporation alone elected the town's two MPs. Each year also, the lord of the castle made a short list of three from which the sovereign was chosen, and no statutes or bye-laws could be made without the proprietor's advice and consent. In practice the corporation came to consist largely of the friends and supporters of the Chichester family, and the MPs elected were always its members or nominees.

One other group is mentioned in the original charter – the 'free commoners' or 'freemen' who could be enrolled by the sovereign (for a fee) if suitably qualified as householders or if they had completed their apprenticeship in the town. Their powers were rather vague but they appear to have acted as grand jurors of the borough court from time to time and had some say in financial assessments but they had little or no political role and by the end of the seventeenth century had lost whatever power of that sort they may have once exercised. The real advantages they enjoyed were economic rather than political – exemption from the tolls that strangers had to pay and protection against unlicensed interlopers illegally selling their goods in the town. For the ambitious citizen, acceptance as a freeman could also be a first step towards possible election as a burgess.[10]

How the new borough developed during the first years of its existence is impossible to trace in any detail, for the simple reason that the records are so scanty. The corporation presumably met from time to time to elect new sovereigns, burgesses and freemen and a record began to be kept from about 1615 in what became known as the Town Book, but the entries for the early years (those that survived at all) were particularly uninformative. For example, the original burgesses were all named in the charter but their replacements thereafter for a quarter of a century were not noted and the next complete list cannot be compiled before 1639. Before 1630, even changes of sovereign were not noted, nor bye-laws earlier than 1633.[11] In fact, on the evidence available Belfast seems scarcely to have existed at all before the 1630s. Whilst there is little to suggest dynamic growth in that decade either, the corporation did show some signs of life. The appointment of a town clerk and two sergeants to enforce its decrees and collect fines from transgressors against a growing number of bye-laws perhaps suggests a greater sense of civic dignity. By 1639 there is even mention of a town hall, presumably rented somewhere opposite the castle gate. Other scraps of evidence suggest that by the end of the thirties the range of occupations among the inhabitants was growing too, if slowly.

Stagnation in an underdeveloped economy which was slow to recover from the effects of war and upheaval was an obvious general reason for Belfast's failure to thrive. The same applied to other Plantation settlements, however.[12] More to the point perhaps, in view of the town's dependence on its founding family, we need to ask how far the slow start in Belfast was caused by the particular circumstances of that family's history under Arthur Chichester (died 1625) and his brother Edward (died 1648). Some negative facts stand out. So far as Arthur Chichester was concerned, having rebuilt the castle, established the borough and built a larger church he seldom found time to visit the north and, when he did, spent more of his time and money in Carrickfergus than in Belfast. Joymount, his great house in Carrickfergus, begun in 1610, took ten years to complete; and when he died in 1625 he was buried in the parish church in Carrickfergus. In his latter years he spent much of his time in England, as a senior privy councillor, or abroad in Germany as James I's diplomatic envoy to the Habsburg emperor.[13] Chronically short of cash, he bequeathed to his brother (along with his estates) very large debts, one of which alone amounted to the enormous sum of £10,000. In short, the founding father of Belfast had neither the time nor the money to spend much on his own town.

In order to reduce the burden of debt on his brother's legacy Edward Chichester sold Chichester House in Dublin, only to contract debts on his own account.[14] The 1630s were an expensive time for him and he was not always able to collect his rents in full. In particular, Charles I's new lord deputy – the formidable Thomas Wentworth – was determined to increase his master's income from Ireland. One lucrative method was the establishment of a commission for remedy of 'defective titles'. Inevitably it found what it was looking for. Chichester's was one of the properties investigated. The outcome was that in order to secure his rights beyond dispute he was obliged to pay a fine of nearly five hundred pounds in cash, to accept more onerous terms for the new patents, and to surrender Lough Neagh with all its valuable fisheries.[15] Numbers of Chichester's tenants among the Presbyterian Scots of south Antrim were affected by the billeting on them of a large number of soldiers to the point where they ran away leaving rents unpaid and crops unharvested. Many of them fled to Scotland when the government tried to force all Presbyterians over the age of sixteen to swear an oath (known as the Black Oath) repudiating the Scottish Covenant of 1638.[16] By May 1641 Chichester was expressing alarm about the poor of Belfast in a letter to the earl of Ormonde.

The repair of the army hither hath been so laid on with numbers that the poor people have not the bedding or merchandise to supply them and by that occasion are so impoverished that they can no longer subsist ... the inhabitants have spent their whole years provisions and have not wherewith to furnish themselves with necessary victuals to maintain themselves and their families.[17]

THE 1641 IRISH REBELLION

A few months later in October, the great rebellion of Irish Catholics, usually referred to as the 1641 rising, burst out. It came as a complete surprise to most of the English and Scots who were settled in the

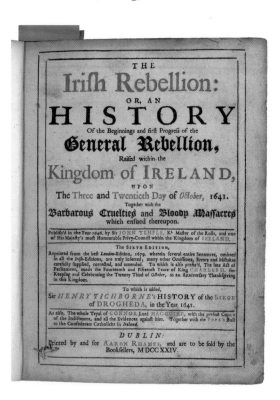

north. Starting in mid-Ulster which was quickly overrun, rebel forces brushed aside most of the opposition as they made their way southward towards Newry and eastwards towards Belfast and Carrickfergus. Unlike Carrickfergus, Belfast was never defended by stone walls. There was panic as an army of rebels approached. Edward Chichester wrote to the king at the end of October to say, 'They are advancing near into these parts and this last night of all there hath been seen great fires so near as were discerned from this place'.[18] An earthwork was hastily thrown up, but as many of the inhabitants fled the fall of the town appeared inevitable – and would probably have come about but for the determined actions of one man.

Robert Lawson had little or no experience of war (he was a merchant and a partner in the iron works at Old Forge on the Lagan)[19] and was staying there when Belfast seemed about to fall. He turned out to be a natural leader. Finding nearly everyone in the town in a panic as he says in his own account, 'the most part of the inhabitants fled and flying … and the old Lord Chichester shipped aboard in a ship'[20] – he mustered and armed a small force of about one hundred and sixty horse and foot and the same day led it to Lisburn, ten miles to the west, in time to rally a successful defence there. This check to the rebel advance saved Belfast too. As one of Lawson's Irish opponents wrote afterwards: 'But for him we had Belfast, we did little dream any such action had been in him, if we had we would have cut him short of his journey, but now no remedy' – remarks echoed by another Irish officer: 'If Captain Lawson had not opposed our cousin Sir Conn Magennis of entering Lisnagarvie [Lisburn], when Lord Conway, his troop of horse, and all the townspeople left it, we would have had Belfast and all those parts in possession!'[21]

WAR, PEACE AND SURVIVAL, 1642–1706

THE OLD LONG
BRIDGE

A painting of the Long
Bridge by Carey, now
in the Ulster Hall. At
three quarters of a mile
(1.2 km) long the Old
Long Bridge in Belfast
was at one time the
longest bridge in the
British Isles. It was even
the subject of the first
photograph taken in
Ireland. It was a popular
landmark in Belfast
and was a favourite
promenade for its
citizens.

BELFAST CITY COUNCIL

THE FAILURE of the Irish rebels in 1641 to take Belfast, Lisburn and
Carrickfergus did not end the threat to the Protestant settlers in Antrim
and Down. On the contrary, elsewhere in Ulster the rebellion spread rapidly,
accompanied in some places by dreadful ill-treatment of civilian refugees – in many
cases, it appears, the work of self-appointed local commanders with old scores to
settle, rather than the result of deliberate policy. Within a short time the plantation
was in ruins; only a few towns and strong points were still able to hold out, and
they needed troops and supplies to continue to do so, let alone to take the offensive.
At Londonderry in January 1642, it was reported, all available ships were crammed
with terrified refugees: 'The terror of the rebellion hath struck such a feare in the
Brittish of these parts that their harts are gone, and, therefore it is to little purpose
to stay their bodyes.'[1]

Although – and also because – the king and his opponents in the Westminster
parliament were preoccupied with the struggle for power between them that was
soon to break out in civil war, they were prepared to co-operate in restoring English

rule in Ireland – up to a point at least. As it happened, the only army immediately available was a force of Scottish Covenanters not yet disbanded after taking part in the defeat of Charles I in the Bishops War. The Scottish authorities readily undertook to supply up to 10,000 soldiers for service in Ulster, to be paid and supplied by the English. Since all the parties concerned had their own particular aims and agendas, however, it took a long time to settle the details. Not until April 1642 did the first of these 'New Scots' under the overall command of Alexander Leslie, earl of Leven, with Robert Monro as major-general, land at Carrickfergus.[2]

The newcomers were at first warmly received by the 'British' – as the troops recruited under commissions from the king by Protestant landowners in Antrim and Down were called. The most prominent and influential officers were Lords Conway, Claneboye and Montgomery, and Colonel Chichester; the last-named commanded in Belfast, since his family owned the town. The two armies combined to move south through County Down, driving back the elusive irregular troops of the Magennis clan, through the Kilwarlin woods and bogs, towards Newry (taken and garrisoned). Dungannon and the strong fort of Mountjoy, near the Lough Neagh shore, followed before Monro turned for home. On the way back the allies rounded up thousands of cattle which provided not only a supply of fresh meat for soldiers soon desperate for food but could also be turned into money: huge numbers were shipped to Scotland from Donaghadee – far more than the Scottish share of the plunder, according to the settlers' reckoning.[3]

The New Scots army under the 1642 arrangement served in Ulster until 1648. Much of the fighting consisted of raids into rebel territory which were met by hit-and-run tactics on the part of the Irish.[4] The rebels were dispirited and on the point of giving up, when the arrival of Owen Roe O'Neill, nephew of Hugh earl of Tyrone and a distinguished soldier in the Spanish service, raised their hopes and transformed the situation. O'Neill was appointed general of all the Catholic forces in the north and set about making a trained army of the ill-disciplined men who flocked to his standard. Monro had strict instructions from his Scottish masters to confine himself to Ulster, fearing what King Charles and his lord lieutenant Ormonde in the south might be up to if the north was left unsecured.[5] The outbreak of the Civil War in England between king and parliament created problems in the other two kingdoms. In particular, neither of these two protagonists could now afford to pay and supply the Scots as regularly as they had undertaken to do.[6] By 1644 the Scots officers were in such despair about pay and supplies and on such bad terms with Ormonde and his 'British' local commanders that they prepared to leave Ireland altogether. The Solemn League and Covenant, by which the majority of Scots presbyterians came down on the side of Parliament in the Civil War and against the king, made a complicated situation even more confused.

In 1643 Ormonde was obliged to seek a 'cessation' or truce with the Catholic leaders (based in Kilkenny). The Cessation (a treaty from March 1646) was condemned by the English parliament and opposed by Monro's Covenanters and also by the rank and file of the 'British' forces in Ulster, most of whose officers however, tried to obey the lord lieutenant's commands.[7] In Belfast, Chichester began to strengthen the defences against his former ally and to lay in whatever supplies he could find. Unscrupulously, though from his own viewpoint sensibly, Monro – by the terms of the Solemn League and Covenant now nominally commander of all the Protestant forces in Ulster – suddenly, on 13 May 1644, sent a force from Carrickfergus which by the treachery of Chichester's scouts (who reported that there was no sign of the Scots) and with the connivance of the guards on the town gates seized Belfast and expelled Chichester's garrison.[8] The fact was that many of the British had become supporters of the Covenant and of Monro; the men of one company tore their colours in the marketplace in defiance of their officers.

They also, in effect, attacked Chichester himself by demanding that all the 'free commoners' should have votes in the election of the burgesses and that everyone elected must be a freeman, a resident and a supporter of the Covenant, which he opposed. 'Malcontents' should be purged.[9] After sitting on this incendiary document for three weeks the sovereign of the corporation, Thomas Theaker, took fright and ran off to Dublin 'to acquaint Collonell Chichester … with the Contents of the said Peticion being still insisted on by the said Comoners'. The secret intrigues of the king with the Catholic leaders, and the attempts of the English parliamentary commissioners to prevent either the Scots or the Catholics or the royalists from gaining complete domination in Ulster complicated matters still further. The strategic importance of the area during this period was shown by Monro's determined attempt to seize Lisburn as soon as he had Belfast and his chagrin when he failed to overawe the parliamentary commander there.[10] No wonder George Benn in the 1870s declared it 'impossible to pursue the perplexing narrative which preceded the peace of 1646' (as the Cessation became).[11] A later and greater authority a century after Benn commented in similar vein that the political and military position in Ireland in the late 1640s quickly reached a state of confusion that defied accurate description. 'Almost every party in the kingdom was divided against itself, and local commanders changed sides according to their own judgement of the situation.'[12]

Sheer survival became a major aim. Seizing the means to keep his troops fed and paid regularly was an essential talent in any commander, more important than the elusive knock-out blow that might end the war. At Benburb in June 1646 O'Neill came nearer than anyone to that, prior to Cromwell, when Monro in one of his sweeping forays stumbled into the main Irish army and, tempted into attacking on ground not of his own choosing, only just escaped with his life, but lost half of his infantry, many of his cavalry, all his field guns, baggage and supplies as well as the thirty regimental colours that proclaimed the magnitude of the disaster.[13] The chastened Covenanter piously excused himself afterwards in suitably biblical terms:

'For aught I can understand, the Lord of Hosts had a controversie with us to rub shame in our faces … till humbled; for a greater confidence I never [did] see in any army than amongst us.'[14]

For whatever reason, instead of pursuing the fleeing Scots O'Neill led his own host south into Leinster where he became embroiled in a struggle for power among the leaders of the Catholic Confederation – a civil war within a civil war – and thus gave Monro some time to recover. The New Scots in Ulster were never again as strong as they had been, however, being hereafter outnumbered by the 'British' of various kinds who were anxious to be rid of them. The most important party in the Belfast area at this stage, once the Civil War in Great Britain was lost by King Charles, was the English parliament; the most important individual was Colonel George Monck (or Monk).[15] A pragmatic professional soldier, Monck had fought for the king until 1644, when he was captured and imprisoned. When released, he offered his services to parliament and in 1647 was appointed commander of the parliamentary troops in Ulster. In September 1648, he carried out a bloodless coup, seizing Carrickfergus (where he arrested Monro), Belfast and Coleraine.[16] Monro was sent to London, where parliament imprisoned him for the next five years.

For a short time a mixed force of 'royalists' which included some Presbyterians and even some Irish Catholics held Belfast, but when Cromwell landed in Ireland in 1649 and stormed Drogheda few dared thereafter to offer much resistance. When Colonel Robert Venables was sent north to subdue Ulster, Newry surrendered to him at once, Belfast after a token siege. In Belfast it was said, '800 Scots were afterwards turned out of the town, whither they had brought their wives and children to plant themselves there'.[17]

To sum up: although the New Scots thus ceased to be of any importance militarily, they left behind an indelible mark on the north of Ireland. Presbyterianism, which had become established under their influence or protection, not only survived, but if the number of clergy is any guide even thrived, despite the hostility of the Cromwellians: the two dozen ministers of 1653 had become nearly eighty within a few years.[18] A different religion, society and culture, neither English nor Irish, has remained a force to be reckoned with ever since. Belfast was fortunate to have survived so many potential disasters during these years. It is true that the cost of maintaining a permanent garrison, as reflected in the number and size of the assessments recorded in the Town Book, was a considerable burden, but on the whole the wealth generated by government contracts and by the constant presence of soldiers with money to spend brought more gain than loss. Also, the Cromwellian settlement of the 1650s encouraged the growth of commerce, both incidentally by the peace it imposed, and also specifically by abolishing or reducing some tariffs. By the end of the decade agriculture was getting back to normal and Belfast's trade had far outstripped that of Carrickfergus and included direct dealings with a number of European ports as well as those nearer home. A few of the smaller ships such as

HIGH STREET AND OLD MARKET HOUSE

High Street was the centre of Belfast administration and society for a significant part of its history. The centre later shifted toward Donegall Square, but only after a new river channel was dredged. The Market House with its tower and arches preceded the City Hall as the meeting place of the Belfast Corporation.

BELFAST CITY COUNCIL

gabarts, employed in the cross-channel trade with Great Britain and Scotland, were not only owned by local merchants but were also built at Belfast.[19]

Although there is no doubt that both the merchant community and the population as a whole grew fairly rapidly from the 1650s onward, it is difficult to estimate actual numbers. The evidence, which mainly consists of lists of citizens assessed for cess, poll tax and hearth money, is difficult to interpret.[20] Benn suggested a mid-century figure of about 1,000, rising to 2,000 by the mid-1680s. More recent analysis favours rather higher figures – at least 2,000 in 1660, 3,200 by 1670 and around 5,000 in 1706.[21] By 1706 Presbyterians alone numbered around 3,000. We know this because the existing meeting-house (though only ten or twelve years old) could no longer accommodate all the congregation; more than a hundred heads of families could not rent pews and a second meeting-house opened two years later.[22] Immigrants to Ulster from Scotland throughout most of this period were attracted to Belfast in particular firstly because the Chichesters were not unsympathetic to Calvinism and secondly because compared with the typical Scottish borough Belfast made entry and advancement easy for enterprising merchants and tradesmen. Besides, in practical terms they found that a single landlord who owned the freehold of the entire town was an advantage to newcomers when seeking leases and negotiating terms.[23] Furthermore the merchants as a community, whether Church of Ireland or Presbyterian, seemed to have good relations with each other, a state of affairs which even survived the testing events of the 1688 Revolution and the Jacobite war in Ireland (1689–91). Thanks to his viceroy, Richard Talbot, earl of Tirconnel, Ireland was the only one of his three kingdoms from which James could mount a recovery with the help of French troops supplied by Louis XIV. Tirconnel had filled the Irish army with Catholic officers and recruits and had also replaced the charters of most of the corporations by new ones in which Catholics and Protestant dissenters were the majority.[24]

In the case of Belfast, there were thirty-five members of the corporation instead of a dozen; eighteen were Catholic gentry (eight were O'Neills); none of them was resident, since there were no Catholic merchants in the town. All the burgesses were named in the new charter, which also appointed as sovereign a wealthy Presbyterian merchant and shipowner, Thomas Pottinger. The Chichesters were thus deprived of control over the choice of burgesses, and the lord of the castle and its constable ceased to be *ex officio* members.[25] Though this might have been expected to please some critics of the old regime who had failed in their attempt to have it reformed in 1671, the seeming liberality of the new arrangements was largely negated by the fact that members of the corporation could be removed at will by the government. A bill of attainder, passed by James's Irish parliament in 1689, named a list of prominent people who had declared for William and Mary (they included the third earl of Donegall and the minister of the Presbyterian congregation in Belfast) or had fled the country without leave on hearing that an army of occupation was approaching.[26] Those who did not submit themselves by a certain date were declared traitors and

BELFAST FROM THE SOUTH

View of Belfast (1805) from the banks of the Lagan by Thomas C. Thompson. Thompson's painting is a valuable record of the town, showing the wide, meandering Lagan and the Long Bridge with its twenty-one arches and Cavehill on the left.

had their property confiscated. The new sovereign sought to persuade the refugees to return, and appears to have been credited with preserving their property, so far as he could; little is known about the details of his administration, since the relevant pages of the Town Book (if any) do not survive. Fortunately, the Jacobite garrison, when it came, behaved well; and when William's General Frederick Schomberg landed nearby in August 1689 the Jacobite commander made no attempt to defend the crumbling old rampart, leaving the town intact. Schomberg at once restored the original charter.[27]

The Presbyterian congregation was itself divided in its views. Few of its members followed Pottinger's lead. At least, so it appeared later, when some of those named in the new charter claimed that their names had been 'made use of' without their knowledge and that they had never actually exercised the powers it bestowed.[28] Although Pottinger got some credit for having used his good offices to protect the property of those who had fled, he was evidently blamed by most of the merchant community for the role he had played. The Williamite government, less condemnatory, appointed him commissioner for prize vessels at Belfast, a post he held from 1691 to 1697. As one might expect in such circumstances, it was hard for people to act both honourably and consistently. Pottinger's brother Edward, for example who was also named as a burgess under the new charter, actually fought against the Jacobites and lost his life in 1690, when, as captain of HMS *Dartmouth*, he was drowned on active service off the coast of Scotland.[29]

By the turn of the century, the town at the mouth of the Lagan was still comparatively small in population and physical extent (though the rampart, which had contained all of it in 1642 – in effect the first 'stop line' – had been breached long before). Its trade and commerce, based upon the export of agricultural products and the import of luxury items, had grown enormously despite various disadvantages ranging from the statutory (the effect of the Navigation Acts which controlled Irish trade in the interests of England) and topographical (awkward landing and loading arrangements at Belfast harbour) to the financial (shortage of easily accessible credit and exchange facilities) and the administrative (limited powers of the corporation to raise money or take initiatives). Direct action by wealthy individuals supplemented the feeble efforts of the corporation in providing some essential public amenities, such as the water supply, funded in 1678–80 by Black George Macartney and Robert Leathes, both of whom were former sovereigns. So too was the other George Macartney, of Auchinleck, who made available premises in High Street for use as a court house.[30] In the early 1660s the Donegalls endowed a classical school, attached to the parish church in High Street. As well as Latin grammar for the sons of the local gentry it taught mathematics, trigonometry, astronomy, navigation and surveying – all of practical use to the sons of merchants.[31]

One measure of the growth of trade, and therefore of the wealth of the community, was the amount of shipping owned outright or in partnerships for individual voyages by the leading citizens (about 80 per cent of whom were merchants). Excluding the smallest vessels known as gabarts, in 1661 there were eighteen ships with a total tonnage of just under 1,000; in 1675 twenty-seven (tonnage 1,527); in the mid-1680s, sixty-seven vessels (tonnage 3,307). By any reckoning, the wealth of Belfast grew faster during those years than ever before.[32]

Reliable estimates of the wealth of the leading merchants are hard to come by. Some impression can be gained from surviving will documents, or from the size of the dowries mentioned in marriage contracts, but the multifarious nature of merchants' dealings, and the complicated networks of credit and debit in which their assets were invested, discourage guesswork. We do know, however, what some of the most successful invested in (as well as trade and ships), namely short-term loans of spare cash (which in Ireland commonly yielded interest of up to ten per cent a year); urban property (George Macartney of Auchinleck, with his four corn mills, and a number of houses is a good example); and, of course, land itself.[33]

Comparatively few of the wealthy Belfast merchants who acquired land retired from trade to live on their estates. One early exception was John Corry (ancestor of the earls of Belmore) who in 1656 bought the manor of Coole in County Fermanagh. Thomas Pottinger purchased a perpetual leasehold or fee farm of the townland of Ballymacarrett, which lay just across the Lagan in County Down, from Lord Clanbrassil in 1672 for £300 and an annual rent of £30.[34] Pottinger continued to trade and his investment turned out to be a good one when the Long Bridge was built in the 1680s. The outstanding example of merchant turned landowner in the late seventeenth century, however, was Thomas Knox (ancestor of the earls of Ranfurly), who bought his estate at Dungannon, County Tyrone in 1692 from the third earl of Donegall and settled there. More typical was William Crawford, who in the same year bought the manor of Florida in County Down but continued to live and work in Belfast.[35]

Some of those who acquired land by investing the profits of trade already had connections with the gentry families of Antrim and Down, most of whom like themselves were still presbyterians in the latter part of the seventeenth century. In the early years of the eighteenth, many conformed to the established church, as later generations distanced themselves from trade and became integrated with the ruling class. Both George Macartneys were from minor gentry families in Scotland, where many younger sons were launched as merchants. The most important late seventeenth-century merchant family in Belfast, in status as well as wealth, was that of Macartney of Auchinleck, who not only prospered financially but went on to confirm his rise in social status by marrying particularly well, registering his arms as a gentleman, and holding several important appointments.[36] Black George, his nearest rival, himself preferred to be called 'merchant' rather than 'esquire', though entitled to that dignity when simultaneously sovereign of Belfast and high sheriff of County Antrim in 1680: 'I intend to continue as I was and will be after,' he

'Belfast is a very handsome, thriving, well-peopled town; a great many new houses and good shops in it ...'

declared to a friend in Dublin.[37] Whether or not these men gentrified themselves, they tended to educate their sons for professions hitherto largely the preserve of the gentry – the law, the church, medicine, the army, Macartney of Auchinleck's eldest and youngest sons both trained as councillors (barristers) at inns of court in London; the first married a niece of the earl of Longford and became a judge, the younger married a well-dowered daughter of the lord chancellor of Ireland.[38] Black George's son George (c.1660–1730) rose to the rank of lieutenant-general in the British army and was commander-in-chief of the forces in Ireland in his later years.[39] The debt-laden earl of Donegall, another career soldier, but of more conventional background also became a general. In command of an army supporting the Habsburg claimant in the war of the Spanish Succession, he lost his life in the assault on Barcelona in April 1706.

Some of the strangers who visited Belfast in the late 1600s and early 1700s recorded their impressions of the place. The Frenchman de Rocheford, who was there in 1672, enthused: 'Here is a very fine Castle, and two or three large streets as in a new built town'. Another Frenchman, Gideon Bonnivert, a Huguenot passing through with William III's army in 1690, was even more polite, calling it a 'large and pretty town' in his journal. Bonnivert also remarked, curiously, that 'the inhabitants speak very good English' – perhaps he thought this odd when so many of them were apparently Scots. The Rev. George Story, one of William's army chaplains and author of one of the best contemporary accounts of the war in Ireland from a Williamite standpoint, was greatly impressed, describing Belfast as a 'very large town, and the greatest for trade in the north of Ireland'; he also remarked that the Long Bridge ('a very famous Stone Bridge') was not yet quite finished, because of the outbreak of the war. The local story later was that the passage of Schomberg's heavy cannon over it in 1689 had damaged the structure. William III's reported admiration for the gardens of the castle, where the Donegalls entertained him – 'a little Whitehall' – is well known. The Dublin scholar Molyneux, in his account of his visit to the north in 1708 wrote, 'Belfast is a very handsome, thriving, well-peopled town; a great many new houses and good shops in it.'[40] A few years earlier, Sacheverell had used similar terms – 'well built, full of people, and of great Trade' – but his impression that Belfast was at that time 'the second town in Ireland' was wide of the mark. (Cork's population in 1706 was more than 17,500, to Belfast's 5,000 or so.) Whatever the quality of these observations, it is at least clear that the town had come a long way since 1604.

MEMORIAL IN CARRICKFERGUS CHURCH

This tablet of white marble is surmounted by a coronet; on the tablet is an inscription to the memory of Arthur Chichester, third earl of Donegall, who was killed in Spain in 1706.

PHOTOGRAPH: CARNEGIE, 2009

A LONG MINORITY, 1706–1760

T HE THIRD EARL of Donegall, who succeeded his father in 1678, inherited along with the title a difficult financial situation. The second earl had challenged the validity of the will left by the first earl who, lacking male heirs, docked the entail and made lavish provision for his two daughters and other relatives. From 1678 the third earl was the chief plaintiff in this suit; the chief defendants were the elder daughter Lady Longford and her husband. Eventually in 1692 a settlement was reached whereby Donegall got most of the property but subject to a very heavy burden of debt. By a stroke of good luck for him Lady Longford died without issue in 1697 and her husband in 1700. The earl had been obliged to sell his Dungannon estate in 1692 in order to meet the immediate costs of the settlement.[1] Thereafter, desperation drove him to depend on borrowing by means of short-term loans carrying penalties of one hundred per cent for late repayment, or by selling cheap annuities, since the canny merchants of Belfast knew better than to lend him their money. Before departing for Spain to take up his new command, he drew up a will that was unduly optimistic about his finances. His death in 1706 at the age of forty left his widow with a large family of young children, the prospect of a long minority, and some looming problems. The most urgent of these was a crisis in relations between Belfast Castle and the town's corporation. Lady Donegall became the children's guardian, while the court of Chancery supervised the financial management. The documents generated by these arrangements provide us with some useful evidence about the estate and its problems in the early years of the eighteenth century.

CASTLE *VERSUS* CORPORATION

Though subject to occasional strains, relations between the Donegalls and the corporation were normally amicable so long as the third earl was in charge. His military duties often made him an absentee however, and though he appears to have kept in touch, by the time of his death in 1706 the situation had changed radically. The very prospect of a long minority seemed likely to weaken the management. At the same time the composition of the corporation was changing as younger and more active burgesses, most of them Presbyterians, found the status quo irksome. These men were unexpectedly disbarred in 1704 by the Irish parliament in Dublin unless they qualified themselves for office by taking communion in the Church of Ireland.[2] So no sooner had the Presbyterians of Belfast become dominant in the corporation than their hopes of exercising power were dashed. The sovereign at the time, David Butle (a presbyterian) resigned from the post immediately, but neither he nor the others affected gave up their seats on the corporation; instead, pending the outcome of a possible legal challenge, they took no active part in its affairs, attending but not voting. This manoeuvre was permitted by Butle's replacement, George Macartney, the youngest son of Macartney of Auchinleck, a barrister by profession, who was already sovereign-elect for the following year.[3] The death of one of the town's MPs in 1707 created an opportunity for Macartney with the help of his brother James, a judge, to challenge the Castle by engineering the election of an English Presbyterian named Ogle instead of the candidate approved by the Donegalls. At the election meeting, when each man got three of the votes cast, the sovereign gave a second, casting vote and declared Ogle duly elected.[4] Having failed to get the better of Macartney in the corporation, Lady Donegall got up a petition to the Irish House of Commons, accusing the sovereign of 'unwarrantable and illegal practices', while her defeated nominee sought to reverse the outcome of the election. After a lengthy grilling, in which he gave a very good account of himself, and threats of violence among rival groups of supporters in the public galleries, Macartney was judged not to have been responsible for the illegalities complained of and was completely exonerated. The validity of Ogle's election was also confirmed.[5] However, parliament declared at the same time that any burgess who failed to take the religious test must resign at once. The remaining presbyterians in Belfast then resigned and in due course the Donegalls regained control of the corporation by filling the vacancies with their preferred candidates. Both of the Macartneys (who were Church of Ireland) remained burgesses; George even remained an MP for Belfast. When he died in 1757 he had been a burgess for 55 years and an MP for more than 40. But neither of the two Macartneys was ever again chosen as sovereign.[6]

Discontent rumbled on for a while. In 1709 the disagreement was over the right to levy and collect tolls from shipping to keep the quay in good repair and the channel clear. When the corporation promoted a bill in Parliament for this purpose, however, the trustees countered by suggesting that a short list of three should be drawn up from which the lord of the castle would select a collector of 'Keyage'. The corporation's reply was sharply worded: 'The naming of three to be collectors will be like the naming of three to be Sovereign. The Lord of the Castle puts a mark upon the one he would have chosen Sovereign and whoever votes for any other is ill looked upon by the Castle. This we have found by experience'. Furthermore, it continued, 'The cause of the present misunderstanding between the Castle and the

Town is because the Town would not consent to give up the entire management of the Corporation in making burgesses, choosing a Sovereign and electing such persons to parliament as were recommended to them by the Castle.'[7] In the end, pressure from the trustees led to the withdrawal of the bill; harbour improvements came about years later through the private initiative of another Macartney, Isaac (a son of the original 'Black George') who built two new quays and persuaded the

THE CUSTOM HOUSE

This is the finest neo-classical building in the city. It was designed by the English architect Sir Charles Lanyon in 1856/57 in the High Italian Renaissance or 'Palazzo' style. On the side facing the river are carved angels and classical deities representing Manufacture, Commerce, Industry and Peace, while the central figures in the pediment are Britannia, Neptune and Mercury. This elegant building conveys the prosperity of the British Empire under Victoria and the commercial success of Belfast as it expanded rapidly in the nineteenth century. Most architectural historians regard this building as Lanyon's masterpiece. It was used for a number of official purposes. The detail (*left*) shows one of the numbered windows on the ground floor. Lanyon also designed Crumlin Road gaol, Queen's University and the Sinclair Seaman's Presbyterian Church.

PHOTOGRAPHS: CARNEGIE, 2009

revenue authorities to move the Custom House to the same quarter.[8] In 1711 there was another election petition which was quashed by the Castle. The last twitch of life from the defeated reformers came at the general election in 1713 when yet another Castle nominee was the target of a petition. Almost everything about this episode was obscure, from the candidate himself – an exceedingly dim Tory squire from King's County – to the nature of the objection raised by his critics and again promptly neutralised by his patron.[9]

There is no doubt that the Macartneys were a real threat to Donegall's control of political power in Belfast at the time. This is how contemporaries saw it too. An account of the hearing of the petition on 24 October, written by Robert Johnson, baron of the exchequer, for the duke of Ormonde described his fellow judge, James Macartney as 'one of the three electors of Ogle, the chief manager for him, who together with his brother, the sovereign, do set up to have the great power over the corporation, to the prejudice of the Countess Dowager and the young Earl.' To conservative minds their actions were all the more reprehensible because, as Johnson went on to observe, the Macartneys had been 'raised by a dependence and by a favour of that family [i.e. the Chichesters].'[10] Had they succeeded, the reformers might have altered the history of Belfast significantly.

Religion

During the reign of Queen Anne (1702–14) Belfast became the cockpit of fierce religious and political controversy between Church of Ireland and Presbyterian clergy and citizens. The leading adherents of both sides volleyed and thundered in pulpit and pamphlet. The Presbyterian ammunition came at first from Scotland, but after 1696, when James Blow set up the town's first printing press, similar controversialist works were also published locally. The High Church vicar of Belfast, William Tisdall, harried the Presbyterian minister, John McBride so mercilessly that he was forced to seek safety in Scotland on two occasions.[11] In the event, Tisdall was thwarted because his bigoted views were detested by most citizens, including members of his own church. For example, in 1713 eighty Anglican merchants publicly testified to the honesty and fair dealing of their Presbyterian fellow traders when the latter were attacked in public; and McBride received warning of attempts to arrest him. The death of Queen Anne the following year and the succession of George I in time brought some relief to the Presbyterians. The Test Act of 1704 nevertheless remained on the statute book (if not always enforced) until 1780. Isaac Macartney's reported joy at hearing the news of the Queen's death – he is said to have capered in the street in his nightgown crying 'Queen Anne is dead' – heralded a false dawn.[12]

As for Catholics, they were scarcely visible at all. When fears of a French invasion alarmed the government in Dublin in 1708 to the point of ordering the local authorities to make a count, in Belfast the estimate for the town was not more than seven, and only 150 in the whole barony. Throughout the greater part of the eighteenth century in and around Belfast, the religious divide that mattered was between Episcopalians and Dissenters, rather than between Protestants and Catholics.[13]

Some echoes of the struggle between the Donegalls and their ambitious tenants in Belfast may be found in the minority accounts, particularly in the form of moneys paid out in lawyers' fees and in travel expenses claimed by agents and officials of the estate. No expense was spared in preparing the parliamentary petitions. The solicitor-general himself, Sir Richard Levinge, was consulted in 1707 for his opinion on the powers conferred by the town's charter, and on whether as a minor Lord Donegall might nevertheless claim a burgess vote.[14]

Other items in the minority accounts refer to the great fire which completely gutted Belfast Castle in 1708, killing three of Lady Donegall's younger daughters and a servant girl. Some of the contents of the house were saved, but by the time the citizens had roused themselves from sleep and had managed to get over the high boundary wall, the main building had gone. Lady Donegall hoped to rebuild but could neither afford to do so at her son's expense nor persuade the government (immersed in a very costly war with France) to fund the work; the desirability of creating a strongly fortified Belfast and downgrading Carrickfergus had evidently faded since Thomas Phillips's plan of 1685.[15]

The urgent need for suitable accommodation for the sadly diminished household was evidently met by moving to Carrickfergus, where Joymount, the great mansion built by Sir Arthur Chichester, lay empty. The relevant entries in the minority accounts are at first sight puzzling. Nowhere is Joymount mentioned by that name, but what is called 'Carrickfergus Castle' must nevertheless be Joymount rather than the royal castle on the rock. 'Repair of the Castle in 1708', the first of numerous sums, cost £28 3s. 10½d. 'Harth money' was assessed at £2 14s. od. Regular bills for 'fireing' the rooms indicate active occupancy over the next seven or eight years.[16] By the end of Donegall's minority, however, if not before, he and his mother had departed to England. So far as we know, neither of them ever set foot in the north of Ireland again

The accounts show that some surviving outbuildings attached to the castle at Belfast were adapted as estate offices. The hearth money assessment on these was eighteen shillings, as compared with £5 10s. od. for the building destroyed. Any material that could be reused, such as bricks and quantities of roofing lead which had melted in the fire and had been 'gathered from the rubbish' of the Castle, were salvaged and sold. The damaged boundary wall was pulled down and where necessary rebuilt, and the view of it as seen from the street was improved by rows of trees planted in boxes. Apart from such minor things, little or no development of the Castle site took place until the late eighteenth century. Lastly, we learn that the work of the estate office was hampered for some time by the large number of leases destroyed or damaged in the fire: one lawyer was paid the substantial sum of £22 for engrossing 153 new ones, not counting the cost of parchment.[17]

The fourth earl's attainment of legal manhood in 1716 increased rather than diminished the anxieties of the people hitherto responsible for him, chief of whom was his mother. The greatest threat was that the new owner's youth, weakness of intellect and want of judgment would make him easy prey for bad companions; worst of all, he might be inveigled into an unsuitable marriage. His social career seems to have begun at an early age, nominally at least, for payments of arrears of pay as an ensign in the Guards amounting to £94, due to him at the end of 1715, are noted in the accounts.[18]

As soon as he came of age the fourth earl was married off to a bride his mother had chosen for him – one, it was unkindly said, who was his equal in intelligence and common sense. As a later agent of the family was to explain, the dowager countess 'knowing the oddity of her son's character was desirous as soon as he became of competent age to have him marry and his estate settled in the strictest manner to avoid the injuries that the Family might receive by his Lordship being imposed on'. Accordingly 'Her Ladyship in the year 1716 had his Lordship married to Lady Lucy Ridgeway, daughter to the then late earl of Londonderry'.[19] Under the terms of a post-nuptial settlement, the estates were vested in three trustees for the use of the earl during his life and thereafter to his sons. In the absence of such issue the property was to pass to his brother John and his sons. In order to prevent the break-up of the inheritance, Donegall was forbidden to sell any of it, whilst his leasing powers were restricted to a maximum of forty-one years. Rents were to be set at the full annual value; 'fines', lump sums in cash, were not to be taken in part-payment, lest debts should accumulate.[20]

All three of the trustees were relations of Donegall. The earl of Barrymore and Viscount Masserene were husbands of his sisters, the third, Richard Rooth, 'gentleman and merchant of the City of London' – was the second husband of the second earl of Donegall's widow, who had a life interest in the estate at Dunbrody in County Wexford that came into the hands of the Donegalls through her marriage. Rooth held a mortgage on Dunbrody.

Management of a great estate by trustees was seldom an easy business. In the case of Donegall the weakness and vacillation of the nominal owner soon led to divided counsels and contradictory policies. The dowager countess, with whom the fourth earl and his wife appear to have begun their married life, was unable to prevent his exploitation by a plausible rogue named Thomas Vigors, who persuaded him to leave home and to give control of his affairs to himself. Under Vigors' tutelage, as leases fell in they were renewed at rents well below current value in return for cash payments which Vigors then misappropriated. Along with others he then proceeded to get his hapless employer's signature to fraudulent contracts for huge amounts. By

1720, when nemesis at last caught up with him, he claimed to be entitled to no less than £60,000. The strength of his case may best be judged by the fact that in the end he agreed to hand over to the trustees all the deeds, mortgages etc. relating to the estate and all other securities given by Donegall to Vigors or to anyone else in trust or in partnership with Vigors in return for the comparatively modest sum of £1,380 (made more modest still by being in Irish currency).[21]

One matter not included in the settlement was a group of debts totalling £4,000 arranged by Vigors and others in a complicated series of moves by which Thomas Vesey, bishop of Ossory, acquired the manor of Abbey Leix in Queen's County (Leix). One of the securities listed in Lucy Ridgeway's dowry, this estate was acquired by the Vesey family and lost to the Donegalls. Sir Thomas Vesey, the Anglican bishop of Ossory, paid a rent of £100 a year to the dowager Lady Londonderry, who was the owner of the long leasehold (the residue of a 95 year term) during her life. Vesey was determined to buy her out and, it was alleged,

THE FIRST PRESBYTERIAN CHURCH

The first congregation was recorded in 1644. The present building dates from 1783. Its attractive boat-shaped interior with handsome dark wood panelling was originally a complete oval.

PHOTOGRAPH: CARNEGIE, 2009

achieved his aim by subterfuge and fraud. In the course of a lawsuit which lasted for more than half a century and ended in the House of Lords, Donegall's advisors produced the following indictment:

> All the said deeds were obtained from the said earl without the consent or privity of the late Countess of Londonderry, or any of the trustees named in the said Earl's Marriage-Articles, or any Friend of the said Earl's and without having been perused by any Counsel on the said Earl's behalf, and Counterparts of the said deeds, or any copies of them, were ever delivered to the said Earl, or to any person for his use.[22]

The bishop of Ossory always maintained that he had actually paid the money he said he had. He stopped paying his rent when Lady Londonderry died in 1724. In the end, whatever the truth may have been (and despite the plausibility of the plaintiff's case), the appeal to the lords in 1769 failed on the ground of long possession. The lapses during which the Donegall case was allowed to sink out of sight because of the fourth earl's inability to direct his affairs and the indolence or ill-will of his trustees to supply that lack, proved fatal to success.

During the 1720s, the earl and countess lived at Broomfield, near Chelmsford in Essex. The dowager countess lived at Abinger in Surrey.[23] When the younger woman died suddenly in 1732, Donegall went back to living with his mother. There were no children of the marriage, so his heir was the elder of the two sons of his brother

John. John Chichester's wife was the eldest daughter of Sir Richard Newdigate, baronet, of Arbury in Warwickshire. The trustees appointed by Chichester included his brother-in-law Sir Roger Newdigate. According to William Macartney, who was appointed agent for the Irish estates in the mid-1740s, it was well known that, following a dispute between Lord Barrymore and his fellow trustee Richard Rooth, Rooth withdrew his co-operation. This left Barrymore in a position to do much as he liked with the estate, underletting in return for cash and becoming indebted to Donegall for a sum of £20,000. Once in control of her elder son again, Lady Donegall demanded that Barrymore's accounts should be audited and no more leases granted without the express consent of Donegall (in effect herself) and her other son. Before her plans could mature, however, she died suddenly in June 1743. For the next three years Donegall lived with his brother, until he too died, then lodged with Mrs Chichester. Meanwhile, one John Ludford, husband of a younger daughter of Sir Richard Newdigate, had gained the confidence of Chichester to such an extent that when the two boys were orphaned by the death of their mother in 1748 Ludford was able to claim guardianship. At the same time he took Donegall to lodge in his own home on advantageous terms; these included a large indemnity, lest the poor man might be enticed away 'by any of his relations ... who might get his lordship clandestinely married for their own private ends'.[24] One such party was his sister Ann, dowager Lady Barrymore, and her son Richard Barry. When an attempt to have custody of the earl transferred to themselves in 1748 failed, they then applied to the lord chancellor to have him declared a lunatic. At the hearing in March 1750, Donegall 'answered the lord chancellor's questions rationally and politely but could not take 60 out of 100 and tell how many remained, but was able to take 7 from 10 and tell that 3 remained'. William Macartney, the author of these words, also said that though the earl was taught Latin, Greek and French he could never be taught even common addition.[25] The application for a commission in lunacy failed, with much acrimony between the Barrymores and Ludford. The boys' uncle Newdigate petitioned against an arrangement to share responsibility. Custody of Donegall was finally given to Lady Barrymore, and he lived his remaining years in her house in Cheshire. Barry and Ludford promoted an application for a private Act of Parliament in 1752, in order to enable the trustees[26] to grant leases in Belfast with terms of up to 99 years. The preamble to the Bill explained that as 'most of the leases granted by the ancestors of the said earl are now nearing expiry the Houses have been suffered to go out of repair, and are so very old, ruinous and unfit for habitation that it is become necessary for the Preservation and Support for the Trade of the Town and for preventing the inhabitants from quitting and deserting the same, that the said Houses should be rebuilt ...'[27]

In a letter to Ludford from another interested party, Donegall's cousin, Lord Masserene, the same point was made, and more pointedly: 'I live in the neighbourhood of Belfast, and know it to be in a ruinous condition, [and that it] will lose its Trade and inhabitants if it is not speedily supported by proper Tenures.'[28] Such talk was not simply scaremongering; the town languished, or at least developed more slowly and to a lesser extent than it might otherwise have done, not just because of the effects of Donegall's incapacity in itself, but because he lived so long. Meanwhile, other, smaller places, such as Lisburn and Newry began to rival or outstrip Belfast, particularly with the growth of the domestic linen manufacture and trade in the mid-century. Even in the 1720s, Robert Green, the agent in charge of Belfast, was pleading with the only effective trustee at the time, Lord Barrymore, to do all in his power to prevent the town from going to ruin. Early in 1725, for instance, he wrote '… the Merchants are dayly with me desiring to putt yr lordship in mind of doing something to preserve if not to increase ye remains of their declining trade which cannot be without great encouragement to build conveniences for trade and to preserve what's already built …'[29] Green reported great complaints about the way the manorial courts were managed, and complained bitterly himself about the high-handed behaviour of the seneschal Banks (who was soon to replace him). In February 1725 Green wrote again to say: 'I have oft writ that the trade of this place decays, the inhabitants are moving hence to Dublin and elsewhere, and have earnestly recommended ye procuring an Act for setting long leases or for lives renewable, that would encourage to build and repair what's most ruinous …'[30] Green was perhaps ahead of his time in recommending substantial investment in setting up a woollen manufacture and providing houses for the families of the workmen and artificers who, if the scheme succeeded, would keep a lot of money in the town' which is now annually laid out in Dublin …'; he offered to subscribe £500 himself. More than a year later, Green was still hoping that the parties concerned might agree to 'get an act for raising rents and money by setting leases'.[31] If the situation was bad in the 1720s it must have been far worse in the 1750s.

Despite the particular obstacles to economic progress that were evident in Belfast throughout the 'long minority' of the fourth earl of Donegall, there was some growth nevertheless. A market in brown unbleached linen developed from about 1720 with some encouragement from the Castle. The preamble to the Bill of 1752 gave 'the considerable trade and commerce' in the linen manufacture that had been carried on in and about the town as the chief reason for the increase in its population (to about 8,500 by 1760). The chief obstacle, it was said, was that the earl of Donegall was 'only tenant for life of the town and estate,' was 'advanced in years, very infirm, and much incumbered with debts and utterly incapable to undertake the rebuilding of the town at his own expense.'[32] A private Act obtained in 1729 to improve the harbour facilities and thus to encourage trade was expensive yet ineffectual, and the town's share in the growth of the linen trade, though not insignificant, was modest enough by comparison with the success of smaller but better administered towns in what became known as 'the linen triangle'. Though said in 1764 to have greatly increased, the average weekly sales of brown linen at Belfast were only half those of Lisburn or

Lurgan and equal to those of Ballymena or Newry. Newry in particular threatened to oust Belfast during the last twenty years as the chief Ulster port when the canal between Newry and Lough Neagh was cut between 1731 and 1742, and a ship canal completed below the town in 1769.[33] Individual Belfast merchants were still able to make fortunes by trade but in the 1720s even the most enterprising of them, such as Isaac Macartney (c.1670–1738) saw some ventures fail. One cargo shipped from Belfast in increasingly large quantities from the early years of the century onward consisted of emigrants to the American colonies.[34] The number of houses in the town in the middle years actually declined. The powers acquired by the trustees under the Act of 1752 were used to some effect in the 1750s when a start was made by replacing old leases with new ones with longer terms up to 99 years or three named lives, in most cases requiring tenants to rebuild or repair decayed properties. Also, several new streets were planned – if only partly constructed – during the years 1754–56. As it happens, none of the counterpart leases surviving from those years has anything like the permitted maximum term.[35] This may suggest that after forty years' experience of a landlord who was both incompetent and invisible and whose agents and trustees disagreed so vehemently among themselves, the substantial citizens were understandably cautious about investing in the future of the Donegall family.

FISHERWICK PARK

Fisherwick Park and demesne in Staffordshire, purchased by the fifth earl of Donegall as his chief residence and transformed by Lancelot 'Capability' Brown. Donegall bequeathed it to his second son, but it was heavily mortgaged and Spencer Chichester could not afford to keep it up. It was sold in lots at auction in 1808 and completely broken up.

Earlier, Isaac Macartney had done well by building the new quays on reclaimed land and new houses in Brunswick Street, making a clear profit of £400 a year in the 1720s;[36] his failure in the end was due more to his involvement in the debts of his brother-in-law than to commercial incompetence. And the capital with which Mussenden's Bank – the first in Belfast – was set up in 1752 was also acquired in what was generally a period of economic difficulty for many people, as evidenced by the distress of the ever-increasing number of paupers that led a committee of concerned citizens to establish the Charitable Society in the same year.[37] In 1756 there were serious food riots in the town, caused by a poor grain harvest.

The veteran MP George Macartney, reported ugly scenes – hungry people with neither food nor the money to buy any when it could be found, roaming the streets, seizing meal and making shopkeepers sell bread at less than the market price. 'All Order and Government here are now at an end,' he wrote on 22 July. Nobody would bring meal to the market till their property was safe, which was impossible to guarantee 'while the Mobb commands as is the present case, for no Justice dare issue a warrant against one of them'.[38] He tried to censor the *Belfast News-Letter*, which had expressed sympathy for the rioters. More disturbances followed in August, when a grain store was looted and the owner, a woman, was ducked in the Mill Dam. The merchants at first reacted by trying to arrest the ringleaders, but after a town meeting a relief scheme was agreed which sanctioned the collection of a special emergency rate.

The new Poor House, though keen to reach a long-term answer to the chronic problem, did not open its doors until 1774.[39] The young lord had to bide his time before putting his plans into action, but he did not waste it, for a preliminary step in the shape of a manuscript sketch entitled 'Plan of the Town of Belfast' is dated 1757.[40] The likelihood is that the anonymous surveyor was an Englishman, unfamiliar with local names and local speech. At any rate, what he heard and recorded as 'Wern Street' was Waring Street; the clipped vowel as characteristic then as now. Whether or not the Plan was commissioned by Donegall after his uncle's death or by the trustees in anticipation of a renewed outbreak of leasing is of no importance, but it may be worth noting here that it was the fifth earl's usual practice when carrying out major improvements on his Irish estates to employ reputable people with whose work in England he was familiar.

CHAPTER FIVE

ARCHITECTS AND AGITATORS:
BELFAST, 1760–1800

ARTHUR CHICHESTER, fifth earl and (from 1791) first marquess of Donegall, was born in England in 1739 and was educated at Eton College and at Trinity College, Oxford. Unlike many noble undergraduates with great expectations he took his studies seriously; at any rate, he graduated MA in 1759 and was awarded the DCL degree four years later. A cultivated Belfast physician, Dr Alexander Haliday, described his new landlord as 'a serious well disposed nobleman'. With this background, and a tradition of absentee ownership, he never contemplated living on his Irish estates; quite the contrary in fact, for his first independent action when he came of age was to buy a place of his own in Staffordshire.[1] Fisherwick Hall was an old Tudor hunting lodge – rather modest and unfashionable in style for such a fashionable young owner but not too dear, for the vendor was content to let two-thirds of the purchase price remain unpaid, on the security of a mortgage for £20,000. As for modesty, Donegall evidently had faith in his own ideas of good taste and could see the capabilities of the place. In due course, after his marriage to the daughter of a (Scottish) duke, Donegall engaged Lancelot 'Capability' Brown himself to design and construct a Palladian mansion in a landscaped park of 400 acres. The main work was finished in 1774 (the date on the pediment of the huge Corinthian portico). Further work was done later, however. Even then, it was said, only half of the original plan was executed.[2]

Described as 'the epitome of Georgian elegance', Fisherwick was made of the finest materials and planned on a generous scale. Its interiors were the work of the leading decorative artists of the time, its libraries stocked with the 'finest editions of the most eminent ancient and modern authors'. Among the cultural objects on display were a virginal once owned by Queen Elizabeth, as well as fashionable cabinets of natural history specimens. As Dr Haliday condescendingly remarked in 1788, the owner had 'expended £20,000 on books not yet opened, and £10,000 on shells not yet unpacked'.[3] The cost of supporting such an expensive lifestyle was very great. The rental of the Fisherwick estate itself did not cover even the interest on the mortgage. Yet the lender, Samuel Egerton of Tatton Park, Chester, did not hesitate

BELFAST FROM THE SOUTH, 1770S

View of Belfast from the south, c.1772, by Jonathan Fisher. In the foreground the meandering river Blackstaff makes its way into the Lagan upstream from the Long Bridge. To the left are the Cromac Woods and, in the background, is the Cave Hill.

© ULSTER MUSEUM, 2008

to lend more when required; the total sum rose at one point to £40,000. In other words, Donegall's credit was excellent, but his cash flow was a problem.[4]

Though Donegall was anxious to replace the old leases, as they expired, with new ones at greatly increased rents, he was also determined to reform the way his property was run. For years, hand-to-mouth renewals of old low-rent leases had widened the gap between potential and actual yields; the main beneficiaries were middlemen (who sublet at a profit rent to under-tenants), not the landowner. On his first visit to Belfast, in 1765, Donegall let it be known that he intended to re-lease his estate, starting with the town itself where most of the leases had already expired or would soon run out. It took two years for James Crow, a reputable English land surveyor with an address in London, to complete his measuring and mapwork and for new rents and covenants to be agreed. The outcome, in 1767, was in effect the blueprint for a new, 'Georgian' Belfast.[5]

By good fortune, the estate papers now in the Public Record Office in Belfast include counterpart copies of most of the new leases – 258 of them, all dated

1767 and all for a term of ninety-nine years or the lives of three named persons (Donegall himself, his wife and his brother). They can be divided into four different kinds. The first simply renewed an existing lease that had run out, with covenants for keeping the premises in good repair and, usually, paying a somewhat higher rent. The second was a full repairing lease, with appropriate adjustment of the rent where necessary. The third – a full building lease requiring the demolition of existing buildings on the site and the erection of new ones within agreed time limits – covered a range of buildings whose differing size and quality reflected current ideas about uniformity of street frontage and so on. In Castle Place, for example, new houses had to be twenty-eight feet high, of brick and stone and lime, all front windows sash rather than casement style, walls to be at least fourteen inches thick, timber to be good oak or fir. The roadway in front of these houses was to be paved and kept clear of 'ashes, dung,, filth or dirt'. Nearby in High Street the standard height was twenty-five feet; in Ann Street it was eighteen; workmen's cabins on Peter's Hill were only ten feet high, and thatched rather than slated. Fourth and last were leases of ground never before built upon, some of which consisted of gaps in streets planned earlier but not completed, such as Donegall Street and what is at present called the Cathedral Quarter, now undergoing its latest transformation. The determination to have a decent uniformity even in streets of the humbler sort was helped by the fact that the tenant of some extensive tracts of this new land, Roger Mulholland, was also both the developer and himself an architect whose work Donegall evidently admired.[6]

left
ARTHUR CHICHESTER, FIRST MARQUIS OF DONEGALL

Portrait of the fifth earl and first marquis of Donegall by Thomas Gainsborough. The *Belfast News Letter* in January 1799 printed an obituary for the first marquess: 'Though an absentee from this country he evinced his attachment to it by a liberal expenditure of large sums for the advancement of the community. In the course of a few years he laid out above £60,000 in the Lagan Navigation and the Public Building in the town.'
© ULSTER MUSEUM, 2008

The timing of what was in other respects a careful, well-planned operation turned out to be rather unfortunate, however. Throughout the eighteenth century there was growing criticism in Ireland of absentee owners of Irish land who chose to live abroad and spend most of their money outside the kingdom. Public criticism was given impetus by the publication in 1729 of a list of the chief offenders and the estimated sums each was thought to be responsible for.[7] The total in that year,

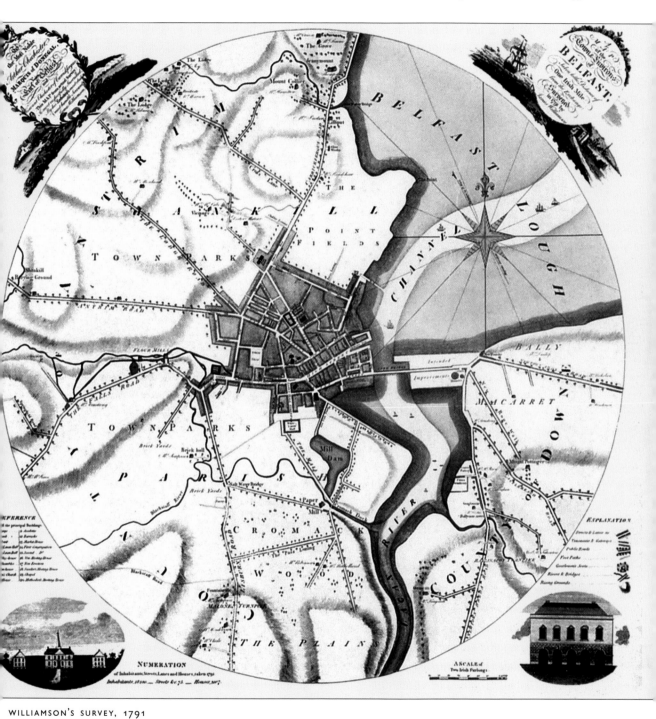

WILLIAMSON'S SURVEY, 1791

Williamson's highly decorative survey of 1791 was drawn with the corners marked by his dedication to Donegall and illustrations of some of the buildings he gave to the town.

THE TOP OF
DONEGALL STREET

In 1774 the 5th earl of
Donegall contributed
the land for the building
of Donegall Street. This
picture shows St Anne's
parish church, the focal
point for the street and
now at the heart of the
Cathedral Quarter.

BY KIND PERMISSION OF THE LINEN HALL
LIBRARY

£600,000, had doubled by the 1780s and a 'Patriot' party in the Dublin parliament was making serious efforts to impose a special absentee tax. As the greatest of the detested species, and the least penitent, Donegall drew particular odium on himself when the releasing of his agricultural holdings in County Antrim, close to Belfast, set off a rural insurrection so serious that the areas affected were rendered virtually ungovernable for more than two years in 1770–72. The agitators, who called themselves the Steelboys or Hearts of Steel, were bold enough at one point to invade Belfast, burn the homes of a couple of rich middlemen who were accused of having taken leases over the heads of the occupying tenants, and – despite the presence of a garrison – force the authorities to release one of their leaders who had been arrested.[8] Contemporary observers ranging from a former lord lieutenant and the liberal newspapers in Dublin to John Wesley (on his last visit to Belfast) gave Donegall a very bad press. In England one prominent political figure even called for him to be expelled from his seat in the Commons at Westminster.[9] Arthur Young, the noted agriculturalist and traveller, was almost alone among contemporaries in doubting Donegall's guilt; and Young's opinion, though weighty, made little difference at the time, and was little regarded by historians later. In 1790 the great absentee was publicly accused of 'draining a manufacturing country ... of £36,000 a year' and of having 'raised fines sufficient to impoverish a province and transported them out of the kingdom to build palaces in another land, where he is unknown or disregarded ...'[10]

The demonisation of Donegall, recent research suggests, was largely unjustified.

right
MARKET HOUSE

In 1769, to mark the
birth of his son and
heir, Lord Donegall
presented to the
town the arcaded
Market House, fitted
out with stalls to
accommodate traders.
For fifty years it was
the gathering place for
local merchants but in
1820 the Commercial
Buildings were erected
nearby in Waring Street
and the Exchange was
thereafter converted
into shops. This
utilitarian building was
greatly improved in
1776, when a second
storey was added to
house stylish Assembly
Rooms to the design
of Sir Robert Taylor,
a leading London
architect, as an upper
storey of the Market
House.

BY KIND PERMISSION OF THE LINEN HALL
LIBRARY

WHITE LINEN HALL

The White Linen Hall was built in 1783, paid for by public subscription. It was used as the venue for the white (i.e. bleached) linen trade and other purposes. The success of the building helped to make Belfast the centre of the linen trade, outstripping all rivals. The old building was demolished and replaced in 1906 by the present City Hall.

The scale of his reorganisation, however, was both alarming in itself and at the same time gave opportunity for agitators to organise opposition. When things had settled down, it could be seen that most of his own tenants had survived all right. A reviving economy and a run of better harvests brought growing prosperity to Belfast in the 1780s and early 1790s. The availability of work in the town brought a rapid rise in population, from 13,500 in 1782 to 19,500 in 1791.[11]

Though seldom seen by the citizens of Belfast, Donegall invested considerable sums in improving the amenities of the town. In 1769 a new single-storey arcaded market house was built entirely at his expense to mark the birth of a son after four daughters. This useful building was greatly improved a few years later by the addition of a second storey, designed by Sir Robert Taylor, Architect of the King's Works, and housing 'very spacious and elegant' Assembly Rooms. The second major gift to the town was a new parish church, St Anne's in Donegall Street, which was designed by a Warwickshire architect named Hiorne or Irons; Roger Mulholland, 'carpenter' as he was described at this stage in his career, was Hiorne's assistant. Other benefactions included the sites of the new Poor House in Donegall Street and the new White Linen Hall (where the City Hall now is). The construction costs in both cases, however, were met by public subscription – £17,000 was raised for the Linen Hall. From the 1780s fine houses were built in Linen Hall Street (now Donegall Place), a street of town houses laid out in the gardens of the old castle. One in particular was said by a knowledgeable visitor, to be 'equal to many in Grosvenor Square' in London. A more ambitious scheme, featuring an ornamental canal around the Linen Hall, never materialised, but Donegall did complete at his own expense a real canal, the last stretch of the Lagan Navigation which ran from Belfast to Lough Neagh. Its construction facilitated the transport of linen from the bleach greens of the Lagan Valley and Lough Neagh basin to Belfast and thus helped to make the town the centre

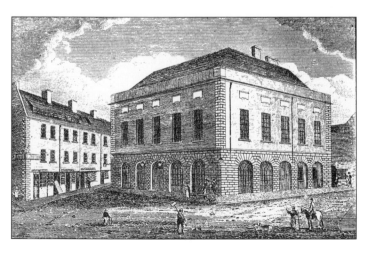

of the northern trade in fine linen. Donegall's purchase, in 1787, of the townland of Ballymacarrett, across the Lagan at the other end of the Long Bridge, had been prompted at the time by his determination to prevent the development of a rival town. Thereafter, let to Thomas Greg, Ballymacarrett became an industrial suburb – with glassworks, a foundry, ropeworks, vitriol works – economically part of Belfast but outside the town boundary until the 1850s. In 1799 it ceased to be part of the main Chichester estate however, passing on Donegall's death to his younger son along with the property in Wexford and the great house at Fisherwick.[12]

The Lagan Canal apart, Donegall's interest in improving the appearance and amenities of his town was essentially a larger-scale version of the urge many great landowners exhibited in making their estate villages a credit to their own good taste. A stronger and more representative corporation in Belfast might have undertaken necessary public projects, but in this respect things had got worse rather than better since the defeat of the Macartneys. Following the outcome of a lawsuit concerning the borough of Newtownards, an Act of Parliament declared the election of non-resident burgesses legal. By the end of the century more than half of the members of Belfast Corporation were non-resident Anglican gentry with little personal involvement in the business life of the town and no desire to take initiatives.[13] The vacuum left by the comatose corporation was increasingly filled by self-help committees of citizens, a typically Presbyterian way of doing things. It was such groups, drawn largely from the same individuals, that built and ran the Poor House, started a dispensary for the sick poor and a

WHITE LINEN HALL

This painting by Carey shows the handsome railing surrounding the hall. The area between the railing and the building was planted, and afforded 'a most agreeable promenade for the inhabitants at all seasons'. A cupola, possibly of wood, with clock and weathervane, was added in 1815.
BELFAST CITY COUNCIL

left
ASSEMBLY ROOMS

This engraving of the interior of the Assembly Rooms was done by Thomas Malton of Dublin. During the late eighteenth and early nineteenth centuries the elegant Assembly Rooms were the main venue for balls, card games, art exhibitions and meetings of various kinds. In 1846 the building became the headquarters of the Belfast Bank.
© ULSTER MUSEUM, 2008

lying-in hospital, undertook to supply the town with water, founded a Chamber of Commerce (one of the earliest), built and administered the White Linen Hall and established the Belfast Academy; the Academy was intended to become a college of higher education as well as a school.[14]

The Chamber's inaugural meeting in October 1783, chaired by Thomas Greg, elected Waddell Cunningham as its first president. Both men had made large fortunes as partners in trading out of New York with the French and Dutch settlements in the West Indies, even during the Seven Years War when penalties for smuggling were severe. Greg and Cunningham retired to Belfast and became involved in a wide variety of enterprises. One of these was the cattle trade, hence the hostility of the Steelboys in 1772.[15]

The Chamber of Commerce, in turn, took the initiative in trying to improve the harbour facilities at Belfast, petitioning the Irish parliament for £2,000 towards the cost of cutting a straight channel from the quays (at low tide these dried up

BELFAST FROM THE SOUTH

View of Belfast from the south, showing the spire of St Anne's church and (*left*) the back of the White Linen Hall which at that time was on the very edge of the town.

JOHN NIXON WATERCOLOUR. © ULSTER MUSEUM, 2008

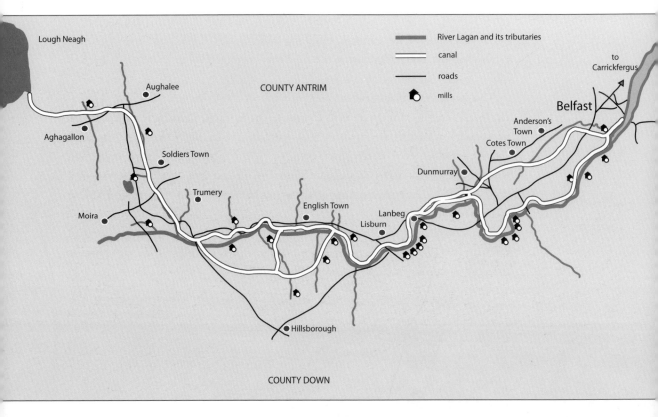

LAGAN NAVIGATION

Plan for part of Lagan navigation (redrawn): 'A plan of the river Lagon [sic] and of the intended navigation canal from Belfast to Lough Neagh. Surveyed by Robert Whitworth, engineer.'

completely, and even in mid-channel the Lagan had only two feet of water) to deep water in the Lough, 'by means of which Vessels of a large burthen would be enabled to pass up or down at high water in common tides'. Parliament gave no money but did transfer responsibility from the useless corporation to the merchant community which had a direct interest in the matter. A 'Corporation for Preserving and Improving the Port of Belfast' – commonly known as the Ballast Board because it provided dredged material as ships' ballast – was established which removed some of the worst shoals, made pilotage compulsory and constructed the first dry dock[16] on part of the foreshore leased from Lord Donegall (he had at first said he would build the docks himself but decided to invest in the Lagan Canal instead).[17]

During the last two decades of the century this economically successful class of merchants and traders was joined by a number of cotton manufacturers. Protected with tariffs by the Irish parliament, cotton was originally introduced into Belfast as a way of employing and training children in the Poor House.[18] Both flax-spinning and the weaving of the yarn were cottage industries until first the one and then the other became mechanised. A textile printer from Lancashire, Nicholas Grimshaw, who settled in Belfast, built the first power-driven mill in Ireland in 1784.[19] The motive power was provided by the short and swift-flowing streams running from the Antrim plateau into Belfast Lough, as at Whitehouse. Thereafter the manufacture

of cotton largely replaced that of linen in the town's economy. By 1791 the spinning mills were producing sufficient yarn to supply nearly 700 weavers, of whom three quarters were producing cotton cloth.[20] Political disturbances and economic depression halted or seriously hampered new investment during the next decade or so, but the establishment of cotton was to turn out to be the initial stimulus to Belfast's later industrialisation.

RADICALISM AND REPRESSION

The first marquess of Donegall, who died early in 1799, was credited by the *Belfast News Letter* with having 'laid out above sixty thousand pounds in the Lagan Navigation and Public Buildings in the Town'. Members of the Church of Ireland minority certainly appreciated the new parish church, for the majority of them were the less wealthy inhabitants. A growing number of Catholics, even poorer, also benefited – in their case by getting a site within the town boundary for their first church, St Mary's in Chapel Lane (1784).[21]

The religious test which excluded Presbyterians as well as Catholics from holding public office was repealed in 1780. Its long-overdue demise made little or no immediate difference to the membership of Belfast Corporation, however, since burgesses were elected for life. The aristocratic and episcopalian monopoly in church and state that Donegall represented became increasingly irksome to the prosperous Presbyterians who owned most of the town's wealth. The general spread of Enlightenment culture in the eighteenth century in the British Isles was encouraged in Ireland particularly by the writings and teachings of men such as Francis Hutcheson, an Ulsterman who was appointed professor of Moral Philosophy in Glasgow University in 1729; Hutcheson's pupil Adam Smith, who transformed economic thought; and the brilliant English propagandist Thomas Paine whose writings inspired the stand of the American colonists in their quarrel with George III. Belfast had close ties of trade and kinship with the American rebels (our 'American cousins' was no mere figure of speech for many Belfast people) who wished them well when they declared their independence in 1776. Lord Harcourt, Lord Lieutenant 1772–77, remarked that all the northern Presbyterians were in their

above

This attractive tea pot is attributed to the Downshire Pottery on the basis of the moulded spout and the decoration. While the flower garlands are adequately painted, the text is misspelt. 'My Grace is suffiant for the Anna Prince' should probably be interpreted as 'My Grace is sufficient for Thee ... Anna Prince'. (In other words commissioned for Anna Prince).

below

Coffee pot and sparrowbeak jug with an attributed 'tortoiseshell' decorated mug

PHOTOGRAPHS: PETER FRANCIS

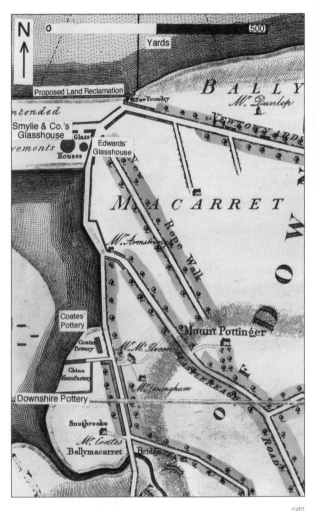

right

James Williamson's map of Ballymacarrett (1791) shows the early development of east Belfast as an industrial suburb with enterprises established in pottery and glass manufacture. Both the Downshire Pottery (1787–c.1806) and Smylie's Glasshouse were initiated by Thomas Greg. Victor Coates's factory produced black-glazed pottery and Benjamin Edwards' Glasshouse produced fine quality Irish table glass. At this date Ballymacarrett was not part of Belfast but had recently become the property of Lord Donegall who sublet it to Greg for development.

ST MARY'S, CHAPEL LANE

On Sunday 30 May 1784 St Mary's was opened in Crooked Lane, now Chapel Lane. It was the first Catholic church in Belfast and was built at a time when there was a strong ecumenical spirit within the town. Indeed its Protestant inhabitants contributed substantially towards the cost of the building, and the First Belfast Volunteer Company under the command of Captain Waddell Cunningham lined the chapel yard as a guard of honour, in full dress and presented arms to the priest as he passed into the church.

PHOTOGRAPH: CARNEGIE, 2009

hearts Americans. The success of the colonists meant that most of the regular troops in Ireland having been transported to America, volunteer regiments were raised by the landowners and middle classes at their own expense to meet the threat of a possible invasion of Ireland by France. In Belfast volunteering was adopted with tremendous enthusiasm; parades and manoeuvres offered the colour and pageantry of war without any of the risks, for the French never came. Instead, the Volunteer corps became middle-class political clubs, in which role they demanded first that the Irish parliament should have the right to make laws for Ireland without requiring English scrutiny and approval; then, when legislative independence was conceded in 1782, they went on to demand a reform of the Irish parliament itself.[22] Liberal opinion in Belfast was enthusiastic for reform of a system which gave one landowner complete control of the MPs representing the borough. The sharp critic quoted earlier gave Belfast as the prime example of a *close* borough in the following terms:

> This residence of numerous, wealthy, and spirited inhabitants remains in abject slavery to the absentee earl of Donegall; electing without enquiry whomsoever he nominates … so that the inhabitants have no more influence in the choice of their representatives than if they were sent over to them, ready elected, by the worthy colony of Botany Bay.[23]

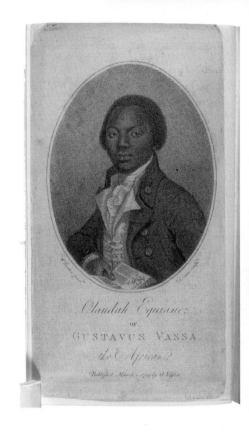

By the mid-1780s, however, the Volunteers were much less united than before. Parliament did not respond well to large crowds wearing military uniform and making demands for still more reforms. Attempts to force the pace in Belfast or Carrickfergus by getting Waddell Cunningham into the Commons, either as a nominee of Donegall or by popular vote, finally failed in 1785.[24] The high-water mark of reform appeared to have been reached.

The outbreak of the Revolution in France in 1789 inspired a renewed agitation. Reformers in Belfast soon divided however, on the issue of whether – and if so when – the Catholics of Ireland should be emancipated from their disabilities. At one end of the spectrum the Northern Whig club, founded in 1790, favoured cautious indeed minimal changes; at the other end radical spirits formed the Belfast Society of United

Irishmen (1791), which agitated for equal and democratic rights for all, propounding their views in a successful newspaper, the *Northern Star*.[25] The outbreak of war between Britain and France in 1793,

DR WILLIAM DRENNAN

Oil painting of Dr William Drennan, one of the founders of the Society of United Irishmen.

© ULSTER MUSEUM, 2008.

right
BELFAST SCENERY

Title page of *Belfast Scenery in Thirty Views*, surmounted by the arms of the Donegall family and enclosed within a classical style setting by Joseph Molloy. The painting shows the towers and turrets of Ormeau House across the river Lagan.

BY KIND PERMISSION OF THE LINEN HALL LIBRARY

however, and the excesses of the Revolution, dampened the enthusiasm of the more cautious among the reformers and hardened the resolve of an alarmed Irish government, which presently forbade reform meetings and Volunteer parades and then proscribed the United Irishmen.

Many of the radicals drew back at this point, but others organised in secret and plotted a rebellion, looking with undue confidence to the arrival of arms and armies from France. A French expedition did indeed reach County Cork in December 1796, but could not land because of bad weather. Though the episode at Bantry Bay was a great disappointment to the plotters, some found it encouraging as well; the United Irishmen's numbers swelled and arms were made or stolen in open defiance of the authorities as it seemed. At last recovering its nerve, the government abandoned conciliation. The brutal but effective General Lake was sent to disarm Ulster with a mixed force of regulars, militia and yeomanry. In Belfast many of the leading radicals were suddenly arrested and imprisoned without trial. Among them was the manager of *The Northern Star*; the paper itself finally ceased publication when its presses were smashed by the military. Even these setbacks and the presence of a large garrison did not entirely deter the most ardent of the local United Irishmen. When the planned rebellion broke out in 1798, however, they could attempt nothing in Belfast itself. A prominent inhabitant later recalled 'the death-like silence which pervaded the streets when the counties of Down and Antrim resounded with the noise and tumult of battle'.[26] Instead, Henry Joy McCracken, a scion of two prominent Presbyterian families in the town, led his rural followers to defeat in a skirmish at Antrim and was afterwards tried by court martial in Belfast and hanged outside the Market House. While McCracken and his friends plotted insurrection, many of the leading citizens volunteered to form a corps of yeomanry to defend the town. The complete failure of the rebellion in Ulster, and the news that in southern Ireland the rebels had massacred Protestants was a profound and bitter disappointment to the radicals of Belfast. It was reported that one of the insurgent leaders said shortly before his

THE POOR HOUSE

The Poor House *circa* 1785 by John Nixon, the earliest view of the town's finest Georgian building. Nixon was an English merchant who came frequently to Ireland and sketched wherever he went.

© ULSTER MUSEUM, 2008

execution that, 'the Presbyterians of the north perceived too late that if they had succeeded in their designs, they would ultimately have had to contend with the Roman Catholics'.[27] Some of those arrested before the outbreak of the rebellion would see out the delusive decade of the 1790s in a Scottish prison. By the time the survivors returned home to take up their lives again, the Act of Union of 1800 had put an end to the parliament they had set out to reform.

Belfast had changed a good deal in the previous half century, during which its population had increased from 8,000 to 20,000. Thanks to its aristocratic owner it

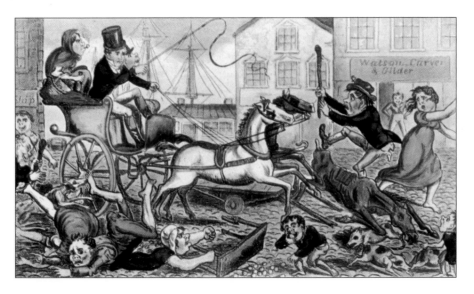

LORD DONE'EM-ALL

Brian Boru's entry into Belfast, a coloured illustration from *Real Life in Ireland by a Real Paddy*. The book was published first in London 1821 and satirised the second marquess of Donegall as Lord Done'em-all.

AUTHOR COLLECTION

LINEN HALL LIBRARY

Established in 1788, the Linen Hall Library is now the last subscribing library in Ireland. The Society declined in the 1790s as it owned no permanent premises, but in 1802 it moved to rooms in the White Linen Hall (from which it took its name), and remained there until 1902 when it lost its premises as the White Linen Hall was demolished to make way for the new City Hall. The Library moved to a former warehouse in Donegall Square which it still occupies. Its collections of Irish material are unique.

had acquired a modestly imposing appearance and one or two fine buildings; thanks to the efforts of its citizens it had become a more important port and commercial centre, the hub of the northern linen trade and the location of a small but thriving cotton-manufacturing industry. Though never perhaps the 'Athens of the North' that a local poet claimed in 1793 (he was really talking about its devotion to political liberty rather than its cultural pretensions), it had a sizeable reading public served by a good library (still in existence as the Linen Hall Library), several newspapers and a well-patronised theatre. It was still, nevertheless, essentially a Protestant plantation town, however fierce the political disagreements among its Protestant inhabitants, and it was still entirely owned by the family which had established it two centuries earlier.[28]

Long before the death of the first marquess in 1799 his life had been made miserable by the behaviour of his elder son and heir George Augustus (1769–1844).[29] Known during his father's life by the courtesy title Earl of Belfast, he was one of the greatest spendthrifts of his day. Within a few months of his coming of age he had contracted gaming debts of £30,000 or more. His father settled these and many other debts but eventually decided to let things take their course. Arrested by some of his creditors, young Lord Belfast was lodged in the Fleet prison for debtors in London. There he came across Edward May, a sharp-witted

Irish attorney, who raised the money to get him released. Without the knowledge or consent of his father, he then married Anna May, the lawyer's illegitimate and under-age daughter. When Belfast became Donegall all the Mays went to live with him. Edward May senior became his son-in-law's chief agent, arranging further loans and, it was said, taking some of the money for himself. By 1802 Donegall's credit in England was completely exhausted but at least as a peer he himself could no longer be arrested for debt. The whole ménage then fled to Belfast, from where with the connivance of the local law officers he fought a long rearguard battle, refusing to pay any debts he considered to have been fraudulent. He became notorious, earning from sporting journalists the nickname 'Marquis of Done'em-all'.[30] He intended his exile in Belfast to be merely temporary; instead, he and his in-laws were to live there until his death at Ormeau over forty years later.

The unexpected arrival of the Donegalls in Belfast caused a tremendous stir. Though apparently almost penniless most of the time, they threw themselves into the social life of the town and were not in the least haughty. The marchioness was particularly affable. A romantic soul, she read the latest French novels, loved the theatre and was fond of dressing up. (an American art gallery has a miniature of her in the uniform of a yeomanry officer). The worst the sharp-tongued Mrs Martha McTier could say of her was that her only failing was 'a too great attachment to most worthless parents'.[31] There were lavish evening functions where as many as a hundred guests sat down to dine and the dancing went on till six o'clock in the morning. Real life in the Donegall saga had as many twists and turns as the plot of a modern soap opera. The most serious one of all came out of the blue when the eldest son and heir, the current earl of Belfast, had just come of age and was about to marry. Shortly before the ceremony the father of the bride, Lord Shaftesbury, received an anonymous letter proving that the marriage of the Donegalls in 1795 had been performed illegally. The match was called off at once, since the intended bridegroom was now illegitimate, with neither wealth nor prospects to offer his fiancée. Lord Donegall himself, as tenant-for-life of the family estates, would not be affected but at his death everything would pass to his nephew Arthur. For the next two or three years the Donegalls tried every court in the kingdom, and every device known to the lawyers, to annul the annulment, but all without success. In the end, the family fortunes were saved by a change in the marriage laws, brought about by the Donegall case and applied retrospectively (which was almost unheard of in those days).[32]

GEORGE AUGUSTUS CHICHESTER, SECOND MARQUESS OF DONEGALL (1769–1844)

The second marquess was a notorious spendthrift who in order to evade his creditors had to flee from England to Belfast in 1802. His portrait is by J.J. Masquerier c.1800. This oil painting is now owned by the City Council and hangs in Belfast Castle.

The immediate political result of the defeat of the United Irishmen in 1798 was the Act of Union (1800) by which the Irish parliament was merged with the Parliament of Great Britain in the parliament of the United Kingdom. The 300 MPs who had represented Ireland in the Dublin House of Commons were reduced to 100. The borough of Belfast lost one of its two MPs. More important, the Prime Minister, William Pitt, who intended that Catholic Emancipation should follow the Union was unable to achieve this aim because King George III absolutely refused to accept it. Pitt could only resign. More than twenty years after the Act of Union emancipation was no nearer. Pitt and the King were both dead but no change had been made. A group of Irish MPs under the leadership of Henry Grattan came close on several occasions to acheiving a majority for emancipation but in the end without success. The Catholics of Ireland were left feeling cheated.

At this point, in 1823, the Dublin lawyer Daniel O'Connell became the leader of the Catholic Association. In 1824 he reformed this body completely and proceeded thereafter to replace the ineffectual parliamentary campaign of Grattan and his friends by mass agitation and organisation of Catholic voters Any man who wanted to join the new Association could do so if he paid a subscription of only one penny a month (known as 'the rent') which was collected by the priests before mass on Sundays. There were meetings and events at many different levels, from single parishes to counties and provinces which attracted enormous crowds, especially if addressed by O'Connell himself. On the whole these huge gatherings were largely peaceable but the sheer numbers and evident determination of those attending were in themselves a threat to the authorities. In 1828 a by-election in county Clare persuaded O'Connell (after much hesitation to become a candidate himself he had hoped to persuade a Protestant instead). The result was a smashing victory for the 'Liberator'. He then refused to swear the three anti-Catholic oaths without which no elected MP could take his seat. With the country in an uproar the Prime Minister, the Duke of Wellington, bit the bullet and chose to grant emancipation rather than risk civil war. O'Connell's triumph was complete. In Ireland this was the background to all politics for the foreseeable future. O'Connell's campaign and its success added greatly to the sectarian animosity in Belfast during the 1820s. Newcomers to the town seeking employment in textile manufacturing tended to settle in particular areas close to their work, many Protestants in Sandy Row, many Catholics in the nearby Pound area. Some brought with them from their rural backgrounds the Orange Lodges and Ribbon Societies – which had enabled them to survive in districts where Catholics and Protestants were competing with each other for the same land and opportunities. In

MATTY McTIER

A pastel copy of a portrait of Martha or Matty McTier (née Drennan) sister of William Drennan, a Belfast doctor. Her correspondence with her brother over many years is a major source of information about radical politics in Belfast and Dublin and about social life in Belfast.

© ULSTER MUSEUM, 2008

the town, especially in times of particular tension, these groups flourished. It was not difficult to organise a riot in these conditions but from the available evidence it is often difficult to find out why one started. Each side provoked the other and both feared that massacres were being planned. Another factor was the work of a group of evangelical Protestant preachers who made a serious effort to convert all the Catholics, This project, sometimes called the second Reformation, had little success, if anything adding to the feeling among the lower ranks of Unionism. By 1830 they felt they had lost a lot of ground to their opponents. To make matters worse, the government banned Orange parades and to the fury of the rank and file their leaders accepted this.

After 1800, Belfast soon faded as a stronghold of radicalism. While not abandoning their liberal principles, most Belfast merchants and manufacturers found that the Union was good for business and welcomed the opportunity to recover their fortunes. One who was particularly successful in this regard was William Tennent — merchant, banker, capitalist, landowner in several counties, in the 1820s purchaser of substantial parts of Belfast from the Donegalls, philanthropist, leading Presbyterian layman, who was released from Fort George in 1801 and who died rich and respected in 1832.[33]

The course of sectarian rioting in early nineteenth-century Belfast has usually been taken to have started in 1813, when a small gathering of Orangemen who had spent the day in Lisburn returned to Belfast and insisted on parading through the town. In North Street they were met by an angry mob and took refuge in a public house from which they fired shots at the besiegers as a result of which two people were killed and others injured.[34] The next recognised major incident was in 1825, but recent research in local newspapers and other detailed evidence has revealed that scarcely a year passed without provocation and violence of some sort. It is far from clear however what some of these encounters were about. Unemployment among textile workers may have been enough in itself to account for trouble without resorting to ideas of economic competition between Catholic and Protestant workers. In some cases the actions of the participants resembled rather those of the Luddites of Lancashire and the north of England with the destruction of machinery and great concern about the price of bread. What is one to make of a curious episode in April 1815 when what was described as 'a mob of apprentice lads, boys and women' protesting about dear bread and low wages, marched off to Ormeau to make their grievances known to Lord Donegall.[35] Finding him proved to be difficult however. He was not at home when they reached Ormeau, nor was he at the theatre in Arthur

ANNA, MARCHIONESS OF DONEGALL

Miniature of Anna, marchioness of Donegall, wife of the second marquess, in the uniform of an officer in the Belfast yeomanry c.1800, probably as part of a demonstration of support for her husband, who wanted to be appointed Commander of the Yeomanry, c.1800. The government had no high opinion of Donegall, but wanted all the votes he could command in the Dublin parliament.

© WORCESTER ART MUSEUM, MA, ARTIST HORACE HONE

Anna, marchioness of Donegall, with the eldest of her seven sons on her back, and dressed as a gypsy, telling the fortune of her own younger sister. The marchioness liked dressing up.

ENGRAVING AFTER THE PAINTING BY J.J. MASQUERIER RA. © ULSTER MUSEUM

Square that was one of his haunts. Thwarted in their quest, tired and hungry, the marchers made their way back into the town, smashing property as they went until the military eventually arrested a dozen of them.

Lastly, a brief comment on the Tory establishment on the eve of the reform of the old corporation. In parallel with its remarkably rapid industrial expansion Belfast also became notable for the frequency and ferocity of its outbursts of sectarian unrest. Donegall and those around him were quite unfit to give a moral lead or even to set an example. The burgesses and officials appointed by the corporation were greedy and bigoted. The Town Clerk had to be dismissed, despite having the backing of the Sovereign.[36] That same Sovereign – Thomas Verner – had held the post in 1813, when his partisanship had enraged the radicals (Liberals) of the town. The fact that Verner was a prominent Orangeman and was married to the marchioness's sister made him important regardless of his behaviour. In 1813 he had been accused of assault and attempted rape of a pedlar woman. Indicted at the Assizes in Downpatrick, he was acquitted after some dubious work. It can scarcely have enhanced his public reputation (or his patron's for that matter) to see the press reports of the Sovereign allegedly succumbing to lust in broad daylight within sight of his own house. The Tory establishment in Belfast had closed ranks on that occasion to ensure that Verner was acquitted whatever the evidence against him.[37]

ORMEAU HOUSE

The second marquess of Donegall came to Belfast in order to escape his creditors. He and his family lived at first in the town, but in 1807 they moved across the river to Ormeau. Ormeau Cottage, a modest country house, was greatly enlarged in the 1820s to give it the appearance of a Tudor mansion. The architect was William Vitruvius Morrison.

BELFAST SCENERY AND THIRTY VIEWS REPRODUCED BY PERMISSION OF THE LINEN HALL LIBRARY

CHAPTER SIX

Industry, trade and politics, 1800–1860

T HE outstanding economic development in Belfast in the early nineteenth century was its rise as a centre of power-driven textile manufacture, first of cotton and then of linen. This was accompanied by, or led to, other economic changes which were to transform the Georgian town into a Victorian city – notably the creation of a superb port and the development of commercial and financial facilities. Such changes, and their social results, and the kind of municipal self-government that grew up to deal with the problems of urban expansion, were not dissimilar to those experienced by other British cities of the time. Indeed, even the tensions created by the sudden influx of large numbers of Irish Catholics into a hitherto Protestant town were not untypical. But only up to a point: in the case of Belfast these tensions were to prove in every way sharper, more persistent and more divisive than anywhere else.

INDUSTRIAL REVOLUTION

Though there were ten or eleven cotton spinning mills in the Belfast area by the end of the eighteenth century, the industrialisation of the town did not begin in a substantial way until after 1800. By 1820 more than 2,000 people were employed in some fifteen mills in or near Belfast. The Smithfield area of the town then became the main centre of new steam-powered enterprises. McCracken's mill there had 14,000 spindles and employed 200 hands. McCrum, Lepper & Co.'s five-storey mill behind the artillery barracks employed 300. Another five-storey mill in Winetavern Street was bought in 1815 by Thomas Mulholland, who later bought a second in Francis Street and in 1822 built a third in Henry Street.[1] By 1824, when tariff protection for Irish cotton ended, there were twenty mills employing 3,500 people, and though its prosperity depended largely on home demand the industry in Belfast was a very successful one. Even compared with Lancashire, it was neither particularly small in scale nor lacking in capital. The cost of raw material was the same everywhere, and while Belfast mill-owners had to import their coal they offset this additional cost by paying their workers less. So it was not, as used to be thought, an inability to compete with British producers after the removal of protection that led to the decline of cotton in the 1830s.[2]

What happened during the next ten or fifteen years was not so much the decline of cotton as its replacement by a more profitable, because modernised, linen industry. (The manufacture of linen, as distinct from the linen trade, had hitherto been largely a rural, domestic industry.) The basis of this change was a technological invention, James Kay's discovery of how to produce fine linen yarn by the wet spinning process, and its adaptation for commercial purposes by Marshalls of Leeds. These developments were observed with great interest by cotton manufacturers in Ulster. When Thomas Mulholland's new mill in Henry Street accidentally burned down one Sunday morning in 1828 he rebuilt it to house 8,000 flax-spinning spindles, after a successful trial of 1,000 in his Francis Street mill. In 1830 there were two linen mills, in 1834 ten (nearly as many linen as cotton); by 1850 only four cotton mills remained, and by the end of that decade only two. By that time there were thirty-two linen mills with over half a million spindles. Apart from slumps in 1854–55 (the Crimean War) and 1857–58 (a financial crisis), linen enjoyed a prosperous period in the 1850s. This textile transfer was to prove enormously important for Belfast. By the early 1860s it was taking over the lead in linen manufacture from Leeds and Dundee and was thus well placed to make the most of the opportunity created by the outbreak of the American Civil War, which caused a cotton famine.[3]

MULLHOLLANDS' MILL

Mulhollands' flax-spinning mill, c.1840. This was the beginning of the York Street flax-spinning enterprise.

ILLUSTRATION FROM A BOOK BY MR AND MRS S. HALL, TOURIST VISITORS TO BELFAST IN THE 1840s. © ULSTER MUSEUM, 2008

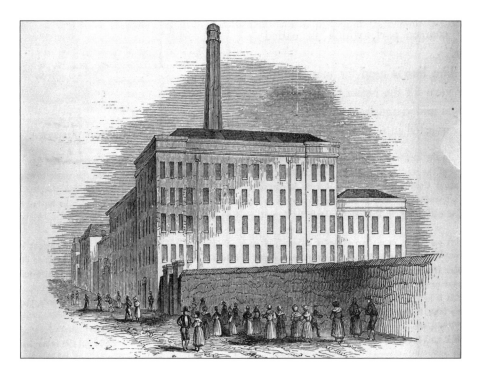

The spread of mechanised flax-spinning ruined not only handspinners but also handloom weavers, since many of the former turned to weaving and thus drove wages down. With weavers plentiful and wages cheap, factory owners had little incentive at first to introduce power looms, especially since the early looms could weave only the coarser types of linen. One effect of the Irish potato famine of the 1840s and subsequent emigration was to force up the wages of the skilled weavers and encourage employers to look for an alternative. In response to this demand power looms were modified to make them more suitable for finer work. By 1850 two Belfast firms had begun powerloom weaving. By 1862 there were nearly 3,000 powerlooms operating in the Belfast area and the production of linen was becoming largely mechanised.[4] Visitors were increasingly struck by the resemblance between Belfast and industrial towns in the north of England – 'a clean Manchester' or 'the Irish Liverpool' – and by an impression of industriousness as well as industry which was thought to be un-Irish. 'The spirit of commercial enterprise that pervades the merchants of this prosperous place,' wrote one visitor in 1834, 'appears to be reflected from the opposite shores.'[5] The Halls, who came to Belfast in 1843, found the place full of English virtues – 'so much bustle, such an aspect of business, a total absence of all suspicion of idleness'.[6]

Such views were shared by the inhabitants themselves. The anonymous local patriot who wrote the entry for Belfast in the *Parliamentary Gazetteer of Ireland*, published in 1844, summarised its standing as the fourth town of the kingdom in amount of population; the third in extent of edified area, and in aggregate value of general trade; the second in comparative regularity and beauty; the first in proportionate spirit, though only the second in actual appliances, of literature and science; and incomparably the first in enterprise, intelligence, and general prosperity.[7]

WILLIAM RITCHIE (1775–1834)

In 1791 this Scottish ship-builder from Ayrshire was approached by some Belfast merchants, and transferred his business to Ireland. At that time there was no tradition of ship-building in the town. By 1811 he was employing forty-four ship's carpenters, fifty-six apprentices, seven pairs of sawyers, twelve blacksmiths and several joiners. Apart from wooden sailing ships, he constructed the first dock in 1800 and later with fellow Scot, Alexander MacLaine, was credited with the construction of the first Irish steamboat. He became an active citizen, notably on the General Hospital Committee and with the Charitable Society.

THE EXCHANGE OR MARKET HOUSE

Starting life in 1769, this was the heart of Belfast social and commercial activity in the eighteenth century.

BELFAST IN 1815

This map, we are informed, was engraved for *Smith's Almanac* of 1815. The earliest regular directories date from about this time. Belfast's population was still growing apace, as the wartime boom attracted immigrants from the countryside.

Apart from important developments in textiles, the basis was laid during this period of the two other great industries that were to sustain the expansion of Victorian Belfast: ship-building and engineering. The building of wooden ships other than very small ones dated from the 1790s, when William Ritchie from Saltcoats in Ayrshire had established a successful yard on the Antrim side of the Lagan. There was a modest expansion of this and other yards during the early nineteenth century, but the crucial development came later, in the 1850s, and in a different place, across the river on the County Down side where improvements to Belfast harbour had created an artificial island. The Harbour Commissioners laid out part of the Queen's Island as a shipyard, with a patent slip and a timber pond, attracting in 1851 one of the builders of wooden ships. Two years later Robert Hickson, proprietor of an ironworks with plating to dispose of, took over a site there to build iron ships. In 1854 Hickson appointed Edward Harland, then only twenty-three, as manager. Harland bought the yard five years later for £5,000 with the help of G.C. Schwabe of Liverpool, whose nephew Gustav Wolff became the other half of Harland & Wolff in 1861.[8]

Industrial growth stimulated a demand for foundry products. Two new firms appeared in the early years of the century, Coates's Lagan Foundry and the Belfast Foundry. Both began to build steam engines. The engine for the first steamboat in Ireland, a wooden vessel, was made by the Lagan Foundry in 1820, and the same firm built the first iron steamship in 1838. The growth of textile factories produced a demand for spinning machinery.[9] The great expansion of heavy engineering, however, was to come later in the century, when both linen and ship-building really took off.

TRADE, FINANCE AND COMMUNICATIONS

In commerce too the early nineteenth century was a time of remarkable growth. By the mid-1830s Belfast was the first among Irish ports in value of trade, £7.9 million compared with Dublin's £6.9 million. By far its biggest export at that time was linen, with provisions a long way behind; the town had become the centre of the Irish linen trade long before it became the chief centre of its manufacture. Most of the finance for this expansion came from local sources, through the medium of the banks

BELFAST FROM THE LOUGH

View of Belfast from the Lough, showing the Long Bridge and some of the buildings in the town.

GEORGE BENN, 1822 HISTORY OF BELFAST, BY KIND PERMISSION OF THE LINEN HALL LIBRARY

BANK BUILDINGS

Artist's impression of
the Bank Buildings, a
well-known emporium
at Castle Junction.

© ULSTER MUSEUM. 2008

which had developed since the early years of the century. From 1797 till 1808 there
were no note-issuing institutions in Belfast, only a Discount Company, founded in
1793, which discounted bills of exchange and took deposits on interest. The business
of the company expanded significantly after 1800, as Irish trade benefited from
the Union and wartime demand, rising from £94,000 in discounted bills in 1800
to over £300,000 in 1806, with a matching rise in deposits. The monopoly of the
Bank of Ireland at that time prevented the establishment of banks except as private
partnerships, so the first developments were on that basis: the Belfast Bank in 1808,
followed by the Northern and the Commercial in 1809. Each of the partners in these
ventures subscribed £10,000. All three banks survived the crisis of 1820, when most
Irish private banks went under. When legislation in 1824 and 1825 ended the Bank
of Ireland's monopoly, first the Northern and then a union of the Belfast Bank and
the Commercial (as the Belfast Banking Company) formed joint stock banks on
the Scottish model, each with a capital of half a million pounds.[10] These two were
joined in 1836 by a third, the Ulster Bank. By the mid-thirties, then, Belfast had the
head offices of three banks drawing funds from substantial depositors throughout

THE DUBLIN TURNPIKE

The Old Turnpike with
Dublin coach on the
Lisburn Road, Belfast.
During the first half of
the eighteenth century
tolls were imposed
along major routes in
Ireland.

BELFAST CITY COUNCIL

the north of Ireland, as well as branches of the Provincial Bank and the Bank of
Ireland. A flourishing Savings Bank served the interests of smaller investors who
could not afford to buy £50 or £100 shares. That some of these humbler capitalists
accumulated surprisingly large sums of money was revealed when they were tempted
to buy the £1 shares of a disreputable bank which collapsed in the 1830s: a coach
porter lost 150 guineas, a street constable £300.[11] The author of the *Parliamentary
Gazetteer* entry loyally noted that the failure of the Belfast branch of the Agricultural
and Commercial Bank was no exception to the general soundness of the Belfast banks
'for the affair was wholly a Dublin bubble'.

Industrial and commercial growth could not have
continued much beyond the 1830s without the transformation of the port and harbour, since the textile industry
(linen no less than cotton) depended on imports of raw
material and all the essentials for ship-building, engineering
and power generation – coal, iron and timber – were
imported. The Ballast Board, the body established in 1785,
had carried out some useful maintenance work on the
channel and had opened a second graving dock in 1826,
but despite consulting several eminent engineers (including
Telford and Rennie) it was unable until 1831 to fix on a
feasible way of tackling the main problem. This was that
the Lagan, instead of running straight into the Lough,
meandered across shallows and mud flats in two great
bends before reaching deep water at the Pool of Garmoyle.
Here large ships had to anchor and transfer their cargoes
into smaller vessels for the last three miles of the journey
to the quays.[12] Human cargo fared no better, according to
the recollections of one traveller:

THE NATIONAL BANK

The National Irish Bank
began back in 1809
with the formation of
the Northern Banking
Partnership in Belfast.
Some 31 years later the
Northern Bank opened
its first branch in what
is now the Republic of
Ireland.

PHOTOGRAPH: CARNEGIE, 2009

It was usually the fate of the old *Eclipse*, the *Rob Roy*, the *Fingal* or the *Chieftain* steamers to miss the tide and stop between Whitehouse and Holywood. Then an open boat would come alongside, and any passenger anxious to get up to town had the offer of being rowed up in no time for a shilling. After the wearying journey of twenty-two hours from Glasgow or Liverpool, many of the passengers were glad to leave the steamer. When the boatmen had secured as many passengers as the boat could carry without the certainty of drowning them, they began their journey, the pleasures of which on a cold wintry morning were not much relished.[13]

In 1831 the Ballast Board accepted a plan by the engineers Walker and Burgess to

THE INTERIOR OF THE ULSTER HALL

This drawing is by W.J. Barre, (1830–67), the architect of the building and keen rival of Charles Lanyon. Other works by Barre include the Albert Memorial.

© ULSTER MUSEUM, 2008

make the first of two cuts, across one of the bends of the river; a second cut, to carry the deep channel all the way out to Garmoyle, was to be made later if necessary. It took six years, however, to obtain an Act of Parliament which conferred powers on the reconstructed Board 'for the formation of a new cut or channel and for otherwise more effectually improving the Port and Harbour of Belfast'. The £200,000 needed to begin the work was raised remarkably quickly by an issue of bonds. Work started in April 1839 and was completed in January 1841. At the same time the last part of the Lagan's course, below the Long Bridge, was deepened to link the town quays with the new channel. Some of the material excavated in the process was used to form an artificial island, at first called Dargan's Island after the contractor but later renamed Queen's Island in honour of Victoria's visit to Belfast in 1849. The private quays and docks down-river from the Long Bridge (which was taken down in 1841 and replaced by the Queen's Bridge) were all purchased by the Ballast Board, which was thus in a position to control the future development of the harbour. Charges for quayage and pilotage were reduced to encourage trade, so successfully that

THE TOWN DOCK

The town dock at the bottom of High Street c.1830. The dock was constructed where the Farset joined the Lagan. By the early nineteenth century the dock was completely inadequate for the needs of the growing trade of the town. In low water only small vessels could get a berth. Instead the cargo of larger ships had to be brought up to the quay in lighters and had to wait in the Pool of Garmoyle

FROM AN ENGRAVING BY T.M. BAYNES. ©
ULSTER MUSEUM, 2008

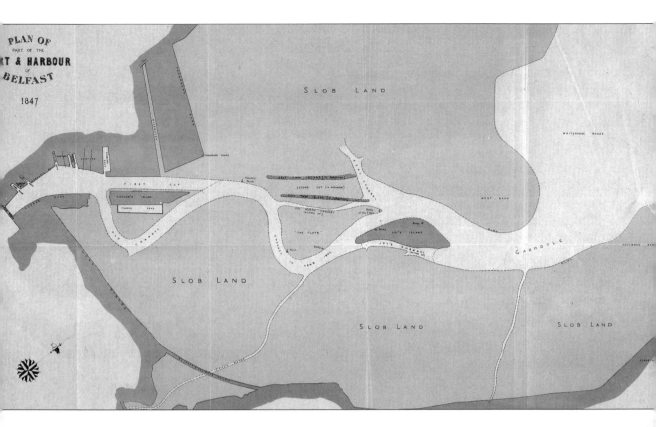

Plan of part of the Port & Harbour of Belfast (1847). This shows the first cut made by the harbour authorities to straighten the channel of the river Lagan. The work created the Queen's Island – here called Dargan's Island – and the line of the second cut was in progress. The port was transformed by these developments.

© ULSTER MUSEUM, 2008.

the Board's successors, the Harbour Commissioners (established under the Belfast Harbour Act of 1847), immediately made the second navigation cut. The resulting Victoria Channel, which carried the deep water all the way out to Garmoyle, was opened in 1849.[14] Thereafter even the largest vessels could come right up into the town and Belfast had one of the finest ports in the world.

During the same period the old docks were filled in, to be developed presently as Queen's Square (formerly Town Dock), Albert Square (Lime Kiln Dock) and Corporation Square (Ritchie's Dock). The transformation of the port's already considerable trade was one of many indications that Belfast was growing into a city. In 1837 the number of ships cleared was 2,724, with a total tonnage of 288,143; ten years later 4,213 ships and over half a million tons; 7,817 ships and 1,372,326 tons by 1867.[15] No wonder the Harbour Commissioners moved from the cramped quarters of the old Ballast Board to splendid new offices (built on the site of William Ritchie's shipyard) in 1854 and the revenue authorities to a palatial new Custom House in 1857.

At the same time as harbour developments were transforming the approach to Belfast by sea, the town's hinterland was being enlarged by the construction of railways. The first line, the Ulster Railway between Belfast and Lisburn with its terminus in Great Victoria Street, opened in 1839 and soon extended to Lurgan and Portadown. Sabbatarians immediately denounced the running of Sunday trains. One clergyman told his flock he would rather join a company for theft and murder than the Ulster Railway Company, whose business was sending souls to the devil at sixpence apiece. 'Every sound of the railway whistle,' he thundered, 'is answered by a shout in hell.'[16] After the Railway Act of 1847 made public money available for railway promotion, the network developed rapidly. Lines to Ballymena and Holywood opened the following year; Coleraine and Dublin were linked to Belfast in 1855, Londonderry in 1860. Communications in the town itself changed little until horse omnibuses began to appear in the 1850s; they scarcely needed to, since most people lived within easy reach of their work. Before that there was scarcely anything in the way of public transport: an old man looking back in the 1870s recalled that 'In addition to the expensiveness of public conveyances in those days, there were very few of them. I remember when Belfast could boast of only four outside cars'.[17]

THE FALCON

The Belfast-owned cross-channel steamship *Falcon* at the entrance to the Mersey. Oil painting by Joseph Heard, Liverpool, c.1835.

© ULSTER FOLK AND TRANSPORT MUSEUM

BELFAST HARBOUR

The old Long Bridge was demolished in 1841 and replaced by the Queen's Bridge, designed by the architect Lanyon at a cost of £20,000. It was regarded as a great success. The new bridge opened in 1842. Doyle's *Tourist Guide* (Dublin 1854) recommended a stroll along the bridge to enjoy the views of the harbour and the new quays and all the bustle of mercantile and maritime activity. The new Custom House can be seen in the background, left.

WATERCOLOUR, © ULSTER MUSEUM, 2008

POPULATION GROWTH AND URBAN PROBLEMS

Industrial and commercial expansion attracted large numbers of immigrants into Belfast, first as labour for the cotton spinning mills and as handloom weavers of cotton, then to the linen mills and later the weaving factories. The large majority were from Ulster, and most of the rest from other parts of Ireland, but there were also a few Europeans – notably some Italian craftsmen associated in one way or another with the arts (drawing masters, carvers, gilders and so on). The population rose from about 20,000 in 1800 to 30,000 in 1815, to over 53,000 in 1831, to over 70,000 in 1841 (when in addition to the 70,747 in the town itself the census-takers felt that another 4,861 living outside the boundary should be added). The rate of growth declined in the next decade, reflecting slower industrial growth and the effects of the great potato famine. Even so, the census figure for 1851 was 87,000. Up to that point the increase had taken place within the old boundary of the town, which enclosed an area of one and a half square miles. In 1853 the boundary was greatly extended to increase the area to ten square miles. By 1861 the population of this larger Belfast had reached 121,000.[18] This phenomenal rate of growth was to be exceeded in the second half of the century, but it was nevertheless already very striking and put Belfast among the major cities and towns of the United Kingdom; in Ireland only Dublin was larger by the middle of the century.

Urban growth created urban problems, especially when expansion was so rapid. Typhus fever, carried by body lice, was endemic but reached epidemic proportions in the famine year of 1847, when the hordes of starving poor who poured into the town from the stricken countryside were easy victims to it. The Poor Law Guardians, who controlled the workhouse (built in 1841 with accommodation for a thousand inmates) and its infirmary, were warned by the fever hospital to expect a plague. In the event, the 1847 outbreak was, in the words of Dr Andrew Malcolm, a plague 'in comparison with which all previous epidemics were trivial and insignificant'. The workhouse infirmary was enlarged and temporary hospitals were provided in huts and tents in several other places. The number of recorded admissions during the year was nearly 14,000. 'Yet hundreds', the *Belfast News Letter* reported on 20 July, 'for whom there remains no provision – are daily exposed in the delirium of this frightful malady, on the streets or left to die in their filthy and ill-ventilated hovels …' Malcolm reckoned that 'one out of every five persons in Belfast was attacked during this year'. The problem for the Poor Law Guardians was made worse by the arrival of several shiploads of Irish emigrants repatriated by the Poor Law authorities of Glasgow and other British cities, for whom Belfast was the most convenient port, regardless of their place of origin in Ireland.

The cholera outbreaks which ravaged the town in 1831–32 and 1848–49 were sadly inevitable in any large port in the early Victorian period and were experienced also in Glasgow and Liverpool. The epidemic of 1848–49, which followed hard on the heels of the typhus, was expected and prepared for. Even so it took a heavy toll in the poorer quarters of the town, killing nearly a thousand people in 1849. The death rate among patients, one-third, was twice that of the earlier outbreak in 1831–32; living conditions for the poor had evidently worsened in the meantime. A Sanitary Committee, with the reforming Dr Malcolm as its moving spirit, produced a damning report in 1849 on the unhealthy condition of working-class districts, in particular the absence of any proper drainage and sewerage; and Malcolm himself in 1852 (in an address to the British Association, meeting in Belfast for the first time) showed conclusively that disease caused far more deaths in houses without proper sewerage than in the better-drained parts of the town. Only 3,000 of the 10,000 houses, he estimated, had piped water, and few of these had cisterns; 3,000 had no yard of any kind; 1,800

DR ANDREW MALCOLM (1818–56)

Malcolm was a pioneer campaigner for improved public health in early Victorian Belfast. He died of overwork and a fever.

© ULSTER MUSEUM, 2008

BELFAST SLUMS

Pepper Hill Court, a row of old slum houses with a steep flight of steps leading down to Birch Street. There the Rev. O'Hanlon in 1850 found the inhabitants indulging in 'whiskey drinking and lewd singing'.

were accessible only by covered archways into enclosed courts; 25,000 people had no privies. Though the science of statistics was in its infancy, it is certain that at this period Belfast had the highest death rate in Ireland and possibly the worst in the United Kingdom. Malcolm produced the extraordinary statistic that, due to the 'absolutely excessive' infant mortality, the average life expectancy in Belfast was no more than nine years.[19] Malcolm's figures confirmed the eyewitness accounts of a Congregational minister named O'Hanlon, who in a series of letters to the Liberal newspaper the *Northern Whig* (subsequently published in book form) revealed horrors that most citizens never saw for themselves.[20]

The presence of vice in the poorest quarters of the town caused more concern than the absence of privies. The extent of prostitution in early Victorian Belfast

is impossible to establish with any accuracy in the absence of statistics, but in a garrison town and port it was inevitably considerable. O'Hanlon did not attempt an estimate but noted that it was rife and listed the areas where he came across it in his 'walks among the poor'. One entry contained 'five notorious brothels', another had nine, while Hudson's Entry near Smithfield was 'A complete den of vice and uncleanness, probably unsurpassed in what is called the civilised world', being filled with 'imbruted, guilty, shameless women' who 'breakfasted upon whiskey'. The fact that half of all the surgical cases in the General Hospital were syphilitic in origin supports O'Hanlon's impression. To their credit, many concerned citizens felt that something must be done. While action at an official level was inevitably slow to materialise, a large number of charitable bodies did what they could to alleviate the situation.

No amount of private charity, however, could deal with such problems adequately. Housing, water, drainage and public health needed laws and regulations for the

BIRD'S EYE BELFAST

This bird's eye view of Belfast, c.1860, is a good example of the fine work produced by the firm of Marcus Ward & Co. Steel engraving not only provided the artist with an excellent proof image but could last longer than most alternatives.

A STEEL ENGRAVING BY MARCUS WARD AND CO., © ULSTER MUSEUM, 2008

common good which would override the selfish interests of property owners. In the absence of an effective corporation, the Police Act of 1800 (40 Geo. III. c.3 7), one of the last Acts of the Irish Parliament, had established in Belfast two elected bodies, the Commissioners of Police (elected for life) and the Police Committee – the first supervisory, the second executive – to be responsible for paving, lighting and cleansing the town and providing it with a fire service and a night watch. A second Act, passed through the Parliament at Westminster in 1816, expanded the powers of the commissioners. Though never very satisfactory – the arrangement was a cumbersome one, with overlapping jurisdictions and frequent complaints from ratepayers about high valuations – this first essay in elected local government was by no means altogether ineffective, and would have been more effective still if its borrowing power had not been limited to £2,000. Within a year of its inception a visitor was praising the labelling of streets and the numbering of houses which 'gave a neatness and city-like appearance to the town'. Thirty years later another tourist remarked approvingly that the streets were 'marked by great regularity, having very good footways, and being, in general, well cleansed and lighted'.[21] By that time gaslight (supplied by the new Gaslight Company, a private concern which opened in 1823) had replaced the four hundred oil lamps purchased earlier.

POLITICAL CHANGE AND POLITICAL POWER

Enlightenment soon extended to politics. But whereas the economic developments so far described, and their social consequences, broadly conformed to the experience of other industrialising British cities, their political consequences were rather more special to Belfast, if not unique. In 1832, by the Irish Reform Act, the Corporation

The unveiling of the statue in memory of Frederick Richard, earl of Belfast, November 1855. This was the first public statue in Belfast. It was erected in front of the Academical Institution, but was replaced in that location by a statue of the Presbyterian minister Henry Cooke (see page 89). The earl's statue was painted black and ended up in the present City Hall.

was deprived of its monopoly in the election of the town's Members of Parliament, now increased to two. Under the new franchise of £10 householders (the same as in Britain) the electorate immediately rose from thirteen to over 1,600. A year later, the Corporation was comprehensively damned in the report of the Select Committee appointed to investigate the municipal corporations of England, Wales and Ireland, which concluded: '... now that the Sovereign and his colleagues have ceased to choose the Representative to Parliament of the Town, they do not appear to exist for any public or useful purpose'.[22] This judgement was echoed by the commissioners who investigated the Irish municipal corporations in 1835. The Irish Municipal Corporations Act of 1840 replaced the sovereign and burgesses by a Town Council of ten aldermen and thirty councillors, representing five wards, to be elected, like MPs, by male

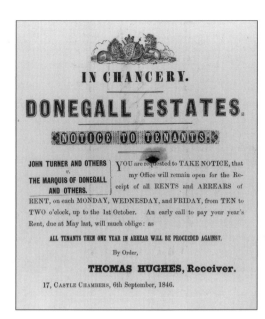

householders owning property valued at £10 or more. This franchise, it should be noted, was narrower than the one adopted in England, where after 1835 all ratepayers had the vote in local elections. The Council met for the first time in November 1842 and elected a mayor. The last sovereign, Thomas Verner, failed even to get a seat – an outcome that caused his patron and kinsman, George Augustus Chichester, the elderly marquess of Donegall, to burst into tears at a public meeting.[23]

This humiliation in fact virtually marked the end of the Chichester family's long domination of Belfast. The loss of political control, or at any rate the complete control formerly exercised through the old Corporation, was inevitable in an age of reform. The simultaneous decline in economic power, however, was a direct result of the second marquess's astonishing career as Lord Done'em-all. After surviving the desperate matter of his marriage, when he could not make full use of the estate's resources, Donegall and his heir Lord Belfast made a comprehensive new settlement in 1822 by which more than £200,000 was to be raised to pay off most of the father's old debts.[24] The money, which in the end amounted to more than £300,000, was raised by granting leases forever at low rents but for large sums in cash. These perpetuities affected almost all the ground of Belfast, as well as thousands of acres in Antrim and Donegal. Only when his father died in 1844 did the third marquess discover that the total amount owing was the immense sum of £400,000. The perpetuities affected almost all the ground of Belfast. The two main exceptions were Ormeau Park and the old Deerpark below the Cavehill. Eventually, under the Encumbered Estates Act of 1849, the whole property was put into the hands of a receiver and as much of it was sold outright as was needed to wipe the slate clean.[25] Paradoxically, whereas his father, the great absentee, had closely influenced the development of the town, the resident second marquess lost control of it.

IN CHANCERY

When the second marquess of Donegall died in 1844 his son and heir inherited the family titles and estates. The late marquess was supposed to have paid off most of the debts he had accumulated during his lifetime, and with his son's agreement had sold off a large part of the estates, so it came as a great shock to discover that most of the old debts were still owing, and the third marquess as he now became had his own debts as well. Altogether it totalled almost half a million pounds. The creditors took the matter to court and receivers were appointed to collect the rents. The receiver in this case was a Belfast banker. Eventually most of Belfast was sold outright.

NOTICE TO TENANTS FROM A RECEIVER

CHAPTER SEVEN

'FIT AND PROPER PERSONS', 1800–1860

T HE new town council was a very different body from the old corporation, not least in its social composition. Of the forty councillors first elected in 1842, twenty-five were listed as 'merchants', eight as 'Esq.' or gentleman', three as 'manufacturers' (two of linen, one of cotton) and one as medical doctor'. Three of the 'gentlemen' probably had commercial interests or connections. Commerce, not industry, was still clearly in the ascendant, one might conclude, though at least one 'merchant', Andrew Mulholland, was also a manufacturer. The really extraordinary thing about the Council, though, was that all forty of its members were Conservatives, despite the fact that a substantial and influential section of the town's middle class was Liberal. Even more extraordinary, not a single Liberal (much less a Catholic) was elected until 1855; of the six then chosen, Bernard Hughes, owner of a large bakery and flour mill, was also the first Catholic.

The virtual absence of manufacturers from the council in the 1840s and early 1850s can be explained by the fact that the old-established textile families, such as the Grimshaws, were Liberals – and Liberals, as we shall see presently, were excluded from the council by their own complacency and by the chicanery of their opponents. Party organisation in Belfast dated from about 1830, when liberal Presbyterians began to agitate for a radical reform of Parliament. These men were the political heirs of the radicals of the 1790s, and had recently, like their forebears, demonstrated strong support for Catholic emancipation, but there was one crucial difference between them and the United Irishmen of a generation earlier: Nationalism had ceased to be an essential element of their creed. This came about because Irish Nationalism after 1800 was, politically speaking, a protest against the union with Britain, yet the union had brought a period of great and growing prosperity for Belfast.[1] These Presbyterian Liberals formed an uneasy alliance with the Catholics, based on a common dislike of the Tory party and the established church with which it was so closely identified.

The Conservatives on the other hand were 'a defensive union of Protestants against the forces of Liberalism and Roman Catholicism', first organised to oppose the radical supporters of political change and thereafter, when the Reform Act became law, to secure the election of candidates to the House of Commons. The alliance consisted of traditional Tories (Churchmen), supporters of the Donegall interest in the corporation and moderate Whigs (Presbyterians). From the start they were more united than their Liberal opponents, who were increasingly divided in particular over the question of the repeal of the union, which Catholics supported and Protestants opposed.

Nevertheless, for the first twenty years Belfast was a keenly contested marginal constituency. The Conservatives won both seats in 1832, largely because the very radical programme of the Liberals did not appeal to the new electorate. Soundly defeated, the Liberals then abandoned radicalism and became a party of amelioration, supporting such local issues as municipal reform. This strategy worked so well that they took one seat in 1835, both in 1837 (when, however, they put up candidates without consulting the Catholics and on a platform which was distinctly Protestant and anti-repeal) and shared the representation again in 1842 and 1847. By 1852, however, the constituency had become a safe Tory one. The Conservatives won both seats in a landslide that year and the local Liberals thereafter disintegrated, being crushed in 1857 and unwilling to make any challenge again until 1865.[2]

The adherence of a substantial number of Presbyterians to the Conservative cause came about despite a history of antipathy between Presbyterians and the established church. A crucial role in this development was played by Dr Henry Cooke, minister of May Street Church (which was built for him) from 1829 till his death in 1868. In October 1834 Cooke took part in a great Protestant meeting at Hillsborough in County Down called by Lord Downshire and other leading Anglicans. In a stirring address, he presented himself as a 'sample' of the Presbyterians of Ulster and advocated the coming together of Presbyterians and Episcopalians, as in 1688, in defence of civil and religious liberty against Catholicism and arbitrary government. He concluded with a rhetorical flourish in which he published 'the banns of marriage' between the two churches. Cooke himself admitted that he was not typical of his brethren in championing the Conservative cause – indeed many of them were scandalised by his action – but beyond a statement from the Moderator saying that Cooke had not been representing the views of the church there was no official repudiation of his performance.[3] Cooke became increasingly influential as the scourge of Liberals and Repealers. When O'Connell paid his only visit to Belfast in 1841, to propagate the cause of repeal, Cooke challenged him to a public debate, which was declined; and

BERNARD HUGHES (1808–78)

Hughes arrived in Belfast as a penniless labourer from Co. Armagh in 1826. By the 1870s he owned the largest baking and milling enterprise in Ireland, introducing innovative production and marketing ideas and providing a cheap basic food at a time when people needed it most, during the Great Famine. He was Belfast's first elected Catholic municipal politician and an industrial reformer. His sharply independent outlook brought him into conflict with the Tory hierarchy of the town and also with the local Catholic bishop and the Catholic press.

COEY ALBUM, © ULSTER MUSEUM

HENRY COOKE

Today the statue
of Henry Cooke
– popularly known
as The Black Man
– stands in the centre
of Belfast, for Cooke
was one of those who
have made Belfast and
Northern Ireland what
they are. Born in 1788,
the son of a humble
Co. Derry tenant
farmer, he became the
most influential Irish
Presbyterian minister of
his age, a great public
figure and the friend
and confidant of British
prime ministers.

PHOTOGRAPH: CARNEGIE, 2009

riotous mobs disrupted O'Connell's meetings till the police escorted him out of town. The identification of repeal with Catholicism and Catholicism with intolerance and lack of liberty which Cooke expounded struck a chord in many Presbyterian hearts and minds, and weakened the Liberal cause. Relations between Presbyterians and Episcopalians were soured in the 1840s by disagreements over education and the validity of 'mixed marriages' between members of the two churches performed by Presbyterian clergy, as well as by the conciliatory policies of Peel's Conservative government towards Irish Catholicism, but on the whole the marriage of interests heralded by Cooke in 1834 increasingly became a reality, in political terms at least.

The failure of the Liberals to gain any seats at all on the Town Council in 1842 was directly attributable to the local party's carelessness and to the astuteness of John Bates, the Tory election agent from 1832 onward. Energetic, determined and unscrupulous – in 1835 he managed to have eighty Liberal voters disqualified because they had described their premises as 'house and shop' instead of 'house, shop' – Bates made himself expert in how to manipulate the voting register in both parliamentary and local elections. Under the terms of the Municipal Corporations Act of 1840, the register of local voters was based upon published lists, drawn up by the church-wardens of the parish, of all the male householders who appeared to be qualified on the basis of a £10 police tax valuation. These lists were then scrutinised by the rival parties, whose agents prepared objections to supporters of the opposing party who seemed to be dubious; four barristers appointed by the government ruled on their validity. On the Liberal notices of objection in 1842 both the name of the agent and his address were incorrectly stated. When Bates challenged them on this ground they were all declared invalid, whereas all the Conservative claimants went on to the roll of qualified voters. The resulting Conservative council appointed Bates (who continued to act as the party's agent) to the posts of Town Clerk and Town Solicitor. As Clerk, he was then responsible for compiling the lists of those who had paid their local taxes and were therefore, barring any other objection, eligible for the burgess roll; anyone who failed to pay any of the five rates could be disqualified. All the collectors appointed were Conservatives who, under Bates's guidance, ensured that as the deadline approached for registration Conservatives paid their rates on time and in full (if necessary they were lent the money to do so, or even issued with receipts without having paid), while Liberals were deliberately neglected. It later emerged that on average every year between 1843 and 1854 nearly half of the people apparently qualified were struck off, most of them Liberals; in 1852 a total of 999 Liberals out of 1,119 were removed, compared with 463 of the 1,322 Conservatives. The Liberals of course complained, but there was nothing much they could do about it. When Bates fell from power in 1855 the collector's office was conveniently burgled and the parish rate books were stolen.[4]

In 1842 the Conservatives were careful to distribute council seats to each of the elements among their supporters. Though Churchmen occupied the leading positions, Presbyterians were nominated for the largest single number of seats. Two supporters of the Donegall interest were also chosen, though not the last Sovereign, who stood as an Independent Conservative and lost. In three of the five wards the Tories were returned unopposed. The Liberals contested only one, St Anne's, where they put up four Protestants and four Catholics. From the start, the Conservative businessmen elected were content to ask no questions and to leave all arrangements to Bates, who, it has rightly been pointed out, came to occupy in Belfast a position not unlike that of a city boss in America. One alderman later confessed that he himself did not know the Conservative ward secretary, never campaigned for votes and did not even know of his election until he was told about it.

JOHN BATES

For many years John Bates (d. 1855) was Town Clerk, Town Solicitor and Conservative boss of Belfast.

FROM A POSTHUMOUS SKETCH, ARTIST UNKNOWN, © ULSTER MUSEUM, 2008

LOCAL GOVERNMENT

Despite the bigotry and corruption that characterised their complete domination of local government in the 1840s and early 1850s, the Conservatives were both energetic and effective in governing the town. Here one must note that the powers given to Irish town councils by the Municipal Corporations Act of 1840 had in fact been quite narrow. One notable omission, compared with the corresponding legislation in England, was control of the police, but in neither country were the new authorities empowered to carry out large programmes of municipal improvement. In Belfast the Police Commissioners (most of whom in 1842 were Liberals) and Police Committee continued to exist and retained responsibility for policing, lighting, paving and so on. One of the new Town Council's first actions, however, was to take over the powers of this rival organisation. The Town Clerk, Bates, secured a legal opinion that the successors to the twelve burgesses of the old corporation, who had been *ex officio* Commissioners, were all the people on the new, Conservative-sifted burgess roll. In January 1843 the mayor summoned these men to what he claimed to be a meeting of the Police Commissioners but which the existing Commissioners held to be illegal. Packed with Conservatives, this meeting swept aside the objections of the Liberals and voted to transfer to the Town Council the powers of the Commissioners

This portrait shows
the earl wearing the
uniform of the 7th
Hussars. He was
later captain of the
Yeomen of the Guard,
Vice Chamberlain of
the Royal Household,
Privy Councillor, Lord
Lieutenant of Co.
Antrim, ADC to the
Queen (1847–83).
When earl of Belfast,
he was described by
the compiler of *The
Complete Peerage* as
a typical easy-going
Irishman: always in debt.
He and his wife, who
was hot-tempered, and
he so handsome, were
known as 'Bel and the
Dragon'.

PAINTING (1824) BY JAMES ATKINS

and the Police Committee. A Liberal appeal to Parliament failed when a similar case in the town of Sligo was decided in favour of the council. So in January 1844 the powers of Belfast Town Council were immensely increased when the transfer took effect. So too were the patronage and influence of Bates, who had managed the whole affair.[5]

Thereafter, as in other cities, additional powers had to be sought by means of private Acts of Parliament (the expense of which until 1847 fell entirely on the town concerned). In this respect the Conservative council in Belfast demonstrated a zeal for improvement that was matched only by the most progressive Liberal corporations in Britain. Indeed by 1847 only 29 of the 178 municipal corporations in England and Wales had applied for additional powers to carry out improvements, whereas Belfast, established later than any of them, had already obtained three improvement acts – in 1845, 1846 and 1847. (Of the usual public amenities, only water never came under council control. Despite several attempts by the council, the water supply remained the responsibility of a separate elected body, which was established in 1840 to take over the task from the Charitable Society.) The aim of the Conservatives, according to the chairman of their local act committee in 1844, was 'to get the largest amount of good done at the least possible expense'. The three elements of the council's financial strategy were to raise revenue from the rates, to finance improvements by borrowing and to make profits from any improvements undertaken. The level of the rates was kept as low as possible, well below the limit allowed and just enough to pay normal operating charges and the interest on loans. Debts were to be paid instead from the returns on 'productive improvements'. The very concept of productive improvement, by which the council financed street schemes and other amenities by taking more land than was necessary and selling the surplus when improved, was anathema to the Liberals, who saw it as speculation by a public body with private property. In a rapidly expanding town it appeared to work, however. By 1850 the Conservatives could claim that the loan of £150,000 raised under the 1845 Act had been met by the sale of surplus land and the profits from the markets that the council had purchased.[6] The 1845 Act granted the power to borrow an additional £150,000 to widen old streets and make new ones, to pave, clean and light parts of the town, to lay sewers, to buy land for new markets and so on, and it also outlawed thatched roofs in all new buildings and forbade such undesirable practices as the keeping of pigs in dwelling houses and offering rotten meat for sale. The 1846 Act 'for the better lighting and improving the Borough of Belfast' gave power to borrow a further

**THE ULSTER BANK
(MERCHANT HOTEL)**

left
The former Ulster
Bank building. In a
competition to design
the Waring Street
head office, the
architect William Barre
was defeated by the
Glasgow architect James
Hamilton. The building
was completed in 1860.

above
The interior of the
building is a splendid
example of the High
Victorian style design
and architecture to be
found in Belfast. It is
now a five-star hotel.

PHOTOGRAPHS: CARNEGIE; NICK AT SYNC
IMAGING FOR THE MERCHANT HOTEL

£50,000 to municipalise the Gasworks. The 1848 Act and another in 1850 authorised further borrowing, mainly to deal with the 'Blackstaff nuisance' – a euphemism for the notorious health hazard created by the frequent flooding of a tributary of the Lagan which had become an open sewer – and laid down minimum standards for all new housing, including notably that each dwelling should have a small yard and an ash pit. Using the powers gained by this burst of legislation, the Council filled in the old docks along the river and created broad new streets, the most impressive of which were Victoria Street and Corporation Street. Using its powers under the 1845 Act, the Council formed a markets committee and bought up existing markets and market rights, paying over £20,000 to Lord Donegall for the ground of the Smithfield Market and his interest in it.[7] Altogether, markets and manorial rights cost £52,000, and a further £38,000 was invested in the creation of new market facilities which centralised trading in livestock and agricultural produce (one must not forget that in becoming a commercial and industrial centre Belfast never ceased to be an important market town) and put an end to the filth and inconvenience associated with street trading in livestock. The proposed purchase of the gas undertaking had to be abandoned, however, for lack of money. The draining of the Blackstaff was not achieved either, foundering on the reluctance of the Council on the one hand to undertake the scheme unless it was given large powers of compulsory purchase (and hence the prospect of large profits from selling off the land when improved) and on the other hand of the millowners using the stream (most of them Liberals), who obstructed voluntary purchase of their rights. The issue was to run and run, a good deal more vigorously than the polluted stream itself.

The Liberals' revenge, and a long pause in the spate of improvement acts, came in 1854, when a solicitor named John Rea filed a suit in the Court of Chancery in Dublin against the Town Council, naming as special respondents Bates, the Treasurer and sixteen leading councillors. The Council was accused of having exceeded its borrowing powers and of using for unauthorised purposes the money raised to buy the gasworks. Bates himself was charged with fraud and with having exacted exorbitant fees for his professional services as Town Solicitor. The Lord Chancellor's verdict, delivered in June 1855, found all the allegations proved and held the respondents personally responsible for the huge sum of £273,000. Bates resigned at once and died three months later, and the Treasurer also gave up his post (he had run an overdraft with the bank of which he was a director). Moderate Liberals were not unwilling to make an accommodation with the Conservatives, but a more extreme group allied itself with Rea. A private bill to indemnify the respondents foundered on the opposition of the no-compromise faction, but the report of a Royal Commission in 1859 was more favourable to the accused: apart from censuring the failure to drain the Blackstaff it spoke approvingly of the Council's improvements and referred to arbitration the question of the £273,000.[8]

These exciting events were not without their political effects. In 1855 the disorganised Tory machine managed to remove only 988 names from the list of qualified persons and the local electorate consequently shot up from fewer than a thousand to over 2,500. In the elections of that year the Liberals got six candidates in, one of whom was Rea himself. As a catalyst he had been superb, as a councillor he was deplorable. In council meetings, his characteristically disruptive and eccentric behaviour (as a solicitor he had a long history of being forcibly ejected from the courts) amused his supporters but alienated moderates, until he was ousted the following year. In an attempt to settle matters the Conservatives, whose electoral machine survived the demise of Bates and soon enabled them to recover their hold on the representation, voluntarily made way for seventeen co-opted Liberals in 1859. Two years later, with half the council seats under their control, the Liberals were able to install their nominee Sir Edward Coey as Belfast's first and only Liberal mayor.[9]

SECTARIANISM

'Apart from one-party dominance and a penchant for corrupt practices, the Council of the era of John Bates exhibited another unpraiseworthy characteristic, sectarianism. In every election of the period, with increasing emphasis, the close connection between civic prosperity and Protestantism was loudly proclaimed.'[10] This judgement may be illustrated by the story of John Clarke, the second mayor (a supporter of the Donegall interest), who was dropped by the Conservatives because he attended the dedication of the new Catholic church of St Malachy's in 1844 (when he helped to take up the collection and personally subscribed £10) as part of his declared policy of showing no partiality to any party or sect. Such was to be the fate of all moderates in the partisan world of Belfast municipal politics. How did this situation come about? And how did it become a permanent feature of Belfast life?

There was little or no anti-Catholic feeling in eighteenth-century Belfast because there were very few Catholics in the town and because, in a largely Presbyterian community, both denominations shared a common sense of being discriminated against by the Anglican establishment. In the early years of the nineteenth century, however, large numbers of Catholic immigrants came to Belfast to work in the cotton mills, altering the balance between the denominations in a short space of time. Whereas the proportion of Catholics in the population had been only six per cent in 1757 and no more than ten per cent at the end of the century, by the 1830s it was one in three.[11] This Catholic counter-colonisation of an area hitherto perceived as Protestant might not in different circumstances have caused such a hostile reaction. It coincided, however, with political and religious developments which polarised opinion nationally, notably O'Connell's campaigns for Catholic emancipation and for repeal of the union with England, the controversialist evangelical movements in both main Protestant churches and, in the 1850s, the appearance of a much more challenging, ultramontane spirit in the Catholic church associated with the leadership of archbishop Paul Cullen – a spirit which many Protestants, evangelicals in particular, interpreted as 'papal aggression'. These reinforced the division in the community. A property-owning franchise after 1832 gave Catholics little direct voice in Belfast politics, since few had sufficient property to qualify, but before the introduction of the secret ballot in 1872 they and their equally voteless Protestant counterparts could have what one sardonic observer later called 'a warm interchange of opinion on a basis of basalt'[12] at election time. Competition between Catholic and Protestant labourers, if not in the early years of the century then certainly later, added an economic ingredient to this explosive religious and political brew; it is sometimes forgotten that a majority of unskilled labourers were Protestants, though the proportion was smaller than in the case of the skilled. By the 1830s most Belfast Protestants believed that the maintenance of the union with Britain was good for business. At the height of O'Connell's repeal campaign in 1843, a petition that in the event of its coming about, the north should either opt to become a separate kingdom or remain within the union was seriously canvassed.[13]

The first reported riot in Belfast was as early as 1813, an Orange and Green affair that was an urban version of the kind of sectarian violence common enough in some rural areas but not typical of the opening decades of the century in Belfast. In fact, apart from a minor scuffle in 1825 between supporters and opponents of Catholic emancipation there were no outbreaks of any significance till the 1830s, the decade when real parliamentary politics arrived in Belfast. In 1832 two mobs stoned each other and four people were killed during the chairing of one of the successful Conservative candidates. The unexpected election of a Liberal three years later caused a clash between rival factions from Sandy Row (Protestants) and Pound Street (Catholics), a sign that the territoriality that was such a striking feature of sectarian strife in Belfast was already becoming established. A similar fracas occurred after the election of 1841. The pitched battle between the Pound Street Boys and the Sandy Row Boys two years later followed the Twelfth of July celebrations rather than an election but happened in the context of O'Connell's campaign for repeal, which reached its climax that year. In 1852 an election held on 12 July, in which the one Liberal member lost his seat, was the occasion of another confrontation in which at least one man was killed, the military had to be called in and (a new feature that was to become a familiar one) numbers of people fled their homes, taking their belongings with them. A much more serious outbreak occurred in 1857, starting with ten days of continuous rioting in which both sides, as well as the armed police who had been drafted in, did a good deal of shooting.[14]

This time the trouble had begun with a fiercely anti-Catholic sermon to a congregation of Orangemen, preached in his own church (which stood on the edge of the frontier or 'shatter zone' between Pound Street and Sandy Row) by the rector of Christ Church, the Rev. Dr Thomas Drew. Drew had been preaching in similar vein at open-air meetings in the town centre since the previous summer, and had been joined in publicising the evils of Romanism by another Church of Ireland clergyman, Thomas McIlwaine, and by a fiery Presbyterian, the Rev. Hugh Hanna. Indeed, the only inhabitants of Belfast entirely safe from sectarian preaching of one sort or another in the mid-nineteenth century were the inmates of the Lunatic Asylum, whose medical superintendent resolutely refused to admit chaplains, on the ground that 'over-zealous pastors might disseminate a wild and dangerous fanaticism amongst the lunatics'.[15] After the initial outburst had subsided the rioting resumed and continued well into September, despite the fact that the police had

THE CUSTOM HOUSE

The Custom House (1857), the finest work of the architect Charles Lanyon, who left an enduring mark on the appearance of Belfast. The steps were the 'Speaker's Corner' of the town and figured prominently in the riots of 1857; the cobbled street in front provided plenty of ammunition for those unconvinced by argument alone.

'THE SPEAKER'

The Custom House steps were used as the place for public speaking in the past. In honour of the fact, the city has erected a life-size bronze statue of a speaker in full flow.

been reinforced by the military. When all was over the Liberals demanded an inquiry, which was granted in the form of a Royal Commission. The Commission's report was rather inconclusive but chiefly blamed Drew's inflammatory preaching and the provocation offered to Catholics by the activities of the Orange Order. It also criticised the Town Police as both inadequate and biased.[16]

The 1857 report was to be only the first of many. Though the circumstances and the details of each outbreak were of course different, the basic cause of the continuing conflict – and the essential shape of 'the narrow ground' on which it was fought – was already fixed by 1860. A recent detailed study of the local politics of the period comes to this conclusion:

Behind the vicious sectarianism there lurked a political question involving a test of strength and a difference of identity: the Roman Catholics, seeing themselves as part of Ireland's overwhelming religious majority, challenged Belfast's identity as a Protestant town where they were regarded as alien intruders; the Protestants, fearful of Ultramontanism and of an Irish identity which Roman Catholics seemed to regard as exclusive to themselves, determined to assert that Belfast remained a Protestant town in a Protestant United Kingdom.[17]

RELIGION AND EDUCATION

There were, of course, many quite normal aspects of religious activity in this town where – as Thackeray remarked in 1842 – no stranger could fail to be struck, and perhaps a little frightened, by the number of churches and the esteem accorded to leading clergy.[18] The number of churches had certainly grown since 1800, but not nearly so quickly as the population. A second Church of Ireland congregation was established only in 1816, when St George's was built on the site of the old parish church at the foot of High Street. By the early 1830s, however, when Christ Church (Drew's) was built, the two buildings could accommodate only 2,300 of the nominal 16,000 members of the established church; in fact, since pews were bought and bequeathed as private property, only six seats were left for the poor.[19] By 1850 five more churches had been built, and by 1861 there were ten. Catholics had even greater difficulty in keeping pace with population. A second church, in Donegall Street, was opened in 1815 (like the first, with the help of Protestant subscriptions). By 1861 there were still only three churches, which with the chapels of a religious order and the diocesan seminary served a population of more than

41,000; the observation made (by a Protestant clergyman) in 1863 that only one-third of Belfast Catholics attended Sunday mass was probably true, if for no other reason than lack of a church to go to.[20] There was no Catholic church on the Falls Road until 1866, despite the numbers of Catholics who had settled there by that time. Poverty was a major cause of this time-lag. The much greater number of Presbyterian churches, on the other hand, was a reflection both of numbers and wealth; indeed Belfast was then, as now, the ecclesiastical capital of Irish Presbyterianism. The normal Presbyterian tendency to divide and form separate organisations in fact operated in reverse during this period, apart from the great split over Arianism at the end of the 1820s: in 1840 the two bodies that claimed the allegiance of most of the congregations in the north – the Synod of Ulster and the Secession Synod (the latter itself only united in 1818) – came together to form the General Assembly of the Presbyterian Church in Ireland. By 1861 mainstream Presbyterianism had no fewer than twenty churches in Belfast. A further twenty belonged to

other dissenting sects. The Protestant churches at that time were still digesting the effects of an extraordinary outbreak of popular evangelical fervour, which reached a climax in the 'Great Revival' of 1859, an experience which transported many worshippers into hysterics. (The typical Belfast converts were evidently unmarried mill girls. Male shipyard workers, despite all the efforts of evangelists, resisted almost to a man.)[21]

The 1861 census revealed that 30 per cent of Belfast Catholics were illiterate, as compared with 10 per cent of Protestants. Religion and public education were of course closely connected. In the early years of the century two undenominational schools for the education of the poor had been established, the Lancastrian school in Frederick Street (founded by the educational pioneer Joseph Lancaster when he visited Belfast in 1811) and the Sunday School Society school in Brown Street. The priest in charge of the Catholic parish from 1812, Dr Crolly, supported both of these schools for many years and was elected to the committees that ran them. In 1822 however, he was not re-elected to the Brown Street committee, and his offer to supply the Catholic pupils with free copies of the Douay version of the Scriptures was also rejected. As a result, he withdrew the Catholic children from Brown Street and set up a Sunday School in the new church in Donegall Street. Distrust of the Sunday School Society's evangelising policies combined with growing numbers of Catholic children (the new school soon had 1,500 on its rolls) to undermine the co-operation that had existed. Nevertheless, in 1825, when he was made bishop of

ROYAL BELFAST ACADEMICAL INSTITUTION

The school which would become 'Inst' was first proposed by a group of well-to-do Belfast merchants and professional gentlemen. The foundation stone was laid on 3 July 1810 by George Augustus Chichester, 2nd marquess of Donegall, who granted the school a lease for the grounds. Money was collected to pay for the building by encouraging rich merchants and businessmen to subscribe 100 guineas each for the privilege of being able to nominate one boy to receive free education. It is still a successful boys' school.

PHOTOGRAPH: CARNEGIE, 2009

Down and Connor, Crolly included many Protestants – including the sovereign, who proposed his health, and leading clergy – among his guests at a celebratory dinner, and was entertained in return by 170 of 'the most respectable Protestant inhabitants'. The fact that as bishop he chose to run his diocese from Belfast, rather than Downpatrick, indicates how significant the Catholic population in the town was becoming. As bishop, and later as archbishop of Armagh, Crolly supported the National Schools, introduced throughout Ireland after 1831, which were intended to be undenominational. However, in practice they became denominational because of clerical pressure from all sides. By 1854 there were 28 National Schools in or about Belfast, most of them under the control of the Protestant churches; at this stage, in the absence of sufficient schools of their own, many Catholic children attended what were in effect Protestant schools.[22]

At the secondary level the only establishment in the early years of the century, apart from a few small private schools, was the Belfast Academy, a Presbyterian foundation. A second, the Academical Institution, was founded in 1810 and opened its doors in 1814; one of its subscribers, incidentally, was the Catholic priest, Dr Crolly. The old radical Dr William Drennan (author, in one of his poems, of the epithet 'Emerald Isle' as a description of Ireland) delivered the opening address; and indeed the Academical Institution represented the liberal hopes of enlightened Presbyterians. It had a collegiate department which it was hoped would develop into a university and which in fact soon largely replaced Glasgow University as the seminary for Presbyterian clergy. The presence on the staff of liberal ministers such as the Rev. Dr Henry Montgomery drew down on the Institution the implacable hostility of the reactionary Cooke, who in 1825 accused them of promoting 'Arian' or unitarian doctrines. Cooke's strictures were not upheld by a government investigation in 1829. He did, however, oblige his opponents and their supporters to withdraw from the main Presbyterian body, which thereafter withdrew its students from the polluted teaching at the Institution.[23] (Following the union of the Synod of Ulster and the Secession Synod in 1840 and the opening of the 'godless' Queen's College in 1849, the orthodox Presbyterians built their own seminary, Assembly's College.) St Malachy's College, established in 1833, was the first Catholic secondary school for boys as well as a diocesan seminary. Victoria College, founded in 1859 by a redoubtable widow, Mrs Elizabeth Byers, was the first secondary school of respectable academic standing for Protestant girls. These sectarian divisions in schooling were by no means peculiar to Belfast, however.

The Academical Institution did not develop, as hoped, into a secular college of higher education, but the need and wish for such a college in the north of Ireland became increasingly strong. Trinity College, Dublin, the only university in Ireland, excluded both Catholics and Dissenters from degrees and appointments. In 1845 Peel's government decided to establish and endow colleges in the Irish provinces. The act establishing the Queen's Colleges did not specify where they were to be, and in the north the rival claims of Armagh and Londonderry were canvassed before Belfast was decided upon. The design of the architect Charles Lanyon for a Tudor-style edifice reminiscent of an Oxford college was accepted; work started in 1846, and the opening ceremony was carried out just before Christmas 1849. Though officially non-denominational, the College inevitably reflected the predominance of Presbyterians among its supporters and students: its first two presidents were Presbyterian ministers and it became in effect the college for Presbyterians, just as the Queen's Colleges in Cork and Galway became colleges for Catholics.[24] At the university level as in primary and secondary education, the ideal of every denomination was to control its own institutions.

The establishment of the Queen's College both confirmed and strengthened the intellectual and cultural interests already evident in the existence of the Academical Institution and other bodies such as the Linen Hall Library, the Literary Society (1801), the Natural History (later Natural History and Philosophical) Society (1821) – which in 1831 established the first museum in Ireland paid for by public subscription

QUEEN'S COLLEGE

The college was designed by Lanyon in the style of an Oxford college. The façade of the building has not changed greatly since the photograph (inset) was taken in the 1880s. The college received its charter in 1845 and opened in 1849. It gained full university status in 1908. The earl of Shaftesbury was the first Chancellor.

– and a Mechanics' Institute (1825). Another self-improvement group, the Historic Society (1810), did not long survive the arrival of real politics in the 1830s. One of its leading lights during its last years was the young Thomas O'Hagan (1812–85), a Catholic educated at the Academical Institution who went on to become Lord Chancellor of Ireland. On the whole, however, Belfast Catholics at this stage lacked either the education or the leisure to take much part in such activities. The town was remarkable in this period for a number of gifted amateur natural scientists, notably the botanist John Templeton, his son Robert, a renowned zoologist, and William Thompson, the leading authority on the invertebrate fauna of Ireland.[25] The visual arts were less well patronised: hopes for an art gallery, first expressed by the promoters of the Academical Institution and later attempted in the Museum, foundered on the philistine indifference of most potential patrons, though there were several local artists of some competence, and the owner of a cotton mill, Francis McCracken, was an early collector of Pre-Raphaelite paintings (unfortunately he had to sell them all when his business collapsed).[26] The linen manufacturers could not even be induced to subscribe half the running costs of a government-sponsored School of Design (1849–55) which aimed to train designers for the textile industry. The theatre in Belfast, formerly well supported, incurred the disapproval of respectable citizens in the 1840s and 1850s (the author of the entry in the *Parliamentary Gazetteer*, for example, remarked that it was 'much neglected, greatly to the credit of the metropolis of the north'). More popular entertainments, however, in the theatre and the Queen's Island pleasure grounds, attracted large crowds in the 1850s and 1860s; so too did the numerous public houses (over 300 by 1861, despite the efforts of the temperance movements that had developed in all the churches during the previous three decades). These diversions, like many other everyday activities, were still common ground in a town which in other respects was steadily growing more divided.[27]

Over the half century or so before 1860, Belfast like other towns in the United Kingdom had been transformed into a major industrial centre. Its urban facilities had similarly expanded as a result of public and private efforts. A social hierarchy of the kind to be found in other industrial areas had also emerged, with a commercial and manufacturing elite replacing aristocratic patronage and pretensions and dominating a growing urban labour force. Untypically, however, in Belfast divisions over nationality and religion were assuming greater importance than those of class and were already stamping their peculiar pattern on the social geography of this great and rising town.

THE OLD MUSEUM

This building, from 1831, is an excellent piece of work in the rare style of the Greek Revival, which was fashionable for a time in the 1830s. The opening was enlivened by the arrival of a genuine Egyptian mummy, which was witnessed by a fascinated audience.

PHOTOGRAPH: CARNEGIE, 2009

Industry, trade and society, 1861–1901

T HOUGH the basis of Belfast's reputation as a great industrial and commercial centre had already been laid by 1860, it was only during the last forty years of Victoria's reign that this reputation was actually given substance, first as 'Linenopolis' and then as the site of the largest shipyard and the largest ropeworks in the world, a major engineering centre and a great port. This chapter surveys these developments and the society, which both produced them and resulted from them.

Linen

The effect of the American Civil War (1861–65) on the Irish linen trade was nothing short of dramatic. With imports of raw cotton from the Confederate states cut off, the demand for linen and also its selling price soared. Both sectors of the manufacturing side of the industry, by then heavily concentrated in the north-east, benefited enormously. In Belfast itself, however, the boom led to the expansion of existing mills and factories rather than the building of new ones: only two mills were built between 1862 and 1871, and by 1866 only twelve of the country's powerloom factories were in Belfast. On the contrary, much of the expansion in production in the 1860s and early 1870s took place in rural areas of Ulster, now well served by railways, where wages were significantly lower than those paid in Belfast. Even so, by 1870 more than 80 per cent of the spindles in use and 70 per cent of the power looms were located in or near Belfast. According to the 1871 census, 8,500 of the town's 'industrial class' workers were employed in the manufacture of flax and linen. The more striking thing in the town, however, was the expansion of the commercial side: by 1870 practically every firm in the country had its warehouse and offices in Belfast and over 99 per cent of Irish linen was being exported through the port; the number of 'linen merchants and manufacturers' listed in the street directory rose from 29 in 1863 to over 150 in 1870. No fewer than 21,000 workers, out of the 50,000 engaged in industry and commerce, were employed in making or dealing in textiles and dress. At the height of the boom some firms made vast profits, in one case equalling the value of the entire premises and plant two years running. The reappearance of cotton caused some recession in the late 1860s, but in general the good times continued until 1873. By that date Belfast had become the largest linen-producing centre in the world, a position it retained until 1914.

A number of firms which had extended too far and too fast in the sixties went bankrupt in the later seventies. The next crisis, in the mid-1880s, was precipitated by the collapse of the great spinning firm of John Hind & Co. – a disaster brought on not by commercial failure but by a lawsuit over a will. No further run of bankruptcies occurred till 1898, when the effects of collapse were worse on firms in outlying areas than in Belfast. In fact the net outcome of these recurring difficulties was the still greater concentration of the industry in and around Belfast, where the surviving firms struggled with some success to keep up their share of a highly competitive market. This was achieved in part by more efficient production – improved hackling machines were adopted, for example, and spinning machinery was speeded up – but also by a determined search for new markets and new uses for linen, and by more aggressive marketing. Though the number of spindles fell from 925,000 to 828,000 between 1875 and 1900, linen at the end of the century was employing slightly more people than in 1868 because powerloom weaving increased.[1]

ARDOYNE MILL

Ardoyne Mill, established 1819, manufacturers of linen and damask.

A LETTERHEAD. ENGRAVING BY J.H. BURGESS c.1860, © ULSTER MUSEUM, 2008

VIEW OF THE

Royal Manufactory, of Linen and Damask, Ardoyne, Belfast.

Established 1819.

RICHARDSON SONS AND OWDEN'S LINEN WAREHOUSE 1861.

This is an appropriate place to add a footnote about cotton, whose displacement by linen was such a striking feature of the decades before 1860. That decline continued so far as manufacturing was concerned: by 1883 only one spinning mill remained and not a single weaving factory. A considerable business developed, however, in bleaching, printing, dyeing and finishing cotton piece goods from England and

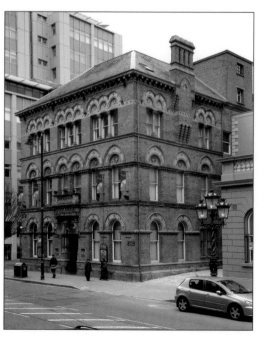

LINEN WAREHOUSE

Richardson Sons & Owden's linen warehouse in Donegall Square, early 1880s. Built in the late 1860s at the time of the great linen boom, this palace of commerce later became the head office of the Belfast Water Commissioners; it is now part of Marks & Spencer's store. This fine building was praised by Oscar Wilde.

R.J. WELCH COLLECTION, © ULSTER MUSEUM, 2008

below, far left
ROBINSON & CLEAVER

This department store was founded in 1870 in a modest way in Castle Place, but soon was so successful that premises in Donegall Place were obtained and in 1888 Messrs Robinson and Cleaver were proud to open the Royal Irish Linen Warehouse. The imposing building established itself as one of the city's landmarks and gained a world-wide reputation for the quality of its linens and other goods. Its patrons were not only Queen Victoria, but a number of the most aristocratic and important people throughout the empire and beyond.

left
BRYSON HOUSE

Bryson House was a linen warehouse, constructed in the 1860s and designed by W.J. Barre. It was one of many in and around Bedford Street.

PHOTOGRAPHS: CARNEGIE, 2009

Scotland; this led in turn to the local manufacture of cotton goods such as blouses, shirts and pinafores.[2]

The evidence of Linenopolis was to be seen not only in the great mills and factories to which the shawled women and girls hurried early in the morning and from which they poured out in the evening, but also in warerooms and workshops where linen was finished and made up and in the warehouses and offices of dozens of firms. Some of the best buildings that survive from this period were built as linen warehouses. When a foreign visitor admired Richardson Sons & Owden's building in Donegall Square (now owned by Marks & Spencer) and asked which nobleman had built it he was told, 'Duke Linen'. The Robinson & Cleaver building next to it, built in the late 1880s, was also a linen warehouse; so too were the Bank Buildings in Castle Place (see page 75), while Bedford Street consisted almost entirely of the imposing facades of such premises.[3]

SHIP-BUILDING

If linen was king in the sixties and seventies, ship-building rose in the 1880s and 1890s to share the throne. During the 1860s and 1870s the firm of Harland & Wolff produced a growing number of iron ships, many of them for the Bibby Line. The three launched for Bibby's in 1867 were constructed to a revolutionary new design by Harland which combined great length with narrow width and a flat 'Belfast' bottom. Derided at first by rivals as 'Bibby coffins', they were later admired as the 'ocean greyhounds' of their day. Harland & Wolff's connection with the Oceanic Steam Navigation Company of Liverpool – the White Star Line – began in 1870 with the *Oceanic*, which made all existing Atlantic liners obsolete, both in performance and in standards of comfort (innovations included cabins amidships, electric bells and lamps instead of candles). By later standards these iron liners were not particularly large (*Britannic* and *Germanic*, launched in 1874, were the first to exceed 5,000 tons), and they carried sail as well as steam, but they were the beginning of real comfort in ocean travel and fast as well. Harland & Wolff were to build increasingly large and more luxurious ships which would make their name and that of the White Star Line famous throughout the world. By 1880 the yard had been extended to forty acres and had ten slips; when it built its own engine works on the Queen's Island in the same year it became practically self sufficient.[4] Great as these changes were, they were only the beginning. Harland

EDWARD HARLAND

This statue of Edward Harland in the grounds of the City Hall is now overlooked by the elaborate steelwork of the Belfast Eye … engineering of a type which probably would have appealed greatly to Harland.

PHOTOGRAPH: CARNEGIE, 2009

himself, replying in 1879 to the toast of 'The Town and Trade of Belfast', indicated as much when he said: 'It is a new town without a history, and in time I have no doubt we will possess a reputation for commerce and industry that will assign us an important place in the history of the United Kingdom'.[5]

By that time Harland & Wolff's was not the only yard in Belfast. Another was founded in the late 1870s by Frank Workman, a local businessman, who was joined in 1880 by George Clark from Glasgow. Workman Clark's 'Wee Yard', as it came to be called, expanded rapidly in the 1880s and 1890s; by the end of the century,

HARLAND & WOLFF

The turning shop in the engineering department of Harland & Wolff, Belfast 1897.

R.J. WELCH COLLECTION, © ULSTER MUSEUM, 2008

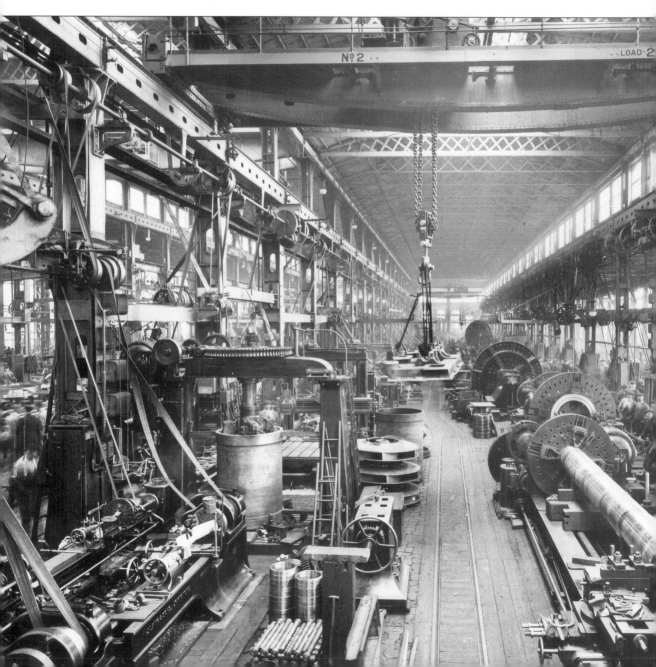

having taken over a third, much smaller yard and built up its own engine works, it was operating on a site covering fifty acres and had attained national importance. Its customers included P&O, Royal Mail, Cunard, Orient, Shaw Savill and Ellerman Lines, for whom it built ships of up to 15,000 tons.[6] Although a serious trade depression in the early 1880s had obliged Harland & Wolff to cut its workforce from 5,000 to 3,500 and to reduce the wages of those who remained, a really spectacular growth of ship-building in Belfast took place in the late 1880s and 1890s. The halcyon era in passenger liners began with the launching in 1889 of the *Teutonic* and *Majestic* for the White Star Line – steel vessels of nearly 10,000 tons with twin screws, triple-expansion engines and accommodation for more than 1,300 passengers.

In the years that followed, Harland & Wolff launches averaged 100,000 tons a year; by 1900 they were employing 9,000 men. Between them the two Belfast yards outstripped those of all other UK regions in their rate of growth right up to the outbreak of the war in 1914, but especially so during the years before 1900.[7] The year 1899, in which Harland & Wolff launched four ships for the White Star Line, including *Oceanic II* – at 17,274 tons the largest ship afloat, and the first to exceed Brunel's *Great Eastern* in length – demonstrated the firm's achievement at the end of the century, when it had become the greatest single shipyard in the world.

Harland himself had begun to withdraw from active management quite early, to enter public life as chairman of the Harbour Commissioners (1875–87), an alderman (1883–87), Mayor of Belfast (1885 and 1886) and finally Conservative MP for North Belfast 1887–95 (when he died). His partner Wolff also withdrew and became an MP, in his case for East Belfast 1892–1910. It was a Belfast man, William Pirrie, who had become a partner in 1874 at the age of twenty-seven, who presided over the firm in its greatest days. The entrepreneurial flair and business acumen of such men were certainly an important factor in the success of Belfast's shipyards. Access to markets, through contacts and connections was vital in what was almost entirely an export industry. Pirrie had many such contacts, and also arranged for established customers to have the benefit of a secret 'commission club' (members could have their ships built at cost price plus a small percentage fixed commission); the advantage to the yard was that orders could be maintained at a high average level. An abundant supply of cheap labour was also important, for though skilled men in Belfast were paid more than the national average, wages for the workforce as a whole were rather less. A reputation for good workmanship, established under the exacting management of Harland, no doubt helped as well.[8]

ENGINEERING

The success of linen and ship-building encouraged the growth of engineering; between 1865 and 1900 the number of engineering workers grew from 900 to 9,000. By 1870 there were twenty foundries in Belfast but, undercut in the making of cast-iron and brass products by English and Scottish firms (both Harland & Wolff and Workman Clark found it cheaper to run foundries on the Clyde), most of them could survive only by making machinery. Steam engines were made by Coates's and Rowan's for use in linen mills (the Ulster Museum has examples of both); Coates's also made water turbines and, at the turn of the century, electricity generation equipment; McAdam Brothers made steam pumps which were used in Nile irrigation schemes; Combe Barbour made engines for cotton mills in India. Even Belfast got its linen looms from Manchester or Leeds, but it became the leading centre in the world for the production of linen machinery for processes which had no equivalent in cotton – hackling, spinning, beetling. The Falls Foundry of James Combe (later Combe Barbour) had been making hackling machines from the 1850s. The Clonard Foundry, established by George Horner from Leeds in 1859, found a world market for its famous 'Duplex' machine, which hackled both ends of the flax. James Scrimgeour, a Scot who came to Belfast to start a textile machinery works, was succeeded when he failed in the Albert Foundry by his manager James Mackie, another Scot, who made a great success of it. Mackie's became a limited company in 1897 and in 1902 took over the Clonard Foundry. By that time Mackie's and Combe Barbour were the largest engineering firms in the city apart from the shipyards, between them manufacturing the entire range of flax-processing machinery. An incidental advantage of having the makers and their chief customers in close proximity was that adjustments and improvements could easily be made.[9]

There were also successful firms in other branches of engineering. Musgrave Bros, for example, became internationally known during this period for its decorative cast-ironwork, patent stable fittings and heating equipment. By the end of the century many of the best stables of Europe were furnished by Musgraves'. The same firm's domestic and institutional heating stoves (the more luxurious in 'ethnic' styles such as the 'Slav', with beautiful coloured tilework) were also to be found all over the British Isles and Europe. By 1900, in which year 'Le Poêle Musgrave' won a gold medal at the Paris Exposition, the firm had a branch in the Rue de Rivoli and was producing a catalogue in French with colour illustrations.[10] One other specialist engineering firm which attained a worldwide reputation deserves mention here. Samuel Davidson spent his early years in the Assam tea plantations, where he devised drying machinery which he patented on his return home. The machines were at first made by a local engineering firm, but when Davidson finally came back to Belfast in 1881 he started his own 'Sirocco' works. By the end of the century Sirocco was

MUSGRAVE BROS STOVE

Le Poêle Musgrave: illustration of stoves from the French catalogue of Musgrave & Co., Belfast Iron Founders. This firm was established in 1855 and developed a lucrative business in cast-iron products of all sorts including stable fittings, cast-iron furniture, and stoves from the utilitarian to the beautiful. It had a branch in Paris in the rue de Rivoli, and produced a French catalogue with coloured illustrations.

© ULSTER MUSEUM, 2008

producing most of the world's tea-drying machinery and a large proportion of its ventilation equipment; most of the ships of the German Grand Fleet, scuttled at Scapa Flow in 1919, were equipped with Sirocco fans.[11]

OTHER INDUSTRIES

Impressive as they were, linen, ship-building and engineering were not the whole story. This period also saw the rise of an extensive ropeworks, formed in a small way near the Queen's Island shipyard in 1873 but rapidly expanded after 1876, when it became a limited liability company with Gustav Wolff as chairman and W.H. Smiles (son of the famous Dr Samuel Smiles, author of *Self Help*) as managing director. An early publicity coup was achieved by persuading the French tightrope walker, Blondin, to use its products. By the turn of the century it was the largest ropeworks in the world, covering forty acres and producing not only rope and twine of all kinds but also sash cord, fishing lines and nets, and binder twine for harvesting machines; the number of employees had risen from only one hundred to 3,000.[12]

Belfast also became a major producer of whiskey, in the days before the Irish variety of the water of life was displaced in world opinion by Scotch. Large-scale production of whiskey began after 1860, when Dunville's gave up their tea business to concentrate on distilling. In 1870 William Dunville, in partnership with James Craig (father of the first prime minister of Northern Ireland), built a huge modern plant on the Grosvenor Road; by 1890 it was producing two and a half million gallons of proof spirit. The Irish Distillery at Connswater in east Belfast was producing two million gallons by 1900, and the Avoniel Distillery about 850,000. In fact Belfast firms were responsible for well over half the total whiskey exports of Ireland.[13]

In a smaller way, soft drinks were also an export success. In the middle of

JOY'S PAPER MILL

The Joy family were significant players in the development of Belfast. They were active in journalism, politics and the cotton and linen industries. Their paper mill at Cromac opened in 1767. Carey's painting drew attention to the huge contrast between past and present in the mill area: Carey painted the Mill in a historical, pastoral setting, but the area was increasingly dominated by offices, warehouses and the Gasworks.

BELFAST CITY COUNCIL

the century there were a dozen small firms producing 'aerated waters' from the exceptionally pure artesian springs on the outskirts of the town at Cromac. The most successful of these were Grattan's, Corry's and Cantrell's (from 1867 Cantrell & Cochrane's), to which was added W.A. Ross & Co. in 1876. Though never so important to the economy of Belfast as extensive advertising and hard selling made them appear, these firms and their products became known throughout the Empire and wherever European settlers found the local water undrinkable. Ross's claimed to have invented the gin and tonic as a way of marketing their tonic water with quinine, Cantrell & Cochrane's to have invented ginger ale (which was also a speciality of Ross's). By the late 1880s, Cantrell & Cochrane's had 500 employees in Belfast and Dublin (the Dublin branch opened in 1869) and was producing over 160,000 bottles of table waters a day; Ross's produced 36,000 a day in Belfast in 1889.[14]

Tobacco, a larger employer of labour, was dominated in particular by the rise of Gallaher's. In 1863 Thomas Gallaher transferred his successful but small-scale operations from Londonderry to Belfast, where his superior pipe tobacco could be produced more cheaply and in greater quantity to meet a growing demand (between 1850 and 1900 per capita consumption of tobacco in Ireland doubled). During the

ROPE-MAKING

Belfast Ropewalk at the Bloomfield Mill of the Belfast Rope Works (1899). In its day this rope works was the largest in the world. The photograph shows fishing lines being made. Overhead is a 'Belfast Roof', a distinctive local style of construction using timber trellis.

© ULSTER MUSEUM, 2008

1870s power-driven machinery began to replace hand-operated methods, and in 1881 Gallaher built a five storey factory in York Street employing 600 people; a still larger one was added in 1896 on the same site. In terms of customs revenue, tobacco became a major import into Belfast; in 1889 Gallaher's alone paid duty amounting to almost half a million pounds.[15] The other notable firm of manufacturers, Murray Bros, expanded less spectacularly than Gallaher's but it too became a substantial enterprise.

Lastly, three Belfast printing firms achieved national or international reputation during this period. Marcus Ward & Co. had started as papermakers before developing as chromolithographers and pioneers of the Christmas card. They exhibited at the Great Exhibition of 1851 and thereafter with increasing success at exhibitions all over the world, notably in Paris in 1867 and 1878 (where they gained the highest awards in all the classes in which they exhibited), Philadelphia and Melbourne. At their peak they employed more than fifty artists and designers at their Royal Ulster Works, and also bought in the services of such notable illustrators as Kate Greenaway. For many years an important bread-and-butter income was derived from a monopoly of printing the Vere Foster writing and drawing copybooks, familiar to generations of schoolchildren. Another firm, McCaw, Stevenson & Orr, which started in the mid-1870s, specialised in commercial and advertising products, such as the 'Glacier' transparent coloured labels which adorned many late-Victorian shop windows. A third firm, David Allen & Sons, became the leading supplier of colour posters for the English-speaking theatrical world. At one point in 1889 it was calculated that they had something like 16,000 theatre posters on London hoardings alone. So good did business become that branches were opened in London and New York, and the firm later transferred its headquarters to the capital.[16]

The phenomenal growth of Belfast industry and commerce during the later Victorian period attracted notice and comment from many quarters. One such source, better informed than most, consists of the reports produced by French consular officials in Dublin for various ministries in Paris. Three volumes relating specifically to Belfast over the period 1861–98 are now on microfilm in PRONI, Belfast. The writers came and went in quick succession on the whole, and some of their work appears to have been of poor enough quality. Agent Villantrey (1863–66) not only surveyed the linen industry in a competent manner but also attempted to analyse the success of this 'Athens of the North'. His summary conclusion was that in contrast to British towns of comparable size and prosperity, Liverpool and Southampton had the advantage of good geographical location, and Birmingham and Newcastle had easy access to rich supplies of industrial raw materials; Belfast on the other hand 'owes its prosperity only to the activity and enterprise of its inhabitants, for, though situated at the northern end of an impoverished land, far from paved roads and deprived of fuel, it has nevertheless become a large manufacturing centre and almost rivals the more flourishing cities of Great Britain, thriving both as a centre of manufacturing and as a port'.[17] In fact the port made the rest possible.

MARCUS WARD & CO.

Title page of photograph album by Marcus Ward & Co., 'embellished with plumage and foliage from many lands' – a superb work.

MRS ANNA STEWART

THE PORT

The continued expansion of the port and harbour facilities was both a condition of all this industrial and commercial growth and a consequence of it. In 1892 exports from Belfast included 35,000 tons of linen, 24,000 tons of whiskey and nearly 9,000 tons of mineral waters, not to mention almost all the output of the shipyards and engineering works. Agricultural exports included 65,000 head of cattle and 11,000 tons of grass-seed, as well as considerable quantities of cured ham. Imports in the same year included half a million tons of coal, 86,000 tons of iron and castings, more than 160,000 tons of wheat and Indian corn, and most of the flax used in the linen industry. By that time the port was clearing nearly 9,000 vessels a year with a tonnage of just under three million, as compared with 1,372,000 in 1867. The

SAIL-MAKING

In port cities in the nineteenth century many riverside properties were given over to ancillary maritime activities such as chandlery or sail-making. This photograph shows the premises of James Tedford & Co. Ltd, a narrow three-storey stucco building on the Donegall Quay upon the gable of which is a stucco lifebelt marked, 'Est. 1851,' and with embossed lettering, 'Ships Chandlers, Sail and Tentmakers' Nearby is a gable fronted warehouse where the canvas sails were sewn. Until recently it was decorated with a gaily painted ship's figurehead. The dates of the buildings are uncertain: the sail loft between 1760 and 1790 and the shop 1843. In 1998 Tedfords Riggers and sailmakers moved to new premises.

PHOTOGRAPH: CARNEGIE, 2009

number of ships handled had increased by less than one thousand but they were much bigger vessels and a greater proportion of their space was devoted to cargo. These larger vessels with their deeper draughts made it constantly necessary to improve the port and harbour facilities, a course which the Harbour Commissioners followed with great energy and foresight. On the County Down side of the Lagan, the Abercorn basin and Hamilton graving dock, started in 1863, were opened four years later. In 1872 the Spencer and Dufferin docks opened on the County Antrim side. The Queen's Quay, completely reconstructed, was reopened in 1877 as part

HARBOUR OFFICE

The headquarters of the Port of Belfast, an imposing sandstone building, built in two sections during the nineteenth century.

PHOTOGRAPH: CARNEGIE, 2009

of an extensive programme which included the rebuilding of the Donegall Quay, the renewal and extension of the Albert Quay and the widening and deepening of the existing channel. During a visit by the prince and princess of Wales and Prince Albert Victor in 1885 the new Donegall Quay was declared open and the first sod of a new graving dock was cut. Albert Victor returned in 1889 to open the Alexandra dock. The century-old connection of the Chichester family with the Ballast Board and its successor came to an end at this point: when the fourth marquess of Donegall died in 1888 the office of president, which he had held by virtue of being lord of the castle, was abolished.

By the time the duke of York came to Belfast in 1894 to open the dock named after him, all the docks, quays and sheds were lit by electric light, produced by a special generating station erected in 1892 at the Abercorn basin. The rowing-boat ferries across the harbour were replaced by steamboats in 1872. The Harbour Office, built in the 1850s, was greatly extended in the early 1890s, to designs by W.H. Lynn, Lanyon's former partner. As the century neared its end the commissioners obtained another Act of Parliament to widen and deepen the Victoria Channel, to make a new cut with a tidal dock at the end of it, to construct two other docks on the site of older existing ones and to build a graving dock on the County Down side. The first part of this ambitious programme was started in 1899 and the new cut, named the Musgrave Channel, was opened in 1903. Compared with other major ports such as Liverpool, Belfast was fortunate in having only a small tidal range. There was no need to enclose the docks by gates; vessels could lie alongside the open quays and wharves to discharge their cargoes and could be berthed, docked and undocked at all times without waiting for high water.[18]

POPULATION CHANGE

In the forty years between the census of 1861 and the death of Queen Victoria the population of Belfast almost trebled, from 121,000 to just under 350,000. Part of the increase can be attributed to a boundary extension in 1896 which expanded the physical area of the borough from ten to twenty-three square miles. Officially Belfast's population became larger than that of Dublin, much to the northern city's satisfaction. Most of Belfast's human growth, however, was caused by the immigration of workers attracted by the dynamic industrial and commercial scene described above: the decades of most industrial growth were also those of greatest increase in numbers. The rise in 1861–71, for example, the years of the linen boom, was no less than 43 per cent, the highest in the town's history after the start of censuses in 1821. By contrast the 1870s and 1880s, with decennial increases of 19 per cent and 22 per cent, were periods of lower (if still substantial) growth. The boom years of the 1890s were reflected in a rise of over 36 per cent, only a small fraction of which was due to the boundary extension.

This late nineteenth-century immigration was largely from the eastern, predominantly Protestant counties of Ulster. The proportion of Catholics in Belfast's population consequently declined during this period, from a fraction over one-third in 1861 to just under a quarter in 1901. Their numbers, on the other hand, more than doubled, from 41,000 to 85,000, and in the circumstances of the time this rise in absolute numbers seemed more significant in sectarian calculations than the proportionate decline. There was comparatively little immigration from further

QUEEN VICTORIA LOOKS OUT OVER BELFAST

Queen Victoria looks out over Belfast. View from City Hall grounds along Donegall Place.

PHOTOGRAPH: CARNEGIE 2009

afield. Though its ship-building and engineering industries attracted skilled workers from Scotland and the north of England (a two-way traffic), Belfast never had any large number of immigrants from outside the British Isles – unlike Liverpool and other places. A few more Italians appeared towards the end of the century.[19] A small Jewish community also developed, starting in the 1860s with a handful of well-to-do families from Hamburg engaged in the linen trade, notably the Jaffe's. Gustav Wolff, Harland's partner, was another prominent member of this group. Around the turn of the century a larger influx of poorer refugees from Russia settled in Belfast. Even so, by 1911 the entire Jewish community numbered only 1,140.[20]

At the turn of the century only one-fifth of the city's householders had been born in Belfast. The proportion of native-born was somewhat higher among Catholics than among Protestants a reflection of the heavier immigration of Protestants (particularly Presbyterians) into the city in the preceding generation or so. Another significant feature revealed by the censuses was the consistently greater number of women. In 1841 there had been 38,000 women and 32,000 men; sixty years later, with 188,000 women and 162,000 men, the ratio was very much the same. Nineteenth-century Belfast in fact provided more employment for females than most other cities in the British Isles, particularly in the textile industry and allied trades; domestic service was less important as a way of escaping from what for some was the unattractively 'restrictive, male-dominated environment of the family farm'.[21] By the turn of the century nearly two-fifths of the city's workforce consisted of women.

HOUSING AND URBAN DEVELOPMENT

The growth of its industry and population led to a great expansion in the physical size of Belfast in the later nineteenth century. The immigrants of the 1860s and early 1870s mostly settled close to the linen mills and factories where they found employment; the working day started early enough without a long walk to reach the mill gate in time to avoid a fine for lateness. In order to have their workers close at hand, especially where mills were situated beyond the built-up part of the town, millowners themselves constructed rows of small 'kitchen' houses. Some of these were so badly built that they were slums almost at once: a medical officer in 1873 described mill houses with walls of single brick only four inches thick and flat roofs covered with tarred felt as 'not fit to afford shelter to domesticated animals, much less to our fellow-creatures'. If built recently, however, these deplorable dwellings were probably outside the town boundary, for an Act of 1864 (unique to Belfast, as the Royal Commission on the Housing of the Working Classes noted in 1885) had made landlords responsible for the cost of rates and repairs for all houses with a Poor Law valuation of less than £8 – in effect, all working-class homes. This and stricter building regulations introduced in 1878 made employers uninterested in providing houses.[22]

right

URBAN IMPROVEMENT

A major improvement in 1878 changed the future geography of a large part of the city centre by taking powers to lay out a grand new thoroughfare stretching from Donegall Place to York Street. In the process the old butchers' quarter in Hercules Street was swept away, along with a warren of rotten slums. The outcome was Royal Avenue, a wide boulevard with buildings of tall, uniform frontages. The Grand Central Hotel was planned as part of a rail link that was never built, but the hotel was still by far the most prestigious in the city.

R.J. WELCH COLLECTION, © ULSTER MUSEUM, 2008

Landowners, even those at a secondary level who held long leaseholds from major proprietors such as Lords Donegall and Templemore, played little or no part in the great building boom of the late nineteenth century; most of those concerned were professionals. A crucial role was played by developers – individuals or companies with land at their disposal who laid out their property in building plots, which were then sold or (more usually) leased to builders; some developers, such as the Methodist College and Cliftonville Football Club, were in the development business only part-time or incidentally. Building societies, of which there were eight in Belfast by the early 1880s, provided capital by lending to builders rather than occupiers. So too did building-society-type investment companies such as the Royal, the Bloomfield (particularly active in east Belfast), the Ulster and the Belfast Provincial, which themselves built and owned houses. Some estate agents, such as William Hartley in the 1870s and R.J. McConnell & Co. later, were also major developers and building entrepreneurs; McConnell's in particular built all over the city and for every class of inhabitant. Large contractors such as H. & J. Martin (who owned 300 acres of building land and brickfields) and McLaughlin & Harvey did the same, not to mention some of the city's 170-odd smaller builders. In the last thirty years of the century the stock of houses quadrupled; almost 50,000 were built between 1880 and 1900, a figure representing more than half of all the houses built in Belfast between 1861 and 1917. In the latter decade alone the number of inhabited houses rose from 55,000 to 67,000; the total stock included several thousand more lying empty, for a notable feature of all housing development at this period was that dwellings were built speculatively, ahead of actual demand, and could remain unsold for several years. Nearly 2,300 new ones were built in 1895, nearly 3,000 in 1896 and almost 4,500 in 1898. By the turn of the century there was no shortage of houses, only a shortage of decent houses that the poorest could afford.[23]

Building costs in Belfast were low, not so much because wages of labourers were in general low, though that was true (the highest-paid bricklayers could not earn more than 35s. for a 56¼ hour week), as because there was plenty of cheap local brick. Indeed ever since Sir Arthur Chichester had fired over a million bricks from the local clay to build his castle, Belfast had been a brick town. By 1900 there were more than thirty brickworks in and around the city producing not only millions of the 'commons' used for general building but also a wide variety of fancy bricks and the terracotta panels and ornaments so typical of the better houses of this period. H. & J. Martin's brickworks on the Ormeau Road, the largest in Ireland, produced 60,000 bricks a day in 1888; their price of a guinea a thousand in 1885 was half the cost of bricks in Dublin. Furthermore, Belfast was very well placed to import cheaply, and in as much variety as anyone could wish, the timber, slates and other materials not available locally. Most timber for houses came from the Baltic and most slates (even the smallest kitchen house needed at least a ton) from North Wales, apart from a few years in the late 1890s when a labour dispute at Penrhyn led to the importation of large quantities from the United States.[24]

By the standards of the time, Belfast in the late nineteenth century was well housed, if rather crowded. It had few if any of the dreadful tenement houses to be found in Dublin or Glasgow, for as the well-to-do inhabitants moved out from the centre their homes were made into offices or knocked down for redevelopment as commercial premises (this is why scarcely anything of the Georgian town survived); while its main growth came late enough to ensure that most of its working-class houses were purpose-built to minimum standards, thus avoiding the cellar dwellings and back-to-backs of Manchester and other cities. The great belt of working-class housing that encircled the city centre by the end of the century consisted mainly of 'kitchen' houses, small terrace houses whose front doors (on the street) opened directly into the kitchen/living room that occupied most of the ground floor; the stairs led from the kitchen to the two bedrooms upstairs, the front one of which was usually much bigger than the back one. Behind the kitchen on the ground floor were a small third bedroom and a scullery. The rent of a kitchen house was 3s. 6d. to 4s. 0d. a week. The up-market alternative to a kitchen house was a 'parlour' house at 4s. 6d. to 5s. 0d. a week. Like the kitchen house this had four rooms and a small scullery, and was of similar size, but the front door opened into a small hall out of which rose the stairs to the two bedrooms (there were only two), and off which were doors to the parlour at the front and the kitchen at the back. Quite apart from its lower rent, the kitchen house was popular because its three bedrooms better accommodated the large families that were the norm at that time in both Protestant and Catholic households. In the 1890s some larger parlour houses, with a third bedroom in a return over the scullery, were built for renting by the highest-paid artisans at 5s. 0d. to 6s. 3d. a week; it was the overproduction of this type of house that mainly accounted for the 10,258 dwellings listed as empty in the census of 1901.[25]

AVA BRICKWORKS, ORMEAU

These brickworks, along with a few other brickfields in the Ormeau area, must have produced a very large quantity of the bricks for the construction of the city of Belfast as the deposits of clay were of a very high quality. There was a huge stone-built kiln and storage building at the back of Deramore Gardens on the riverside with the large flooded dam on the lower slopes nearer the Lagan. H. & J. Martin's brickworks on the Ormeau Road were producing 60,000 bricks a day in 1888. Their price of a guinea per thousand in 1885 was half the cost of bricks in Dublin.

© ULSTER MUSEUM, 2008

TRANSPORT

The growth of public transport during the later nineteenth century had little effect on the pattern of development of working-class housing in Belfast; most people lived near their work and in any case could not afford to spend money on fares. Cheap and reliable public transport did a great deal, however, to encourage growing numbers of business and professional people to live at a considerable distance from their work. The flight from the town centre had begun earlier with wealthy merchants and manufacturers who had built country villas on the outskirts, at Malone, Strandtown and the Shore Road. From the 1840s the railways enabled such people to commute easily. It was horse-drawn omnibuses, however, that first conveyed passengers in large numbers across the town and served the nearer suburbs as they grew; by 1870 there were regular services as far as Windsor in the south, Fitzwilliam in the north and Sydenham in the east. From 1872 omnibuses were increasingly challenged by trams, also horse-drawn. The Belfast Street Tramways Company, set up in that year by a group of London businessmen, ran single-decker, one-horse trams to begin with, but introduced double-deckers drawn by two horses from 1878. By that time the lines extended to Dunmore Park on the north side and on the south to Ormeau Bridge and the Botanic Gardens. The omnibuses held their own comfortably enough until the early 1880s. Then a new manager, Andrew Nance, transformed the operation of the tramway company by introducing a two penny fare for any length of journey and a five-minute service on the main routes. Additional lines soon extended the network in all directions and it was also linked to the Cavehill and Whitewell Tramway (set up in 1882) which served the upper reaches of the Antrim Road. The introduction of a penny stage fare finished off the competition: the last omnibus service ended in 1892. The Corporation, which had an option to purchase the Tramway Company after twenty-one years, postponed the purchase (and the necessary electrification of the system) for another fourteen years, till forced by public pressure for purchase to do so in 1904. By the turn of the century the Tramway Company had almost a hundred tramcars and 800 horses. The number of passengers it carried each year had risen from one million in 1881 to ten times that figure in 1891 and to 28 million by 1904.[26] The vast majority were residents of the new lower-middle-class suburbs of small villas and terraces which had grown up beyond the solid ring of working-class houses that enclosed the city centre.

SANITATION AND HEALTH

Though the majority of working-class houses at the end of the century had been built in the previous twenty or thirty years under regulations that should have ensured reasonable standards of construction. Some of them had nevertheless been built in

NORTHERN CYCLING CLUB

Members of the Northern Cycling Club in Ormeau Park c.1880. Note the fashionably healthy clothing and uniform headgear. At meetings the members of the club were marshalled by bugle calls (the bugler is on the right). These men were the fitness fanatics of their day, able to cycle as far as Portrush on the north coast of Antrim, though usually content to stay the night before returning home. The new safety bicycles were soon to make the penny farthing obsolete.

PHOTOGRAPH BY ROBERT SEGGONS, © ULSTER MUSEUM, 2008

ways, and in places, that were anything but salubrious. Giving evidence in 1896 to a public health inquiry, the assistant town surveyor admitted that one site on the Shore Road was 'an enormous dunghill' composed of 'horse manure, cow manure, human excrement; everything of the most abominable character … you would have to go on stilts. No language is too strong to describe it'. One of the chief offenders was Sir Daniel Dixon – seven times lord mayor, knighted in 1892 created a baronet in 1903 and later Unionist MP for North Belfast – whose property company made a fortune by buying large tracts of slobland, filling it with anything that came to hand and creating the maximum number of building plots, which were then leased to small builders for the highest possible rents; 75 acres of mud near the Connswater in east Belfast were thus made to yield ground rents of almost £3,000 a year. A Labour councillor rightly lambasted such 'rack-renters, land speculators, jerrybuilders, usurers, etc.', who acquired swamps and then used their positions on the corporation 'so that the swamps are filled up at the corporation's expense by ashpit refuse, road scrapings, etc.; after which, street upon street of doggery houses are erected thereon, irrespective of the grave and imminent danger to the public health'.[27]

Apart from such unsatisfactory new houses there were many older ones that caused concern on grounds of health. The 1878 Act ensured that all houses built after that date had back access, but houses without access remained a high proportion according to the Medical Officer of Health in 1892:

> At present some 40 per cent of houses in the city have the system of privy and ashpit combined in the small back yard, immediately contiguous to the rooms in which the inmates live and sleep. In thousands of cases there is no back passage or means of access to the yard … save through the house, and hence all the accumulated filth must be removed by carrying it through the kitchen.[28]

In 1896 a special corporation committee, set up to inquire into the city's high death rate, was told by the Sanitary Officer that there were still 20,000 houses (out of a total of about 70,000) without back passages. Until well into the 1890s it was apparently not uncommon for the contents of the cleared privies and ashpits to be left lying in the street to await collection.

Conditions in the old, pre-by-law slum areas off the city centre were worst of all. In the opinion of one witness a piggery in Barrack Street was more fit for human habitation than some of the houses in Millfield Place nearby; and the only sanitation in St James's Square, a foul little court of six houses in the area between York Street and Corporation Street, which had an entrance too narrow to admit a wheelbarrow, was a common pit in front of the dwellings. 'You could not walk through the little narrow passage between the common pit and the houses', reported one who had not forgotten his visit to the place, 'without going over your shoe mouth in human excrement.'[29]

BELFAST TOWN HALL.—Mr. A. T. Jackson, Architect.

THE TOWN HALL

The Town Hall, Victoria Street, c.1900. Opened in 1871, the building was too small and deemed too modest in style for the activities of the City Council (1888), which set about acquiring a site for a new City Hall. At the height of the Home Rule crisis in 1913–14 these premises were the headquarters of the Ulster Volunteer Force.

Very few houses in working-class areas had water closets at that date. Belfast's unique addiction to the old dry closet system was to some extent caused by recurring crises in the supply of water, which could not keep pace with the constantly increasing demand, despite the efforts of the Water Commissioners. In dry summers there was never enough: by 1890 the city was using 9¼ million gallons a day, twice as much as in 1880. Drinking water was sold round the streets from horse-drawn carts, and in desperation even the filthy river Lagan was used. Not until 1893 was the problem tackled in anything other than a piecemeal way. An Act of that year authorised the Commissioners to commence a long-term scheme to draw water from the Annalong valley in the Mourne Mountains, thirty-five miles away. The first Mourne water, both abundant and pure, arrived in 1901.[30] In anticipation of this happy outcome to an old problem the Corporation in 1899 took powers to compel the owners of houses with cesspits, privies and pail closets to provide them with water closets. All or part of the money could be borrowed from the Corporation, which for its part undertook to provide the necessary sewage works.[31] Under this

ARHogg

20

legislation most of the old privies were replaced by backyard water closets within the next twenty years.

Victorian cities imported their water but exported their waste as manure or sewage. Belfast was as slow to solve the latter problem as the former, mainly because public health was not taken seriously in official circles until late in the century. It was 1865 before the Corporation appointed a sanitary committee, and the first Medical Superintendent Officer of Health was not appointed until 1880 (following the Public Health (Ireland) Act of 1878). At last in 1887 an Act of Parliament was obtained to sanction the construction of a main drainage system. From the dispersal point at Duncrue Street the untreated sewage was carried, by means of a wooden 'shoot', across the mud flats and out into deep water in the Lough. As early as 1897 the shoot was said to be unsatisfactory because of leaks and bursts, and there were complaints about the smell at low tide. The small tidal range in the Lough, so beneficial to the development of the port, here made matters worse. Nevertheless, and despite continuing problems with flooding in some of the very low-lying areas near the Lagan and along the course of the Blackstaff (which was culverted in the

1880s), the construction of the sewerage system was a major achievement; though much improved and extended later, it is only now being replaced.[32]

As well as human and industrial waste there was a great deal of animal waste to be disposed of. Inevitably in a world of horse transport, the growth of the city added enormously to the problem, but horses were by no means the only source of it. In 1896 there were more than 800 dairies within the boundary, and many people in the poorer areas kept pigs and fowl. Evidence was given to the 1896 special committee about the danger to health of keeping livestock in densely inhabited streets; one small yard in Percy Street contained 60 pigs and 30 cows, the sewage from which oozed through a wall into the street.[33] Dairies and cowsheds were at least subject to regulation and inspection by the Corporation. The numerous stables were not; the Tramway Company, whose horses were for many years stabled in Wellington Street in the city centre, was merely the largest of many.

The first Medical Superintendent Officer of Health, Dr Samuel Browne, was an elderly former naval surgeon who had been mayor of the town in 1870 and was its Sanitary Officer at the time of his appointment in 1880; he died in office ten years later at the age of eighty-one. His successor, Dr Henry Whitaker, was both elderly and poorly qualified, though an enthusiastic writer of reports. Unfortunately, like most doctors at the time he believed that miasma (polluted air) was responsible for the transmission of infectious diseases such as typhoid fever, which was not only endemic in Belfast but actually increasing in the 1890s. A seven-year delay in adopting the Infectious Disease (Notification) Act of 1890 masked the true scale of the problem; as soon as the Act was implemented there was an immediate huge rise (or apparent rise) in the number of cases, from 219 in 1896 to 3,269 in 1897. In the following year there were nearly 6,500 cases; 662 people died. The epidemic was largely blamed on the consumption of shellfish, which were gathered from the sewage-polluted shores of Belfast Lough by the poor and sold from barrows in the street, until sale was forbidden by a by-law.[34]

The great killer, however, was tuberculosis, which caused as many deaths as all the other communicable diseases put together, over a thousand a year in most years between 1889 and 1906. The death rate from tuberculosis ('phthisis' to doctors, 'consumption' to most laymen) for Ireland as a whole at this period was higher than for the rest of the British Isles. Arguably Belfast was no worse than other parts of Ireland, except in one respect: the very high death rate among women in the age-range 25–44. This was one of the occupational hazards of working, as so many Belfast women did, in the linen mills and factories. The risk of industrial accidents was much the same in Belfast as in any other manufacturing city of the period. Like factory owners elsewhere, Belfast employers opposed the introduction and enforcement of legislation requiring them to fence off dangerous machinery; in 1855 the linen manufacturers had affiliated to the Manchester-led National Association of Factory Occupiers, the body Dickens styled the 'Association for Mangling

Operatives'.[35] Shipyard accidents were also common; working with red-hot rivets on high scaffolding was particularly dangerous. The leading ophthalmic surgeon in Belfast during this period made his professional name with an operation to remove metal fragments from the inner eye of a Harland & Wolff apprentice by means of a magnet.

Working conditions

Conditions of labour in the Belfast linen industry may not have been exceptional in United Kingdom terms – in the Lancashire cotton industry the hours of work were just as long, the workers contracted similar occupational diseases and the risk of accidents with machinery was just as great – but they were altogether exceptional in Ireland, and there can be no doubt that their effect on the health of women and children in particular set Belfast apart. About 70 per cent of all linen workers were female, about a quarter juveniles under the age of eighteen. The proportion of children under thirteen increased during this period from 2 per cent in 1868 to 9 per cent in 1890, then began to fall. Hours of work in linen spinning mills and weaving factories were restricted by the same factory acts as in the cotton and woollen mills of England, and reductions were greeted with similar cries of woe by the employers ('It will ruin our trade, and perhaps leave Belfast a forest of smokeless chimneys', said the president of the Belfast Chamber of Commerce of the 1874 Factory Act, which limited the working week to 56 hours).[36] Workshops, as distinct from factories, were not covered by this legislation until 1878. Till then, certain linen operations continued to demand very long hours; the linen lappers in 1861 complained of being made to work sixteen or seventeen hours a day.

But it was the risks and dangers to health specific to the various processes of spinning and weaving linen that drew the attention of factory inspectors and medical officers. The effect of fine dust on the lungs of workers was worst in the processes by which flax was prepared for spinning. Hackling (which involved roughing, machine combing and sorting) was carried out by men and boys; the certifying medical officer for the Belfast factory district remarked in 1877 that roughers and sorters were so well known to have bad lungs that the Army was forbidden to recruit them. Preparing (which involved spreading, drawing and roving) released even finer, and therefore more dangerous, dust. To make matters worse, the temperature in the preparing rooms was kept high. The women in these departments were subject to dreadful attacks of coughing and diseases of the lung; one manager described spreading in particular as 'sure death'. The carding of tow (a by-product of hackling), which was done by young women, was described in 1867 as the 'dirtiest, most disagreeable as well as the most unwholesome and most dangerous of all the departments connected with the spinning of flax'; the average working life of a carder was reckoned to be only seventeen years or so. Many workers, male and female, could get through the day only by drinking large quantities of alcohol, which added to the already considerable risk of accidents with the machinery.

The hot and moist conditions needed for the wet-spinning process produced anaemia and 'mill fever' among the women and girls who formed the vast majority of the workforce in the mills. The spinners were also liable to get a very particular occupational condition known as onychia, a painful inflammation of the big toe nail which was caused by working barefoot on floors covered with hot contaminated water. Onychia became less common with better drainage and the more frequent wearing of shoes (though bare feet were often safer than shod ones in the wet conditions). The process called dressing – treating the yarn with a mixture of carrageen moss, flour and tallow prior to weaving it – was a very unhealthy one because of the high temperatures used (90–125° Fahrenheit); only fit adults were employed, and they were paid much higher wages than the rest. Even weaving, regarded as more desirable work, was pretty unhealthy. Workers frequently suffered from chest trouble caused by the hot and damp atmosphere in the weaving sheds and the stooping posture they had to adopt. The death rate in weaving was high partly because women whose health had already been ruined in the preparing processes were recruited to it. Not all employers were indifferent or hostile to attempts to make working conditions less unhealthy. In the 1870s one large firm pioneered the use of steam to purify the atmosphere in its hackling, preparing and carding departments (many workers in these dangerous areas resisted well-meaning attempts to make them wear respirators), and it was the largest, the York Street Flax Spinning Co., that introduced localised exhaust fans over the hackling benches, long before such measures were made compulsory in 1906. Nevertheless, at the turn of the century the certifying officer of health for the Belfast factory district (Dr H. S. Purdon, who succeeded his father in the post) found still rife all the diseases and ailments reported a generation earlier by his predecessor, with the sole exception of onychia.

Whatever the effect on their health, and despite the low wages they earned (linen was a low-wage industry, even compared with jute), women were glad to be employed in flax-spinning and weaving and anxious not to lose their jobs. In many poorer households, where the husband had an unskilled labouring job or none, the wife's wages from the mill were essential to keep the family out of the workhouse. As little time as possible was taken off to have children. The children themselves, often raised by 'baby farmers' on a diet of tea, whiskey and laudanum, were taken to work at the mill as soon as they reached (or would pass for) the minimum age (before 1874 eight, thereafter ten).[37]

EDUCATION

Being employed at the mill did at least ensure that children received some schooling, as 'half-timers'. One Belfast millowner, giving evidence to the Powis Committee in

1870, thought half-timers would be better employed and educated on alternate days rather than half-days, being 'not in a proper state of dress when leaving work to go into school, and vice versa'. And indeed the Committee's report found that the mill children were separated from other pupils not only by educational backwardness but also by the disagreeable evidence of their employment:

> … the afternoon set come to school in a state of personal dirt and squalor, which makes association with them disagreeable and offensive in the extreme. The room is pervaded with the nauseous odour of the oil with which flax is impregnated; the children's faces are smeared with the oil and dust which adheres to their fingers after their work; their scanty ragged clothing, with an old shawl thrown over their shoulders to protect them from the rain, distinguishes them painfully from their companions, who are apt to shun them as an inferior class.[38]

After 1874 alternate days became the rule. The system began to decline when the Education Act of 1892, which made full-time attendance compulsory to the age of eleven, took effect, but it was not officially abolished until 1920.

Attendance might be compulsory, but the National Schools in Belfast at the end of the century were in general so badly financed, staffed and equipped and so lacking in adequate accommodation that they could scarcely cope with the numbers on their rolls. Some millowners provided schools for their half-timers, and a few were owned by trusts or individuals, but the great majority belonged to and were run by churches. In Belfast in the 1860s the Presbyterian church owned and ran most of the National Schools – 70 out of the 80, according to the new Catholic bishop, Patrick Dorrian, who was greatly concerned at the number of Catholic pupils attending them, for want of schools of their own.

Dorrian's resolve to change this state of affairs was strengthened by Pope Pius IX's official condemnation of the 'mixed' principle in December 1864. His success during the next twenty years in establishing schools under church control, though naturally a source of great satisfaction to the Catholics of Belfast inevitably also brought about what lack of resources and the caution of his predecessor Bishop Denvir had hitherto prevented – namely the more or less complete separation of Catholic and Protestant schoolchildren. On a practical level, some schools in poor areas faced severe problems. An extreme example, perhaps, was one described by an unsympathetic critic in 1868 as having 64 Presbyterian and 18 Catholic pupils, more than half of whom were illegitimate and 'hard to manage', and an assistant teacher who was reputedly a prostitute.[39] In the absence of school boards, such as existed in Great Britain after 1870, no local body – least of all the Town Council with its concern for the rates – was prepared to take responsibility for schooling. It is only fair to note that, despite all the difficulties, real progress was made. In 1861, according to the census, 30 per cent of Catholic children were illiterate, compared with 8 per cent of Presbyterians; the figures in 1891 were 14 per cent and 5 per cent.

Secondary education expanded to meet the needs of a growing professional and commercial middle class, also along sectarian lines (the tutorial colleges which crammed candidates for entry to the armed forces or the civil service were perhaps an exception). The Methodist College, opened in 1868, was in its early years both a seminary for theological students and a secondary school for boys and girls. Campbell College, a Presbyterian foundation for boys on the lines of an English boarding school, was established in 1890. On the Catholic side, St Malachy's College was enlarged and rebuilt in 1867 and St Dominic's High School for girls was opened on the Falls Road in 1870. The Christian Brothers, invited to Belfast by Bishop Dorrian in the 1860s to provide primary teaching for poor boys, later offered secondary-level instruction as well.[40]

CHURCHES AND CHARITIES

As the city grew, all the main denominations built new churches (often with schools attached) and scores of gospel halls and mission huts sprang up as well. The late nineteenth century, in fact, was the greatest church-building period in Belfast's history, as Christians of all kinds strove to catch up with the needs of an ever-increasing number of adherents – not to mention the many lost souls who had no connection with any organised religion. The Church of Ireland, which had eight or nine churches serving a nominal membership of 30,000 in 1861, built another sixteen during the next four decades and laid the foundation of a new cathedral (which replaced the eighteenth-century parish church). Mainstream Presbyterianism started the period with twenty churches for 42,500 people and finished it with 47 congregations for a membership of 120,000. The Roman Catholic community, with five churches and 41,500 members in 1861, built another six, including the pro-cathedral of St Peter's in Derby Street; in 1901 there were just under 85,000 Catholics in the city. All denominations sought to organise into regular membership the irregular or unattached. Church-going may have become almost universal among the middle classes and the respectable working class which adopted middle class morals and ethics, but it was far less common among the working class in general. In 1888, when Methodist lay missioners surveyed the situation in the Shankill area, the very heartland of militant Protestantism, they found scores of homes with no church connection and where no clergyman had ever called; in one street alone, 55 of the 110 homes were 'unchurched'. All the denominational missionaries, in their quest to reach these lost souls, had to face the realities of life at the lowest level of urban society. The annual report of the Belfast Central Mission for 1893 refers to 'work in slumdom' among people who were 'debased and debauched to the last degree'; volunteer workers were said to 'descend into hell every Saturday afternoon'. As well as the moral squalor in which the inhabitants of the poorer quarters lived, their physical condition became a matter of immediate concern to mission workers.[41]

The poor, the sick and disabled, and those who had fallen on hard times were the objects of charity for the many voluntary societies that operated to alleviate the lot of the deserving poor. The most successful in attracting general public support were those which dealt with the victims of natural handicap, such as the Society for Promoting the Education of the Deaf and Dumb and the Blind, the Association for the Employment of the Industrious Blind and the Cripples' Institute. Even the most successful societies brought relief only to small numbers, however; Prison Gate missions for released prisoners, the Home for Friendless Females, Lady Johnston's Bounty and other such, however well intended, made little impression on the problems they attempted to address.

As in the provision of schools, the main impulse of those concerned in charitable work was religious; and because this was the case, charity, like education, became largely a denominational matter. In a city where most of the population belonged to one or other of the Protestant churches, and where most of the wealth was in Protestant hands, the main voluntary societies were inevitably controlled by Protestants. Few, apart from avowedly denominational organisations such as the

MAGDALEN LAUNDRY

'Fallen women' or 'penitent victims of seduction' at work in the laundry of a Presbyterian institution recently transferred from grim-looking premises in Brunswick Street in the city centre to these more agreeable quarters in Sunnyside Street off the Ormeau Road.

A.R. HOGG COLLECTION, © ULSTER MUSEUM, 2008

orphan societies, excluded Catholics from benefit, with the exception of the Cripples' Institute, but the Deaf, Dumb and Blind School in practice required all its boarders to attend Sunday worship at either St George's Church of Ireland or Fisherwick Presbyterian church. A recent study has concluded that by the end of the nineteenth century in Belfast 'the division between Catholic and Protestant benevolence was almost complete'.[42] Apart from occasional co-operation, as when Bishop Dorrian sat on the committee of the Coal Relief Fund in 1879, the Catholic church set up its own structures. Catholic charity was organised through the religious orders and the lay workers of the Society of St Vincent de Paul. The first St Vincent 'conference' was established in 1850; many more appeared after 1860. Their work covered a wide range of the activities undertaken by a number of separate Protestant-controlled societies; women volunteers assisted the efforts of the Sisters of Charity and the Sisters of Mercy. In 1867 Bishop Dorrian invited the Good Shepherd Sisters to come to Belfast to work among fallen women. Their convent on the Ormeau Road, built in 1867, was enlarged and rebuilt in 1893 and again in 1906. Like the Presbyterian-controlled Ulster Female Penitentiary and the Anglican-controlled Ulster Magdalene Asylum, the Convent of the Good Shepherd ran a profitable laundry. Whatever their religious denomination, fallen women did a lot of washing.[43]

The late nineteenth century brought a great expansion in hospital services. Apart from the workhouse infirmary, the refuge of the desperate or the fever-stricken, most of the public hospitals were charitable institutions dependent on subscriptions and donations; patients who could afford to pay were treated in private clinics or nursed at home. The main hospital was the Belfast Royal Hospital in Frederick Street, an institution which had started as a fever hospital in 1817 and had later become a general hospital (it got its royal charter in 1875). The growth of the city made its facilities increasingly inadequate, until at last plans to replace it got under way in the late 1890s. The new Royal Victoria Hospital was named in 1899 and opened four years later in the grounds of the County Antrim lunatic asylum on the Falls Road (the 'insane poor' were removed to Purdysburn, a 300-acre estate acquired by the Corporation from the Batt family in 1895). Even medicine could not entirely escape the tendency towards sectarian organisation: a second general hospital, the Mater Infirmorum on the Crumlin Road, originating in the work of the Sisters of Mercy, was established in 1883 under Catholic control. Apartheid did not extend to admissions, however.

A number of specialised hospitals also appeared. The Hospital for Sick Children, originally established in King Street in 1873, acquired new premises in Queen Street in 1885. The Hospital for Skin Diseases (1865) was given a fine new building in Glenravel Street in 1875 by a notable benefactor, Edward Benn. The Ulster Eye, Ear and Throat Hospital (1871) was nearby in Clifton Street. The Ophthalmic Hospital in Great Victoria Street (1867) replaced an earlier Ophthalmic Institution. The Samaritan Hospital for Women, on the Lisburn Road, another of Edward Benn's gifts, was founded in 1872. The Samaritan charged 9s. or 10s. a week for each of its intern patients. The Throne group at Whitehouse comprised a children's hospital, a convalescent home and a small hospital for consumptives endowed by Forster Green, another notable benefactor. Lastly, the Ulster Hospital for Children and Women, in Fisherwick Place provided twenty beds for children and ten for women.[44]

A particular medical problem arose from the scale of prostitution in the poorer quarters of the town. Poor Law records suggest that there were 500 or so full-time prostitutes in Belfast in the latter part of the century; in Ireland only Dublin had more. The Guardians were so concerned about the spread of syphilis in the Union Infirmary that they twice tried to have the Contagious Diseases Act (under which, until 1886, prostitutes in garrison towns could be compulsorily examined by doctors) extended to Ireland. Objections from local clergy and others, however, overrode even arguments based on the likely saving to ratepayers. In the 1880s the Infirmary alone was treating about thirty patients a week, and the General Hospital, which had closed its doors to such cases 'on moral grounds', had to admit them again. One indication of the scale of the problem is the fact that in 1880 the Belfast garrison had the highest VD rate of any of the main Army establishments in the British Isles – no less than 428 per thousand – and was always among the first six. So far as possible, official Belfast preferred not to face such unpleasant realities.[45]

By the end of Victoria's reign in 1901 Belfast had become a city of 350,000 people, the major port in Ireland and one of the leading industrial and commercial cities of the United Kingdom. Its linen, ships, ropes, tobacco and mineral waters were known throughout the British Empire and the trading world. Though not equally notable for cultural interests and achievements, except in natural and applied science, it had a high opinion of the value of education (and self-education). A lively press reflected these achievements, but also reflected (and at times exacerbated) ever-sharpening political and sectarian divisions within local society.

CHAPTER NINE

PARTY POLITICS AND LOCAL GOVERNMENT, 1861–1901

Economically and physically, and in the matter of municipal enterprise, Belfast during the latter part of the nineteenth century developed in very much the same ways as other British industrial cities. Politics was another story altogether. Here sectarian and ethnic considerations increasingly distorted the picture in a way that made Belfast different to the point of being unique.

SECTARIAN VIOLENCE AND PARTY POLITICS, 1861–86

The rituals of sectarian conflict which had become established during the decades before 1860 continued after that date, with some significant variations which reflected the development of the town itself and of the national political scene. The next major outbreak after 1857 occurred in 1864, when at least a dozen people were killed and hundreds injured in rioting which went on for ten days in August. The trouble began on 8 August with the return from Dublin, by train, of a large party of Catholics who had attended a great Nationalist demonstration to mark the laying of the foundation stone of a monument to Daniel O'Connell. The Sandy Row Protestants particularly resented such a display at a time when Orange parades in the north were illegal under the Party Processions Act of 1850, and showed their displeasure by burning a huge effigy of the Catholic hero at the boundary between Sandy Row and the Pound. Though the occasion of the clash was novel, in that it arose out of a national political event rather than a local one, the conflict that ensued between the two sets of partisans at first followed the now traditional pattern, escalating from mutual provocation, through increasingly serious confrontations between rival mobs, to armed skirmishes with the police and military who tried to restore order.[1] What was different, however, was the more widespread nature of the disorder and the significant part played in it by Catholic navvies and Protestant shipyard workers.

The navvies had come to Belfast to work on the construction of new docks. On 15 August, a Catholic holy day, they ransacked the town centre, seizing guns and looting shops before marching to the Shankill Road and attacking Brown's Square

National School. This foray led to a Protestant attack on St Malachy's church and a convent nearby. An attack on Bishop Dorrian's house was answered by one on the home of Dr Cooke, the Presbyterian divine. Next day the Protestant shipwrights marched into the town centre and plundered gun shops and hardware stores before attempting to attack the Catholic pro-cathedral in the Falls, where a Methodist church had been the target of a Catholic mob. When thwarted by the military they demolished Malvern Street National School, working (as the principal said later) 'calmly and deliberately … like furniture removers'. The day after, the navvies were caught at work by the shipyard workers and, their retreat cut off, had to flee across the mud flats or swim the harbour; one man was killed by a blow from an adze, many were wounded.[2] There was little sympathy for the navvies from any shade of Protestant opinion. The Liberal newspaper, the *Northern Whig*, had observed the previous day:

> The prosperity of our town, which is the envy of the rest of Ireland, brought to it for the formation of our new docks this horde of assassins; and the

HARLAND & WOLFF WORKERS C.1912

A fleet of open-top trams awaits some of the thousands of workers leaving the Harland & Wolff shipyard after their nine-hour day. Some would have cycled (cycle racks were provided), but many others were on foot because they lived in the terraced houses within walking distance of the yard.

© SEAN SEXTON COLLECTION_CORBIS

greatest punishment that could be inflicted upon them would be, not to send them to jail, but to dismiss them, and send them starving from our town, as starving they came to it.[3]

The 1864 riots, like those of 1857, were the subject of an official inquiry, this time conducted by Serjeant Barry, QC. The Conservative magistrates came in for much criticism for failing to take prompter action against Protestant mobs. The Town Police were particularly censured for their highly sectarian composition (all but half a dozen of the 160 were Protestants, some of them Orangemen) and their partiality. Recent research however, suggests that their failure to do better was due less to partiality (for which there is little evidence) than to the inadequacy of any untrained local force to deal with prolonged conflict between two determined sets of urban rioters. Nevertheless, the main recommendation of the inquiry's report was that the Town Police should be disbanded and replaced by a much larger number of men from the national police force, the Irish Constabulary (or Royal Irish Constabulary, as it presently became).[4] The recommendation was promptly carried out. The 480 constables subsequently stationed in Belfast, the majority of whom were Catholics from the south of Ireland, were resented by the Town Council and most of the Protestant population; as it turned out, they were no less a target in future confrontations than their predecessors had been in earlier ones.

In local politics, the Conservative stranglehold on the Corporation, which had been interrupted briefly by the co-option of a large number of Liberals in 1857, soon resumed as strongly as ever. Co-opting Liberals had not proved to be an effective strategy. Early in 1861 five of them refused to act (although the Liberal mayor, Coey, managed to persuade four to change their minds) and another two had to be replaced later in the same year. One even went so far as to get himself struck off the burgess roll so that his resignation would have to be accepted. The return of Rea to the Council further discouraged moderate Liberals from attending. From twenty in 1860 their numbers fell to twelve in 1863 and eight in 1868.[5] The report of the inquiry into the 1864 riots remarked that the Town Council was then, and appeared likely to remain, anti-Liberal; the chairman of its Police Committee, Samuel Black (who was later for many years Town Clerk), startled the inquiry by stating that he could usually tell a man's religion by the look of him. In the general election of 1865, even with a single candidate untainted by local associations (Lord John Hay), the Liberals failed to get sufficient support among Presbyterian and Catholic voters. On polling day, thoughtfully fixed by the Conservative mayor and returning officer, John Lytle, for the Twelfth of July, there were rowdy scenes inside the Court House, which Lytle allowed to be taken over by a crowd of Conservative supporters, described by the Liberal press as 'a gang of ferocious Orange ruffians armed with bludgeons of a most formidable character'; outside, a Catholic mob wrecked Protestant houses and stoned the constabulary.[6]

After 1865, however, there was a brief Liberal revival. An Ulster Liberal Society was formed to look after the registration of voters and to bring together Liberal Protestants and Catholics. A young solicitor named Charles Brett took responsibility for registration in Belfast and managed it with uncustomary efficiency. When the 1868 election came the Liberals had a single, local candidate, Thomas McClure, while their opponents were for once seriously divided. The Belfast Conservative Association had nominated the architect and former mayor Sir Charles Lanyon and the millowner John Mulholland for the two seats, despite the presence in the field of an existing Protestant candidate – a leading Orangeman named William Johnston, who was proclaimed at a mass meeting of Protestant working men at which the dictation of the Conservative clique in the Town Hall was denounced. The Conservative vote was inevitably split and McClure and Johnston (who had made contact with the Liberals and received a contribution from them towards his expenses) were elected.

The election of McClure was to be the last Liberal success in Belfast and did not last long (he lost the seat at the next general election in 1874). The election of Johnston, on the other hand, signalled the emergence of a new force in local Conservatism. The Irish Reform Act of 1868, by reducing the borough franchise from £8 to 'over £4' and extending the boundaries of the Belfast parliamentary constituency to the municipal boundaries of 1853, increased the number of voters by about 7,000 to just over 12,000 (there were 3,243 municipal electors).[7] The majority of the newcomers were skilled working men, the kind of unionised craftsmen who in England would probably have voted Liberal but who in Belfast espoused Toryism or a populist Orangeism – working-class, democratic and sectarian – which opposed a Liberalism that embraced Catholic voters. Thus the arrival of democracy increased rather than diminished the sectarian nature of Conservative rule in Belfast.

The membership and influence of the Orange Order had grown considerably since the middle of the century, when it had 35 lodges and some 1,300 members in the town. In 1864 a separate Belfast Grand Lodge was formed, and by 1870 there were more than a hundred lodges and over 4,000 members. During the later 1860s the national leaders of the Order, predominantly episcopalian clergy and gentry, accepted the Party Processions Act and were more concerned about the threat to disestablish the Church of Ireland than about the right to march. Many Belfast members, on the contrary, deeply resented the Act and welcomed the defiance of it (and of their own leadership) organised by William Johnston in 1866 and 1867. Hence the establishment of the Ulster Protestant Working Men's Association (UPWA) in 1868, when Johnston was arrested and jailed, and its support for his candidature. Johnston of Ballykilbeg, as he was usually called, was a somewhat impoverished small landowner from County Down, a law graduate of Trinity College, Dublin and author in his early days of several anti-Catholic novels; in 1852 he joined the Orange Order and by the mid-sixties was a district master in Belfast and prominent in both the County Down Grand Lodge and the Grand Lodge of Ireland. As MP for Belfast he introduced the private member's bill that led to the repeal of the Party Processions Act in 1870, supported the secret ballot the following year (even resigning from the Orange Order for a time because it opposed the reform), spoke in favour of the extension of the 1874 Factories Act to Ireland, to the delight of Belfast linen workers and the chagrin of the millowners and the Chamber of Commerce, and voted for the Merchant Shipping Bill (which established the Plimsoll Line).[8]

The Conservative leadership in Belfast was obliged to come to terms with the forces that had ensured Johnston's election. In 1872 it was agreed that in future the UPWA would be consulted about the selection of candidates. This arrangement worked well in the general election two years later, when Johnston and a leading shipowner, J.P. Corry, were chosen and easily elected. Four years later, however, when Johnston created a by-election by resigning to take up a post as inspector of fisheries (which he had accepted because of financial embarrassment), the

Conservative leadership in Belfast engineered the nomination of William Ewart, owner of a large spinning mill, by calling a meeting at short notice and at a time inconvenient to working men. The UPWA retaliated by putting up a candidate of its own, a barrister named Seeds. Seeds was no Johnston, however, and Ewart beat him by more than 3,000 votes. Seeds was nominated again at the general election in 1880. This time it took all the efforts of the Conservative bigwigs to get their two candidates, Corry and Ewart, safely in; Ewart topped the poll with 8,132 votes, Corry got 7,638, Seeds 6,119.[9]

By that time, however, the political battleground was changing. In 1880 the Irish Home Rule party won more than half of the Irish seats and chose Parnell as its leader. Thereafter the politics and parties of Belfast were increasingly dominated by national politics and parties, to the virtual exclusion of local issues. This development was not the cause of the elimination of the Liberals in Belfast, however; that had already happened by 1874, as their inability to take advantage of the division in Conservative ranks after 1868 demonstrates. They not only failed to attract a sufficient number of the new working-class Protestant voters, they failed to keep the support they had had among Catholics and even among the Presbyterian middle class. After McClure's defeat in 1874 the *Northern Whig* wrote despairingly: 'Five years ago the Liberal party was thoroughly organised. Yesterday there seemed no organisation at all. Nobody seemed to know what to do. It was painfully evident there was no directing mind.'[10] But it was more than a matter of organisation. The Tories received increasing support from influential groups such as shipowners (alienated after 1852 by the stance of the Liberals on free trade and further alienated later by Liberal backing for Plimsoll's legislation) and new entrepreneurs in ship-building and engineering. More and more professional men, dependent for business on goodwill, followed this lead; it is a striking fact that by 1874 the Conservatives could call on the free services of fourteen Belfast solicitors, whereas the Liberals had two. Even the linen barons who had been the backbone of the party became less and less willing to finance it. McClure spent nearly £5,000 in 1868 but less than half that much in subsequent contests.[11]

The ruin of the Liberals was completed in 1885–86. In the early 1880s they had made belated, and half-hearted, attempts to secure the support of the more liberally minded working-class voters. The first Liberal Working Men's Association did not appear till October 1885, however, and its inaugural meeting, addressed by speakers who were all employers, made no reference at all to working-class grievances.

SIR JAMES HORNER HASLETT

He was Lord Mayor of Belfast in 1887 and 1888. It was during his term of office that Queen Victoria conferred the status of city to Belfast. Sir James was also an MP for Belfast North and represented Belfast West from 1885 until his death in 1905.

PHOTOGRAPH: CARNEGIE, 2009

THE GASWORKS

The gasworks provided light and heat for the city for more than 150 years. The year 1810 saw the first recorded use of gas in Belfast. Work on this building on the Ormeau Road began in 1822. It was privately owned until 1874, when it was bought by the Corporation. Under Corporation ownership the Gas Department produced enormous quantities of gas and the profits were so great that they subsidised the rates, electricity, parks, libraries and public baths and were still able to pay part of the cost of building the City Hall. It is worth noting that the price paid by the consumer was perhaps the lowest in the UK.

PHOTOGRAPH: CARNEGIE, 2009

Following the reforms of 1884 and 1885, which quadrupled the number of Irish voters and redistributed the seats, in the general election of 1885 Parnell and his party won every seat in Munster, Leinster and Connaught and 17 of the 33 in Ulster. In Belfast the redistribution created four seats in place of the previous two – the constituencies of North, South, East and West Belfast. West Belfast, which contained Sandy Row, Shankill and Falls Road, emerged as a marginal seat, a prominent Orange merchant, J.H. Haslett, just defeating the Home Rule candidate, Thomas Sexton. The other three seats were won easily by Conservative or Independent Conservative (i.e. Orange) candidates: Ewart in North Belfast, where his opponent, Alexander Bowman, secretary of the Belfast Trades Council and a former employee in Ewart's mill, was the first working-class candidate in Irish history; the revenant William Johnston without a contest in South Belfast, which he was to hold unopposed until his death in 1902; and E.S. de Cobain in East Belfast where he defeated the official Conservative, Corry, in a close contest. Since the Home Rule Party held the balance of power in the new House of Commons, home rule at once became the leading issue in British politics. In 1886 the Liberal leader, Gladstone, announced his conversion to the policy of granting home rule, came to power with the support of Parnell and introduced a bill to bring it about. This virtually destroyed the Liberal party in Belfast. Faced with the prospect of a Dublin parliament dominated by Catholic nationalists with little appreciation of the vital interests of northern industry and commerce, most Liberals became Liberal Unionists almost overnight and made common cause with the Conservatives against home rule. In May 1886 a large majority at a meeting of Liberals in the Ulster Hall condemned Gladstone's new policy as one 'fraught with danger to the industrial, social and moral welfare of the country'. The Town Council and other bodies such as the Chamber of Commerce and even the General Assembly of the Presbyterian Church – to say nothing of dozens of Orange and loyalist meetings, including a monster demonstration in the Ulster Hall at the end of February addressed by Lord Randolph Churchill – had already expressed their opposition. From 1886 onward Belfast elections were fought by parties organised on national lines and campaigning on national issues.[12]

The first Home Rule Bill was defeated in the House of Commons on 8 June when 93 Liberal MPs joined the Conservatives in voting against it. The tension its proposal had created in Belfast had already started what were to be the most serious riots of the century. After the outbreak of 1864 things had been comparatively quiet until 1872, when thousands of Belfast Catholics took part in a great Nationalist parade and demonstration. This event marked the first public appearance of the hitherto shadowy Ancient Order of Hibernians, a secret, oath-bound society as exclusively Catholic and Nationalist as the Orange Order was Protestant and Unionist; 'Lady Day' (15 August) was to become the AOH equivalent of the Orange Twelfth of July.[13] Attacks on the 1872 parade by Protestants were followed by a week of rioting in which five people were killed, more than 200 injured and hundreds driven from their homes. On the occasion of a similar 'Lady Day' (15 August) procession in 1880 two were killed and ten injured in four days of rioting. Now, on 4 June 1886, shipyard workers attacked Catholic navvies working on the Alexandra dock who had expelled a Protestant navvy with the message that, once home rule was achieved, 'none of the Orange sort would get leave to work or earn a loaf of bread in Belfast'. One young Catholic drowned trying to escape and ten others had to be taken to hospital.

SHANKHILL RD BARRACKS FROM WHICH POLICE FIRED & KILLED EIGHT PERSONS JUNE.9.

The mayor, Sir Edward Harland, sent to Dublin for more police and soldiers. The constabulary had no sooner arrived than they were sent into action against Protestant looters. Battles between police and Protestants, rather than those between Catholic and Protestant mobs, became the predominant pattern of these riots. The worst of the early fighting took place on 9 June when police, besieged in their barracks by a mob of 2,000, fired indiscriminately and killed seven people, five of them perfectly innocent. The Presbyterian minister of St Enoch's, Dr Hugh Hanna, denounced from his pulpit this massacre of 'seven martyrs … sacrificed to avenge the resistance of a loyal people to a perfidious and traitorous policy'.

There was a lull until July, when another general election was held in which Ewart, Johnston and de Cobain were returned without a contest; so too was the Nationalist, Sexton, in West Belfast (his election gave Parnell's party 86 of the Irish seats – the '86 of '86'). Thereafter rioting was sporadic until mid-September, when prolonged heavy rain dampened the ardour of the mobs; the riots petered out altogether the following month. The worst of the bloodshed occurred in this later period, which featured a Catholic attack on a Sunday School outing (St Enoch's) accompanied by Orange bands and a Protestant attack on a Catholic outing the following day, as well as the sacking of York Street, the expulsion of Catholics from the shipyards and determined assaults on the police. When all was over, about 50 people had been killed (including a soldier and a policeman) and 371 policemen had been injured; 31 public houses had been looted and property worth £90,000 destroyed. The report of the inquiry into the riots, which with the minutes of evidence ran to over 600 pages, put much of the blame on the politicians and other public leaders who had earlier talked of resorting to force to oppose home rule. As a Liberal Unionist witness remarked, it was 'exceedingly unwise on the part of respectable people' to use such words, 'as they were likely to cause the poorer classes to carry out what they had only talked about and threatened'.[14] Quite apart from the widespread fear that Home Rule would mean Rome Rule, Protestant workers feared that it would destroy the manufacturing industry which made Belfast prosperous and gave them their livelihoods: in the mid-1880s, a period of recession in ship-building and engineering during which Harland & Wolff laid off hundreds of men, locked out the riveters for a month and reduced everyone's wages, it must have seemed a serious threat when William Pirrie, the chairman of the firm, let it be known that he would transfer the shipyard to the Clyde if home rule became a reality.[15]

TOWN GOVERNMENT

While all this was going on, municipal affairs on a practical level were developing in ways similar to those in other great urban centres of the period. The chancery case was at last laid to rest in 1864 by the Belfast Award Act, which implemented the recommendation of arbitrators that the Corporation should be responsible for debts of £120,000, while the respondents should pay their own costs and those of Rea (about £50,000 in all). Resisting compromise to the last, Rea had to be forcibly removed by police from a House of Lords committee hearing.[16] Almost everyone, including most Liberals, greeted the settlement with relief. The way was thus clear for further improvement acts. In 1866 powers were taken to establish the first municipal cemetery, outside the town boundary on the Falls Road. More important than this act of colonisation by the dead, local Acts in 1865 and 1868 extended the responsibilities of the Corporation over parts of the borough which lay in the counties of Antrim and Down and had therefore been subject in some respects to the county grand juries and liable to pay county taxes.[17] From 1866 the town had a separate Quarter Sessions court, presided over by a Recorder. In 1869 a new public abattoir was opened, after a deputation of councillors had visited Paris and other continental cities to view the facilities there. Expanding functions and civic pride justified not only jaunts to Paris but also the building of a new Town Hall, which was opened in 1871 in Townhall Street. (Anthony Jackson's designs, appropriately enough, were for a building in Franco-Italian Chateau style). Three years later powers were taken to purchase the gas undertaking, for £386,550 (the final cost, with interest, was £430,000). This was a lot more than the £50,000 secured for the purchase in 1846,

Sir Edward Coey (right) ex-mayor of Belfast with the current mayor John Lytle wearing his chain of office and the future mayor William Ewart. On the left is James Gutherie, Town Clerk. The photograph was taken in London c.1864, at the time of the Chancery case, begun ten years earlier.

COEY ALBUM, © ULSTER MUSEUM, 2008

the diversion of which had been one of the charges in the chancery suit. It was to prove an excellent investment nevertheless: the profits from the Gasworks later paid for the City Hall and other things. The corporation had a Sanitary Committee from 1865, but it was not until 1877 that some limited improvement on sanitary grounds was undertaken in the Smithfield area, and then under Local Government Board legislation dealing with artisans' and labourers' dwellings, rather than the usual private act. Such general acts were to be increasingly important as a spur to social improvement; left to themselves the town fathers were slow to do anything that would add to the burden of the rates.

The enormous and rapid growth of the town, and the desire to emulate more enterprising places such as Birmingham, nevertheless made activity unavoidable. A major improvement Act in 1878 shaped the future street geography of a large part of the centre by taking powers to lay out a grand new thoroughfare between Donegall Place and York Street, sweeping away in the process the old butchers' quarter in Hercules Street and a warren of alleys and entries. Royal Avenue, as it was named, took shape during the 1880s, and very impressive it proved to be with its tall uniform frontages, even if the central railway station that was planned by

VICTORIAN CIVIC SPLENDOUR

Visitors to the City Hall enter through an impressive stone *porte-cochere* and marble-lined vestibule. Like the main entrance hall and landings, the grand staircase used four types of marble, three from Italy and one from Greece. The Great Hall was destroyed during the Blitz and was subsequently re-built.

© GERAY SWEENEY/CORBIS

developers did not materialise (beyond a Grand Central Hotel which was a notable feature of the street until fairly recent times). Under the same Act the long-standing nuisance of the Blackstaff river was at last tackled, the old mill dam near its mouth drained and Ormeau Avenue and the streets between that thoroughfare and Donegall Square completed. Ann Street, Cornmarket, Millfield and the street along Donegall Quay were also widened and improved. Another Act in 1884 led to the widening of the Queen's Bridge, the enlargement and improvement of St George's Market and the improvement of Arthur Square, Rosemary Street, North Street, University Road and Stranmillis Road. This fury of paving and sewering continued into the 1890s as more and more houses were built and as action on the grounds of public health became ever more necessary and unavoidable. In this respect the Main Drainage Act of 1887 was a major (and long overdue) achievement. Apart from the powers it

ROYAL AVENUE,
BELFAST C.1900

In 1880–81 the Town
Council and its surveyor
J.C. Bretland demolished
the old streets between
Donegall Square and
York Street and allowed
developers to build with
different materials, but
all to a standard height.
Royal Avenue became
an important extension
of the business district.

R.J. WELCH COLLECTION, © ULSTER MUSEUM,
2008

gave to construct a proper system of sewers it also contained public health provisions such as a prohibition against carrying the corpses of victims of infectious diseases in public conveyances.[18]

The Main Drainage Act is of interest in another, rather curious way: it led to the introduction of household suffrage in local elections more than ten years sooner in Belfast than anywhere else in Ireland. Though Catholics had no direct representation or influence on the Town Council after 1878, when the last remaining Catholic member died, the power of the Nationalist party at Westminster could be exerted on their behalf whenever the Corporation sought an improvement act. The price for allowing the Main Drainage Bill to pass into law was an amendment to the Municipal Corporations (Ireland) Act of 1840, so far as it related to Belfast, enabling any householder (including women) to be burgesses without the £10 property qualification.[19] A new Council was to be elected, one-third of its members retiring in rotation. It was not until the boundaries were extended and the wards changed, however, that the next Catholic councillors were elected.

Improvement during these years was not entirely a matter of drains and paving stones, though no fewer than 857 previously private streets were handed over to be 'sewered and paved' between 1878 and 1896. In 1869 the Corporation acquired the abandoned demesne of the Donegalls at Ormeau and made part of it into the first public park, thus doing what Professor James Thomson (father of the future Lord Kelvin) had advocated nearly twenty years before. Other parks followed – Alexandra Park in 1885, Woodvale three years later, Dunville and Victoria in 1891, the Botanic Gardens (in existence since the late 1820s but not in public hands) in 1894. A new cemetery for the eastern part of the city was opened at Dundonald in 1899.[20]

For most of the nineteenth century Belfast had no separate provision, under its own control, for the insane poor, as lunatics in public care were called. So far as numbers would allow, these unfortunates were lodged in the County Antrim Asylum on the Falls Road or in the County Down Asylum in Downpatrick. In 1892, however, under the will of the last member of the Batt family to own the property, the mansion and three-hundred acre estate at Purdysburn was inherited by the Board of Belfast General Hospital 'for whatever use they see fit'. The upshot was that the land became public property and a new purpose-built mental hospital was erected in the spacious grounds and opened in 1895. Most if not all of the places were filled with charity cases. There must however have been numbers of people who needed treatment and could afford to pay for it, yet there is little sign of private institutions of a suitable kind in the Belfast area. At the turn of the twentieth century there appears to have been only one private licensed asylum in the Belfast area, a small establishment for up to five men run by a Ligoniel doctor. When inspected by the commissioners of lunatics in 1895 it had only two patients, and by 1900 it had closed altogether. Presumably there were discreet, unlicensed places as well; if so, they are undetectable in the directories. Outside the Belfast area, institutions of a genteel kind, officially inspected and approved, can be found such as the Retreat in County Armagh which published a detailed prospectus (illustrated) in Bassett's *County Armagh* (1888, pp. 128–9). There is evidence that patients were sometimes placed farther off; in one case at least a Belfast patient was looked after by a hospital in Dumfries. Another possibility must

MENTAL HEALTH CARE

The Retreat, Armagh, founded in the 1820s by the Allen family, Quakers, was well known and well regarded.

ADVERTISEMENT

THE RETREAT, ARMAGH.

A HOUSE OF RECOVERY FOR MENTALLY AFFLICTED AND NERVOUS INVALIDS OF BOTH SEXES.

THIS Institution has enjoyed the confidence of the Medical Profession and the Public for nearly sixty years. The greatest care is taken to render it a Domestic Home and House of Recovery rather than an Asylum, in the general acceptation of the term.

The inmates receive the mildest and most careful treatment, and enjoy the greatest liberty compatible with their condition.

Terms from £15 to £20 per Quarter for Ordinary Patients, and from £25 to £35 for those requiring a separate Attendant, paid quarterly in advance.

ALEXANDER D. ALLEN,
PROPRIETOR.

Visiting Physicians—
W. W. LEEPER, M.D.; J. G. ALLEN, L.K.Q.C.P.I., &c.
Telegraphic Address—LOUGHGALL.

have been Dublin, where Dr Stewart's 'Asylum for Lunatic Patients of the Middle Classes' was well known and well regarded.[21]

Another municipal service which was overhauled and expanded at this time was the fire brigade. In 1891 it consisted of 40 men, only ten of whom were full-time. Following reorganisation in 1892 it was staffed by 40 full-time officers and was housed in a new headquarters in Chichester Street. The brigade was responsible for a public ambulance service (horse-drawn waggons to begin with), an arrangement which was copied by cities throughout the kingdom and remained standard until the coming of the welfare state. The Fire Brigade is a good example of the expansion of municipal employment as the Corporation took on new functions or developed existing ones. The wages paid were actually higher than in Great Britain; by 1912 a first-class fireman had a basic 30–34 shillings a week plus allowances and a possible bonus for good conduct, at a time when the average unskilled wage was 15–18 shillings.[22]

Extension of the boundary had been advocated on a number of occasions before 1879, when the lord lieutenant agreed to a public inquiry into the subject. The Council argued for the inclusion of new suburbs at Strandtown, Ballyhackamore, Knock, Malone and Ballymurphy on the usual grounds, namely that they were a danger to public health because they had no sewerage and that they ought to share the burden of the rates because they shared many of the town's amenities. The commissioners agreed, and also proposed increasing the number of wards from five to eight. Nothing was done, however. In 1885 the area of the parliamentary borough was extended by 15,000 acres. Three years later Belfast was granted the dignity of a city, after the Council had assured itself that this could be done without incurring much expense, and in response to pressure from the Chamber of Commerce; the mayor became a lord mayor in 1892. These developments increased the demand for an extension of the boundary. Eventually in 1895 a bill was prepared to extend the municipal boundary to correspond, more or less, with the parliamentary one, a move which would increase the area of the city from ten square miles to twenty-three and its electorate from 39,603 to 47,294.

In political terms the 1895 bill proposed the creation of fifteen wards, based on population and valuation, radiating from the centre. This was immediately seen by Catholics as a threat to their interests. A Catholic Representation Association, presided over by Bishop Henry (who played a dominant role in Catholic politics in the city), drew attention to the fact that they had had only three councillors elected in fifty years despite being a quarter of the population, that the proposed new wards would all have a Protestant majority, that Protestants would not vote for Catholics, and that Catholics were virtually excluded from Council employment. When questioned by a Select Committee, the Liberal Unionist lord mayor, William Pirrie, had to admit that under the new scheme the Catholics could not be sure of a single seat, and that so far as he knew not a single Catholic contractor was employed by the Council. The solicitors largely responsible for drawing up the Catholic case claimed that they ought to have control of at least two wards. Following a meeting with a deputation from the Catholic Association the Council capitulated: two wards, Falls and Smithfield, were to be so drawn as to ensure a permanent Catholic majority. Joseph Devlin, active earlier in the protest but excluded from the deputation, who was later to become the Nationalist boss of Belfast, thought this arrangement was the worst possible outcome because it was sure to perpetuate sectarian politics in the city – and so it proved. It is hard to see what else was practicable in the circumstances, however.[23]

The first general municipal election under the new arrangements was held in November 1897. Only Catholic candidates came forward in Falls and Smithfield, only Protestants elsewhere. Nearly one-third of the sixty seats (three entire wards) were uncontested; henceforth, indeed, local elections were to be of interest only for the internal squabbles of the two main blocks or the efforts of a third force such as Labour to break the sectarian stranglehold. Catholics, for example, were for some time sharply divided between Bishop Henry's Catholic Association and the Irish National Federation (the central Nationalist organisation). The Nationalists put up candidates in Falls and Smithfield but all eight seats went to the Association. Among Protestants the Liberal Unionists remained nominally separate from the Conservatives. All five of their candidates were elected, including the lord mayor, Pirrie, and a future lord mayor, Otto Jaffé, the only Jewish holder of the post. The Conservatives got 33 seats, Independents (basically Conservatives) eight. The six 'Labour' candidates nominated by the Belfast Trades Council to promote action on social issues were also successful; Alexander Bowman was one of them. Neither they nor the Catholic group, even acting together as they often did, could make any impression on the entrenched Conservative majority which, whatever may be said about it, undoubtedly represented the will of a large majority of the citizens.[24]

SECTARIAN POLITICS AND THE LABOUR MOVEMENT, 1886–1901

National politics, and therefore inevitably local politics, were dominated in the early 1890s by the renewed hope or threat of home rule. In 1892, when the Conservative government resigned and Gladstone again sought office, promising to introduce home rule if elected, local Conservatives and other supporters of the Union again organised themselves to oppose it. Well aware that their cause had been damaged in Britain by the disgraceful scenes in 1886, they arranged a great demonstration in Belfast in June 1892 which was impressively orderly and well behaved. The rowdy scenes that usually accompanied gatherings such as the Twelfth of July celebrations were entirely absent, along with bands and party songs. Instead, 12,000 delegates from all over the province met in a huge, specially constructed hall (said to be the biggest temporary structure in existence). Before the political speeches started the assembly listened to prayer and bible reading by the Church of Ireland primate and the ex-Moderator of the Presbyterian Church and sang the hymn 'God is our refuge and strength'. Afterwards, crowds estimated at anything up to 300,000 thronged the Botanic Gardens. In the general election that followed, Wolff, Johnston and Harland were returned unopposed and the Nationalist, Sexton (an anti-Parnellite in the recently divided Irish party), was beaten in West Belfast by a Liberal Unionist, H.O. Arnold-Foster.[25]

Gladstone came to office nevertheless, and the second Home Rule Bill passed the Commons in April 1893, only to be thrown out by the Lords. This time there were no riots in Belfast. All four Belfast members were returned without a contest in 1895, when the Conservatives began another spell in office which was to rule out

any likelihood of home rule for the next ten years. In the general election of 1900 there was again no contest in three constituencies; in the fourth, North Belfast, Sir J.H. Haslett (who had succeeded to the seat on the death of Harland in 1896) easily defeated an independent Liberal Unionist.

The sectarian basis of politics and the intensity of feeling on the national question effectively prevented the development of a strong class-based Labour movement in Belfast. The year 1893 did indeed see the formation in the city of a small Independent Labour Party, whose meetings – regularly the target for anti-socialist objectors – were addressed by Tom Mann and other notable cross-channel evangelists of socialism. The leading local activists were William Walker, a member of the Carpenters Union and John Murphy of the Typographical Association. Even if no more than a distraction, sectarianism interfered with normal union activity. As a great industrial centre with an unusually high proportion of skilled craftsmen, Belfast should have been a stronghold of the craft unions that dominated the Labour movement in Britain in the later nineteenth century. In addition to many small local bodies, the 'New Model' British unions organised in Belfast from the 1850s. Engineers were followed by lithographic printers, boilermakers, carpenters and joiners, cabinet makers and bricklayers; and a Belfast United Trades Council was formed in 1881. There was a rapid growth of unions in the 1890s, among the increasing number of municipal employees for example; by the end of the century there were 57, with a membership of 19,000, affiliated to the Trades Council. The importance of Belfast in the movement was recognised when the Trades Union Congress met there in 1893. However, dissatisfaction among Irish delegates with the scant consideration given to the concerns of their members led to the formation in the following year of an *Irish* Congress of Trade Unions. At the time this was not regarded as a particularly Nationalist organisation, and was not intended to supersede the TUC itself, but inevitably it soon began to reflect the diverse opinions of its membership on the national question.

The extent to which Belfast craftsmen were part of the British labour scene as well as players in the drama of Irish politics is well illustrated in the events of the 1890s when contradictory policies were sometimes pursued. In 1892–93 the shipyard engineers were an essential element in the Unionist opposition to the threat of home rule, yet in 1893 (a period of recession), they were obliged to accept reduced wages. Subsequently the ship-building section of the Belfast Engineering Employers Federation entered into an agreement with the ship-builders on the Clyde jointly to resist wage demands. Thus when engineering workers in Belfast in 1895 demanded an increase of two shillings a week in order to recover what they had earlier lost, the employers refused to negotiate except through joint machinery which included the Clyde employers. And when the union called an official strike in November of that year (which went on into the new year and put out of work large numbers of unskilled men as well as the craftsmen), Clydeside employees were dismissed in order

left
FALLS ROAD PROCESSION

Nationalist procession along the Falls Road in 1898, to celebrate, in the rain, the centenary of the rebellion of the United Irishmen in 1798.

© ULSTER MUSEUM, 2008

to put pressure on the union. Following a joint intervention by the lord mayor of Belfast and the provost of Glasgow, the union eventually accepted a slightly better offer from the employers and cut off strike pay from its members to force them back to work. Belfast prided itself on its good industrial relations, however, and the action of the employers – and of the local MPs, two of whom were Harland and Wolff – did not escape criticism in the press. One way or another trade union activity in the 1890s did very little to advance the cause of socialism as such.[26]

The cause of labour in general at the turn of the century was affected by renewed stirrings of sectarian feeling, which had on the whole been notably absent during the previous decade. Catholic celebrations of the centenary of the 1798 rising had provoked controversy but confrontation had been prevented. In 1900, however, the Boer War provided a focus for conflict. The news of the defeat of British armies was greeted with bonfires on the Falls Road. In reply, when Pretoria fell to the British, Protestant workers left work to parade the streets and sing patriotic songs, bonfires were lit in Sandy Row and the Shankill, and some minor rioting took place. The dominant role of the Catholic Church in local Nationalist politics provoked increased support for the extremist Belfast Protestant Association, which preached anti-popery and organised an attack on a Corpus Christi procession in 1901. When the Association's leader was arrested and imprisoned there were attacks on Catholic navvies and shipyard workers. Against such a background, the sole working men's candidate in the general election of 1900 was easily defeated in North Belfast, despite massive support from his fellow trade unionists for a prolonged strike of carpenters and joiners which was going on at the time.[27]

In 1899 the *Belfast News Letter*, the organ of the Conservatives who controlled the city, could write with some justification: 'We Belfast people are proud of our city and its many activities. We are in the very front of the race of civic development ... and we have a laudable ambition to keep there.'[28] That pride in economic and social advancement could have been shared by many Catholics, who despite great disadvantages had also come a long way, but, whereas in other British cities politics and cultural pressure had operated to assist the assimilation of an important minority, in Belfast the opposite had happened.[29] By the end of Victoria's reign the Catholics as a community had become both more deeply embedded in Belfast and also more separate and distinct from the majority of its inhabitants.

CHAPTER TEN

HEYDAY AND CRISIS, 1901–1914

IN RETROSPECT, the period in the history of Belfast between the death of Queen Victoria and the outbreak of the First World War reveals more clearly than any other the contrast between social, economic and municipal advance – the 'British' aspects of the city – and the effects of sectarian and ethnic division – its Irish or at any rate Ulster character.[1]

THE SOCIAL PYRAMID

The population of Belfast continued to rise in the early years of the twentieth century, though at a much less spectacular rate than in previous decades. Reaching 349,000 in 1901, it was 386,000 in 1911 and by the outbreak of war three years later must have been about 400,000. The rate of increase between the censuses of 1901 and 1911 was 10.8 per cent, compared with 36.4 per cent in the 1890s; this reflected slower economic growth after 1900 in the linen industry and the less skilled sectors of other employment, such as building, which had attracted so many immigrants in the late nineteenth century. The continued importance of linen, however, was still reflected in the preponderance of women in the population – 188,000 women as compared with 162,000 men in 1901 – and in the large proportion of households (a quarter of Protestant, a third of Catholic ones) headed by women. Among all immigrants in the age-range 15–24 the ratio of women to men was 100: 71, among those of them who were Catholics as high as 100: 58. The population as a whole was youthful – 77 per cent were under the age of 40 – the marriage rate high at 8.2 per thousand (the figure for the whole of Ireland in the 1890s was 4.8) and the birth rate correspondingly high at 30.4 (23.1 for Ireland in the decade 1901–11); the first evidence of birth control, by middle-class Protestants, can be found in the low figure of 20.1 in the College district in 1914.[2]

Many such details about Edwardian Belfast can be gleaned from the records of the censuses of 1901 and 1911, which are available to historians in full manuscript form as those for other British cities are not (the detailed nineteenth-century records for

Belfast, on the other hand, were all destroyed). At the apex of Belfast society was a solitary aristocrat, the ninth earl of Shaftesbury (his mother, the only surviving child of the third marquess of Donegall, had inherited the Donegall estates in 1883), who kept up a residence in Belfast Castle with a staff of nineteen indoor servants and played an active part in public affairs; he was lord mayor in 1907 and first chancellor of the Queen's University from its creation, out of Queen's College,

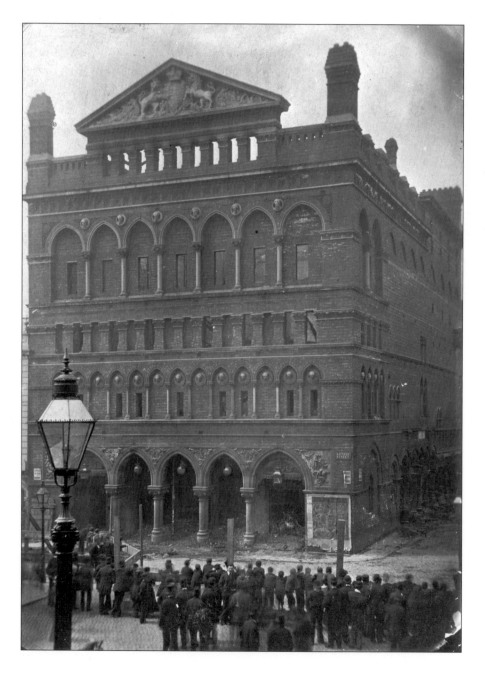

THE ROYAL

The Theatre Royal, Arthur Street, after being gutted by fire in 1881. It was replaced by an equally fine building. Respectable citizens, much influenced by evangelical clergy, were for a long time hostile to the theatre – the Royal was the only one until the Grand Opera House opened in 1895.

R.J. WELCH COLLECTION, © ULSTER MUSEUM, 2008

in 1908. It is worth noting here that few of the men who made fortunes in Belfast felt the need to gentrify themselves to the extent of withdrawing from business. For instance Andrew Mulholland, proprietor of the York Street Flax Spinning Company, who became a major landowner in County Down in the 1840s, remained in control of the firm; more remarkably, so too did his son John, who was raised to the peerage as Baron Dunleath in 1892. Dunleath died in 1895 worth nearly £600,000.[3] His nearest, but even wealthier, equivalent in the late nineteenth and early twentieth century was William Pirrie, chairman of Harland & Wolff, who achieved a peerage in 1905. The Pirries could, and quite often did, sit 160 guests down to dine at Ormiston; and for a banquet in 1896 Pirrie chartered an entire ship to sail from London to Belfast, complete with all the staff, cutlery and linen needed for the feast. When the Pirries set out to dazzle London society in 1898 they rented Downshire House in Belgrave Square, and the head office of the firm was removed to London in the same year. Pirrie subsequently purchased an estate in Surrey, where in later years he entertained most of his guests, including employees of the shipyard, so he and his wife were seen less often in Belfast.[4] At least two other Belfast businessmen of the period, both of them distillers, left over a million each; neither made any attempt to match the conspicuous consumption practised by Pirrie, however.

Below this thinly inhabited stratosphere of the seriously wealthy, 'the social profile' of the city was dominated by a group of three hundred or so families. They formed a tight-knit community of family and business interests, were much intermarried, controlled interlocking companies, were members of the same golf and sailing clubs, and sent their children to the same boarding schools in England or Scotland. Many belonged to the same church congregations, usually Presbyterian, the wives and daughters meeting constantly in church activities and charitable work as the husbands and sons did in the Ulster Club or the Reform Club. Most of the men personally managed their own businesses. These families lived in substantial villas in the spacious suburbs to the east, north and south of the industrial and commercial centre and employed gardeners and coachmen as well as indoor servants (mostly female, though there were 283 butlers, valets and footmen in Belfast in 1911).[5]

Next in the scale were five or six thousand families of the middle classes – an elastic term which included everything from 'aspiring barristers to gasworks' clerks'. They were distinguished from those below them not only by their white-collar occupations but also by the incomes (anything from £200 to £500 a year) that enabled them to buy or rent suburban houses, to send their children to fee-paying schools,

to employ at least one maid (there were 6,360 female domestic servants in 1911) and to save something for seaside holidays, sickness and retirement.

The working classes which formed the large majority of the city's population were sharply divided between the skilled on the one hand and the semi-skilled or unskilled on the other. Skilled artisans – the labouring elite of apprentice-trained ship-building, engineering and building craftsmen who made up 26 per cent of the male and 16 per cent of the entire manual workforce – earned wages of 35 to 45 shillings a week, enough to enable their wives to stay at home instead of going out to work. Typically such families lived in a terrace house of five or six rooms, costing five to six shillings a week in rent, and the children attended the local National School and perhaps went on to study at the Technical College; holidays were an occasional day trip to the seaside at Bangor. The father belonged to a trade union which protected his rights both against the employer above and the encroachment of the unskilled (and generally unorganised) workers below. His spare time might be spent on union or church business, attending meetings of his Orange lodge or cultivating an allotment. Except for the manual nature of their work and their membership of a trade union such men conformed more to the beliefs and outlook of the lower ranks of the white-collar middle class than to those of the working class as a whole.

JENNYMOUNT MILL

left
Jennymount Mill, on North Derby Street, as it looked in 1908.
© ULSTER MUSEUM, 2008

above
... and as it looked, restored, 101 years later.
PHOTOGRAPH: CARNEGIE, 2009

The remaining 40 per cent of the population – those who, as one historian has pointed out, could not afford to buy a £3 plot in the city cemetery but had to rest content with a public grave – were much less well-off. Whereas the wages of the skilled in Belfast were at least as high as those of similar workers elsewhere in the United Kingdom, the unskilled were often paid less, no more than half the earnings of the craftsmen they worked with. Since their numbers were constantly being added to by new arrivals, and since they were scarcely unionised at all till after 1907, they could put little pressure on employers. Even at the best of times, unemployment and casual employment were more likely for labourers than for craftsmen. House-building, which traditionally provided for many, was at a low ebb during this period. Even when in work, only those who worked with craftsmen (who had a 54-hour week) could be sure of reasonable hours; tram conductors worked 60 in all weathers, carters 68. Such families could not avoid destitution without the earnings of wives and children; in bad times they could afford only a share of a kitchen house.[6]

In recent years the census figures of 1901 and 1911 have been analysed in particular for evidence as to the social and economic position of the city's Catholic minority. As far as social class is concerned, one study concludes:

The figures demonstrate ... that the Catholic population of Belfast did not occupy an inferior class position in relation to Britain as a whole, but rather that the Protestant population had obtained for itself a relatively advantaged position.[7]

Protestant workers as such did not constitute an aristocracy of labour. Within the working class the majority of both Catholics and Protestants were semi-skilled or unskilled in 1901. But whereas few Catholics belonged to the elite of skilled craftsmen, substantial numbers of Protestants did – and were much better placed, through the way the apprenticeship system operated in most firms, to transmit these skills to the younger generation. There is no doubt that the high-wage industries were predominantly Protestant and that Catholics were under-represented in them in proportion to their numbers, as they were also in the better-paid linen jobs; they were correspondingly overrepresented in the unskilled, less secure and less well-paid occupations such as carters, dockers, tailors, shoemakers and hairdressers. It is worth noting that Presbyterians were significantly better placed than other Protestants, to the extent that 'Episcopalians as a group could have found a basis for feeling under-privileged had they had any ideological stimulus to seek one'.[8]

WASHERWOMAN

The scullery of this middle-class home, c.1905, is relatively well equipped; note the double taps, evidence of both hot and cold running water. This is probably what is now called a Belfast sink. This is one of a number of similar studies of working women that Hogg made into lantern slides.

A.R. HOGG COLLECTION, © ULSTER MUSEUM, 2008

STANDARDS OF LIVING

While many of the working classes, when in work, could afford to shop at the new chain stores such as Lipton's and the Home & Colonial for groceries, or the Co-ops with their better bread ('the same quality all year round') and more hygienic milk, and even to sample the novel delights of the new Italian ice-cream and fish-and-chip shops (there were nearly fifty of these by 1914), many others were restricted to the staple labouring-class diet of tea, white bread, sugar and condensed milk, occasionally supplemented by margarine and American bacon and cheap foreign meat bought from barrows in the street. Women who worked in the mills had neither the time nor the facilities to do much in the way of cooking. In 1901 only a quarter of the kitchen houses had a gas supply. The free installation of coin meters by the Gas Department two years later encouraged the use of gas lighting and, more slowly, gas cooking. Another measure of domestic comfort was the number of fixed baths, far more common (one in six) in Protestant than in Catholic homes (one in sixteen) – another illustration of relative economic and social status and of the high concentration of

Catholics in the old slum areas of the city. Many kitchen houses, especially in these areas, remained without water closets, despite earlier by-laws; nearly one-third still had ashpits in 1914.[9]

Prices rose faster than wages in the years after 1900. The decline in real wages made life even harder for the families of poorly paid labourers. When the pawnbrokers (whose numbers rose from a hundred in 1900 to 117 in 1914) and all other sources of temporary help had failed, the Poor Law Guardians might have to be resorted to. The Guardians were permitted to give outdoor relief but, under Local Government Board regulations, as little as possible and to as few as possible. They excelled themselves in this task, publicly displaying in each district the names of recipients. By such means Belfast maintained the lowest pauper rate in the United Kingdom. The numbers did in fact rise, from 238 in 1901 to 888 in 1914, but the figure for Glasgow was in the region of 18,000.[10] One category of pauper was largely removed, in Belfast as elsewhere, by the granting of old age pensions in 1908, for which some 7,000 people qualified, but that was no thanks to local charity.

Children who came under the care of the workhouse were treated better after 1900, most of them being transferred to foster homes, some apprenticed, others helped to emigrate. But the workhouse was a last resort for any family, and many children ended up on the streets instead, practically encouraged to beg by being licensed, under a by-law of 1903, as street traders, or working as errand boys or flower sellers. Many came before the courts if they evaded the sheltering care of the missions and sought a precarious independence in the numerous filthy lodging

ABBEY STREET SLUMS

Houses in Abbey
Street off Peter's Hill,
photographed 26
April 1912 for a slum
clearance scheme. The
sash windows are badly
rotten and broken, but
the overall structure
does not appear
completely decayed.

A.R. HOGG COLLECTION, © ULSTER MUSEUM,
2008

houses. Even these were beyond the resources of those who slept rough. The Central
Mission dealt with scores of them every night, such as a group of sixty-five, average
age twenty, in the Springfield brickworks. The Mission's 'waifs' excursion' to the
seaside in 1914 catered for 2,600 children, and in the same year it dispensed 50,000
free meals. One nameless infant rescued from a lodging house by a Mission Sister,
and passed on to Barnardo's, was baptised Grosvenor Hall.[11] Newsboys acted as
runners for illegal street betting; betting shops were also illegal, and the public
libraries even blacked out the racing news in the newspapers. There are no reliable
statistics of the extent of prostitution during these years, but it remained considerable.
A vigilance committee forced the police to close brothels in the city centre, but this

PUBS OF ALL SHAPES AND SIZES

A significant number of Belfast's historic pubs still exist today, some dating back to the seventeenth century.

left

McHugh`s Bar and Restaurant is the city's oldest bar, dating back to its establishment in 1711, and is now a Grade A listed building.

below left

Bittles Bar in Victoria Square: this is a triangular building, dated 1861, which is decorated with gilded shamrocks. It now houses a pub with a literary theme.

below right

The Crown Liquor Saloon on Great Victoria Street, the only pub owned by the National Trust, is a unique Victorian gin palace whose interior contains scalloped gas lights, gleaming brasswork and a glass-inlaid bar. It was restored in the 1970s.

PHOTOGRAPHS: CARNEGIE, 2009

MILITARY PRESENCE

Here the Essex
Regiment are encamped
at Ormeau Park in
1907. There was a lot
of rioting and the police
were constantly on duty
and exhausted. When
they complained, at
least half of the total
force was transferred
to the south of Ireland
and the troops were
sent over to keep order
during the dockers'
strike of that year.

R.J. WELCH COLLECTION, © ULSTER MUSEUM,
2008

only moved the problem to streets farther out. The Irish Council for Public Morals blamed the situation on the extreme condemnation to which unmarried mothers were subjected and on low female wages, especially when the linen mills worked short time.[12]

Drink was the refuge for many. There was one public house or off-licence (the latter used mostly by women) for every 328 inhabitants, and whiskey cost only a penny a tot. The prevalence of drunkenness and its deplorable effects on the morals and living conditions of the poor stimulated the efforts of the temperance reformers. The Pioneer movement, established in 1901 by a Jesuit priest, had considerable success among the devout Catholics at whom it was exclusively aimed (Catholic piety, total abstinence and Nationalist fervour were a potent combination). Protestant churches had their own, such as the Catch-My-Pal movement, launched by an Armagh Presbyterian minister in 1910, which was so successful that the Orange parades that year were remarkable for their sobriety. Missioners working among the poor, such as the Rev. William Maguire of the North Belfast Mission, were fervently opposed to liquor and campaigned hard for its restriction. The Corporation was even persuaded in 1906 to issue municipal temperance posters. In fact the licensed vintners in that year complained that Belfast had 'the most aggressive so-called temperance party to be found anywhere'. Nevertheless, those who stood as temperance candidates in the municipal elections in 1902 and 1904 were notably unsuccessful, despite strong support from Presbyterian clergy. It is true, however, that when William Walker was trying to become MP for North Belfast in 1905–07 he sought support from the temperance bodies in the constituency by stressing his own teetotalism.[13]

right
BALMORAL INDUSTRIAL
SCHOOL

This is a boot-making
class, c.1910. The
Balmoral School, the
only one in Ireland for
Protestant boys, was
certified for 400 pupils.
The object of the
school was described
as 'rescuing orphan,
homeless and destitute
street arab and criminal
lads from the perils
and temptations of
street life – to educate
them and teach them
useful trades so that,
instead of becoming a
terror to society, they
may be brought up in
health and happiness,
to lead honest, useful
lives in this world, and,
with God's blessing be
fitted for another and a
better.'

A.R. HOGG COLLECTION, © ULSTER MUSEUM,
2008

Religion and education

The influence of the churches, based upon strong, even fervid, religious faith in a host of individuals, pervaded public life. Almost everyone claimed to belong to a church of some sort; in the 1911 census only 620 people refused to answer the question about religious affiliation and scarcely any claimed to be atheists or free-thinkers. Church attendance was almost universal in middle-class and Catholic areas and high among the respectable working class in general, but it held little appeal for many sinners; it was estimated in 1908 that only one in fifteen of the population of the parish of Ballymacarrett attended church. The building of churches continued though at a much slower rate than before. The first part of the Church of Ireland cathedral was consecrated in 1910, and a new headquarters for the Presbyterian Church – built in Fisherwick Place in the city centre, on the site of a church which had migrated, like its congregation, to the suburbs – was completed in 1904.[14]

Sectarianism in education, long almost universal in primary schools, extended to technical education in the early 1900s. From 1901 the Corporation was responsible for technical schools, and proceeded to build a splendid new College of Technology to house classes hitherto held in scattered unsatisfactory premises. Staffed by Protestants (almost inevitably, since most industrial skills were at that stage in Protestant hands), the new college was not welcomed by the Catholic authorities, who set up a trades school in Hardinge Street, run by the Christian Brothers. The Brothers' constant emphasis on the importance for Catholic boys of becoming skilled workers was to bear fruit in a growing number of apprentices. The extent to which the Municipal Institute, supported by the rates of the population at large, was regarded as Protestant territory was strikingly demonstrated during the Home Rule crisis of 1912–14 when – in common with the City Hall and other Corporation property – its resources were put at the service of the Unionist cause; there exists a photograph of Sir Edward and Lady Carson inspecting an Ulster Volunteer Force bakery on the premises.[15]

A happy exception to the sectarian trend was the Queen's University, as Queen's College became under the Irish Universities Act of 1908. Independent status and an

right
ULSTER DAY, 1912

The Ulster Covenant was signed by just under half a million men and women on 28 September 1912 in protest against the Third Home Rule Bill. Sir Edward Carson was the first person to sign the Covenant at the Belfast City Hall, with a silver pen. The signatories were all against the establishment of a Home Rule parliament in Dublin. By far the largest turn-out was in Belfast.

© HULTON-DEUTSCH COLLECTION/CORBIS

PAUPERS AT THE WORKHOUSE

In July 1903 Edward VII and Queen Alexandra visited Belfast to unveil the statue of Queen Victoria in front of the new City Hall. This photograph shows paupers outside the Belfast Union Workhouse having tea while awaiting the royal procession. In the background some elderly women in white bonnets are just visible.

A.R. HOGG COLLECTION. © ULSTER MUSEUM

MASS MEETING

The evening before the signing of the Covenant a mass meeting was held in the Ulster Hall. Carson, the chief speaker can be seen in the middle of the front row.

accompanying gesture of goodwill by which a department of scholastic philosophy was established with a Catholic priest in charge brought to an end the ban on Queen's hitherto proclaimed by the Catholic bishops. The proportion of Catholic students soon rose rapidly, from 5 per cent in 1909 to 25 per cent in 1915. In the education of women too Queen's was comparatively enlightened, taking its first female undergraduates in 1881 and admitting women ten years later to the medical course (its dissecting rooms were the first in Europe to be shared by students of both sexes). By 1911 just over a quarter of the 585 students were women.[16]

INDUSTRY AND TRADE

The industry and trade of Belfast continued to expand between 1901 and 1914, but growth was uneven. Apart from the contraction in house-building already mentioned, ship-building experienced difficult times after the end of the Boer War, which had caused a boom in demand for merchant ships. Concerned about the future, and determined to preserve his own freedom of action in a period of intense competition and threatened mergers, Pirrie diverged from the policy adopted by the owners of other British yards and in what was seen by some as an unpatriotic move negotiated with the American tycoon J. Pierpoint Morgan to form a syndicate called International Mercantile Marine. Pirrie operated brilliantly in these shark-infested waters, though international dealings and his own social ambitions meant that he spent more and more of his time in London rather than Belfast. His style of management became increasingly autocratic, and no-one but himself and one trusted subordinate had access to the financial records of Harland & Wolff.

THE PARTNERS OF HARLAND & WOLFF, c.1880

From left to right, Gustav Wolff, W.H. Wilson (designer), William Pirrie and Edward Harland.

© ULSTER MUSEUM, 2008

During 1904 and 1905 Pirrie saved the business by accepting orders at or below cost and by building ships for which Harland & Wolff would not normally have tendered. Of the twenty vessels delivered during those years nine made a loss. Output slumped from 73,264 tons in 1903 to 48,404 the following year and workers had to be laid off. Refit work and Admiralty orders helped to keep the yard going, though the collapse of part of the Alexandra graving dock meant that some work had to be sent elsewhere. Despite this, Pirrie invested heavily in modernisation – a new generating station in 1904, which enabled all the tools to be electrified the following year; new engine shops; higher gantries to accommodate even larger vessels the year after that. At the end of 1907 Harland & Wolff was employing nearly 9,500 men (2,429 in the engine works). The fluctuation of the labour force even in busy times is shown in the fall in numbers to 5,785 in 1909–10 as finishing work ran out; by the end of 1910, however, the figure was up to 11,389, and it reached 14,000

TITANIC UNDER CONSTRUCTION, C.1910

Titanic's keel was laid on 22 March 1909. For the next twenty-six months, Harland & Wolff's shipyard workers laboured nine hours a day, six days a week, to construct her massive hull.

© RALPH WHITE/CORBIS

by 1914. Repair yards had earlier been acquired at Liverpool and Southampton. Now in 1911, at the height of the boom, another ship-building yard was bought in Govan on the Clyde (Pirrie had already sold a majority shareholding in his firm to John Brown). In 1912–13 he planned the expansion of work there, lest civil war should break out in Ulster and he might have to close the Queen's Island. The climax of this era of ship-building was the launch of the 45,000-ton *Olympic* in 1910 and her even larger sister-ship *Titanic* the following year. The other yard, Workman Clark & Co., did not approach this tonnage in individual ships – its largest before 1914 were the 14,500-ton *Ulysses* and *Nestor*, built for the Holt 'Blue Funnel' Line – but its total yearly output was the sixth largest in the United Kingdom and it achieved an enviable reputation for excellent design and workmanship, especially in the construction of the specialist ships used to carry frozen meat from America and Australasia and fruit from the West Indies. By 1914 the combined output of the two Belfast yards was nearly one-eighth of the world's production. Between them they

were then employing some 20,000; their weekly wages bill, £15,000–£18,000 at the turn of the century, rose to £35,000 in 1915.[17] Splendid as all this achievement was, and much as the work and wages of the shipyards contributed to the prosperity of Belfast, it is well to remember that it was not only hard and dirty but also frequently dangerous work: nearly half of the fatal accidents in Ulster in an average year happened in the Queen's Island.[18]

The continued growth of the shipyard was matched by the continued expansion and improvement of port and harbour facilities. The annual tonnage of shipping cleared, nearly 2.5 million in 1900, rose to 3.2 million by 1913. Over 200 ships, totalling more than 300,000 tons, belonged to Belfast owners, which created a lot of business for local repairers, chandlers and agents. Though not always willing to respond to the pressure for additional space for ship-building (Pirrie even tried to bully them by making well-publicised approaches to the Dublin port authorities), the Harbour Commissioners made further major improvements. The Musgrave Channel, begun in 1898, was opened in 1903. The Thompson graving dock, the largest in the world at the time and costing over £300,000, was opened in 1911; its

OLYMPIC AND TITANIC

Olympic (right) and her sister ship *Titanic* (left) in the slips at the Queen's Island. The largest ships afloat when they entered service, these huge liners were built for the White Star Line by Harland & Wolff. *Olympic* was launched in 1910, shortly after this photograph was taken by R.J. Welch, the official photographer for Harland & Wolff.

first occupant was the liner *Olympic*. A giant electric floating crane was acquired. As
well as being what a French visitor, L. Paul-Dubois, described in 1908 as 'amongst
the most thrilling industrial centres of Britain', Belfast in its heyday was, above all,
a great port.[19]

INDUSTRIAL RELATIONS

Relations between employers and skilled workers such as shipwrights and engineers
were good for most of the Edwardian period. After the bitter strike of 1895–96
Pirrie was careful to ensure that the unions were consulted about important matters
affecting their members' interests. Harland & Wolff refused to take part in the
national lockout of engineers in 1897 instead, Pirrie stole a march on his competitors
by conceding a shorter week of 47 hours in return for three-shift working. Two
years later, when the Shipbuilders' Employers' Federation was formed, both Belfast
yards refused to join. Demarcation disputes between the many shipyard unions
were a likelier source of industrial strife during these years than confrontations
with the management. The numerous craft unions not only secured good wages for
their members when in work but also provided them with benefits when laid off.
However, the attempts of labourers to secure higher wages and better conditions
through unionisation were seen by the craft unions as a threat to their privileged
position. From the early 1890s the National Amalgamation Union of Labour had
some success in organising shipyard labourers, but there was no great improvement
in the relative position of the unskilled working for the skilled before the First World
War. In 1907, when engineering labourers at the Sirocco works went on strike and
set up a branch of the union, they were locked out and only allowed back if they
signed a document repudiating their membership.

Linen workers, who could easily be replaced, were in an even weaker position.
Despite attempts to organise them, by 1914 only about one-tenth belonged to any

union. Apart from the hostility of employers, occupational jealousies made organisation difficult. The women who worked in the spinning mills, weaving factories and warerooms were intensely conscious of differences in status between those three workplaces and between the various occupations within each. In the mills, for example, reelers (who wore coats to work as a mark of their superiority) looked down upon the shawled spinners. An economic upturn from 1906 nevertheless encouraged an outbreak of militancy amongst unskilled workers. In May 1906 a strike in the linen mills, the first in ten years, secured a wage increase, and in the spring and early autumn of 1907 there were strikes by engineering labourers and coal heavers (as well as by bakers, printers and machine makers). These conflicts reached a climax in the dockers' and carters' strike of 1907, which was led by the charismatic labour organiser James Larkin, who came to Belfast in January of that year as an official of the British-based Transport and General Workers Union.[20]

In 1907 there were 3,100 labourers employed (or sometimes employed) at the Belfast docks. Just over a thousand of them were permanent, the rest casual, none a member of any union. There were also 1,500 carters, a few of whom belonged to an ineffective union. The dockers were to a considerable degree divided along religious lines: most of those employed in the cross-channel docks, where work was constant and regular, were Protestants, while the deep-sea docks, where work was more occasional, were manned mainly by Catholics. It was among the cross-channel

CONWAY MILL

This flax-spinning mill was established in 1842 by James Kennedy. It is currently undergoing a massive refurbishment due to be completed in June 2010. The aim is to protect and preserve one of the most important historic buildings in Belfast. It will be a social, cultural and economic asset for the local community and for greater Belfast.

PHOTOGRAPH: CARNEGIE, 2009

dockers that the dockers' part of the great strike was concentrated, hence Larkin's boast that he, a Catholic and a Nationalist, led a band of Orangemen in the cause of labour. Within a short time of his arrival he had persuaded all the carters and all but a couple of hundred of the dockers to join the union. Larkin's chief opponent among the employers was Thomas Gallaher, the tobacco magnate, who was also chairman of the Belfast Steamship Company. As a large employer of women and casual labourers, Gallaher saw 'Larkinism' as a threat to all his interests. A number of dock employers were willing to recognise the union, but Gallaher refused to have any dealings with it. When some of the dockers employed by the Belfast Steamship Company struck at the end of May in favour of a closed shop he brought in labour from Liverpool and refused to take the men on again when they tried to return to work.

Larkin's answer to this early setback was to rouse all unorganised workers to give their support. Thousands attended the strike meetings at which he thundered against the employers, Gallaher in particular, and encouraged militant action. The employers in their turn formed an Employers Protection Society and imported more blackleg labour. Sympathetic strikes by the carters and coal heavers, with active picketing to prevent the movement of goods about the city, stretched the resources of the police and soon threatened Belfast's trade and industry. Cavalry were drafted into the city in July to protect vans from interference by pickets, and there were some minor outbreaks of violence. At the end of that month half of the constabulary in Belfast attended a meeting to protest against the long hours of unpaid extra duty they were obliged to work because of the strike whereupon three hundred of them (mostly from the Falls area) were transferred to other parts of the country and replaced by 1,200 troops. The first serious rioting began on 11 August in the lower Falls, where vans were overturned and police and soldiers stoned. Next day two people were killed and many injured when the army fired into a crowd.

When the master carriers conceded both union recognition and a wage demand (though their right to employ non-union labour was accepted by the men), the strike was quickly settled by union officials from England who excluded Larkin from their negotiations. The dockers were then obliged to accept an unconditional return to work. Larkin's expressed belief that the cooperation of Catholic and Protestant workers during the strike meant that 'the old sectarian curse had been banished for ever from Ulster' was soon proved to be a delusion. When he went on in 1908 to establish the Irish Transport and General Workers Union the Belfast dockers divided, Catholics joining the new, Nationalist-led body, Protestants not; the Belfast Trades Council also split on the national question.[21]

Any hope of replacing sectarianism by working-class unity was finally demolished when the home rule question approached its dramatic climax. After a lull of several years, broken only by a two-day riot in 1909 caused by an attack on an Orange procession along the Grosvenor Road, Catholic workers (and Protestant socialists as well) were expelled from the shipyards in 1912. Pirrie and other employers

BELFAST DOCKERS AND CARTERS STRIKE 1907

NOT AS CATHOLICS OR PROTESTANTS NOT AS NATIONALISTS OR UNIONISTS BUT AS BELFAST WORKERS STANDING TOGETHER

disapproved of this action but there was little they could do. There was little they could do. Even in normal times the police hardly dared enter the yards. As the Belfast Commissioner of Police testified at the time:

> In ordinary times they did not do duty in the shipyards and their presence there was regarded as an intrusion and an insult. Even in ordinary times, a policeman in uniform has missiles frequently thrown at him if he has to go down about the Queen's Road. Missiles were thrown at the police marching to and from duty by men working on the ships.[22]

The belief, expressed by most Nationalist and labour commentators, that recurring riots were the result of clever manipulation by bourgeois politicians who wanted to thwart home rule and socialism by keeping workers at each others' throats, greatly underestimated the genuine strength of sectarian feeling among the Protestant working classes – an attitude of mind matched, in truth, by that of their opponents. The proclamation in 1908 of the papal decree *Ne Temere*, which applied new, strict, and exclusive, canons to the validity of marriages between Catholics and Protestants, roused great resentment in Protestant circles, especially when the new regulations were held to have been responsible for a Belfast Catholic named McCann deserting his Presbyterian wife in 1910. The McCann case was widely reported and was debated at some length by the Presbyterian General Assembly. Not surprisingly in the circumstances of the time, the issue strengthened Protestant fears that Home Rule would indeed mean Rome Rule.[23]

DOCKERS' STRIKE MURAL

The first major confrontation between the forces of labour and capital in Ireland occurred in 1907. The Belfast dockers' and carters' strike saw the emergence of the working class as an independent force. The police, exhausted by unpaid overtime, protested. Any who took part were posted to remote parts of the island and troops had to be brought in. The power of the employers was all but broken in Belfast as the workers, Protestant and Catholic, inspired by the charismatic labour organiser James Larkin, united behind the banners of the developing labour movement.

PHOTOGRAPH: CARNEGIE, 2009

MUNICIPAL ENTERPRISE

BELFAST CITY HALL

The new City Hall photographed in 1904, when the exterior was nearly finished. It is a magnificent Edwardian 'wedding cake', built to reflect Belfast's newly won city status. The dome is 53 metres high, and the building dominates the heart of Belfast.

The Edwardian period was, as it turned out, the heyday of Belfast. In municipal affairs nothing symbolised better its prosperity and civic pride than the splendid new City Hall, opened in 1906. Designed by a young London architect, Arthur Brumwell Thomas (who was knighted on its completion), and built by the Belfast firm of H. & J. Martin, it cost the enormous sum of £360,000, twice the original estimate. The increase was due partly to the fact that only the finest and most expensive materials were used – the marble work alone cost over £21,000 – and partly to the insistence (by Labour and Nationalist councillors in particular) that Corporation labourers and

local contractors should be employed on the work, despite the fact that Corporation wages for labourers were on average three shillings a week more than usual and that English firms sent in lower tenders for furnishings. 'A precious stone, I suppose?' said the Local Government Board inspector when told that the foundation stone cost £500. The architect subsequently had to sue the Corporation for the balance of his fee.[24] Another major building achievement, completed in 1907, was the College of Technology, built on a city-centre site unwisely sold by the governors of the Academical Institution, the view of which has been spoiled ever since. The College, which also housed the former Government School of Art, was equipped with the latest facilities for teaching engineering and science (it was the Tech that provided practical courses for the university). A third building was the Fever Hospital at Purdysburn, opened in 1906. The Ulster Hall in Bedford Street, the usual venue for large public meetings as well as for concerts and exhibitions, was purchased by the Corporation in 1902 for £13,500. In the same year the Corporation opened its model lodging house for working men, Carrick House, which was twice extended within a few years because of the demand for its 6d. (2½p) a night accommodation. Additional branch libraries were also provided and, not before time in 1913, a new abattoir. From 1910 the horse-drawn engines and ambulances of the Fire Brigade were gradually replaced by motorised ones. Money had to be spent also on improving the new drainage system, after a combination of heavy rain and high tides flooded the whole city centre with a mixture of sewage and sea water in 1902.

The greatest extension of the Corporation's responsibilities, however, was its acquisition of the tramways. The main part of the system, belonging to the Belfast Tramways Company, was purchased in 1904. A separate system, operated by the Cavehill and Whitewell Tramway Company along the upper part of the Antrim

Road, was bought six years later. The bill to authorise the purchase was held up by the Nationalist party at Westminster until the Corporation agreed to include forty acres of recreational land at Bellevue – an example of the minority group's power in anything requiring legislation. The electrification and extension of the tramways cost well over a million pounds but greatly increased the service and the number of passengers.[25] The employment of Corporation labourers on the electrification of the trams was a convenient response to public pressure during a slump but, as in the case of the City Hall, it made the work more expensive. The lavish scale of municipal entertainment during these years was less justifiable.

Critics accused the Council not only of extravagance but also of incompetence. The Citizens' Association, a pressure group of businessmen and professional people formed in 1905, was particularly concerned about public health and was partly responsible for persuading the authorities in Dublin to set up the Vice-Regal Inquiry of 1906. Its report, published two years later, was pretty damning, though it must be said that by comparison with ten other major cities Belfast was found to have a lower overall death rate than Dublin and about the same as Manchester and Liverpool. The death rate from typhoid, however, was very much higher than anywhere else and the tuberculosis rate was higher even than that for Dublin. 'Inefficient sanitary administration extending over many years' was found to be the main cause. The

QUEEN VICTORIA

This statue in front of the City Hall was unveiled by Edward VII and Queen Alexandra on their first royal visit to Belfast, on 27 July 1903 and, according to an account in the *Belfast News Letter*, he 'looked back over his shoulder at his mamma as the carriage was receding after the ceremony, and exclaimed "couldn't be better"'.

ULSTER HALL,
BEDFORD STREET

Built in 1862, the Ulster Hall has been entertaining the citizens of Belfast for almost 150 years. In its first fifty years it played host to such luminaries as Charles Dickens, Ellen Terry, Lord Randolph Churchill and Caruso. In 1902 the building was sold to Belfast Corporation. To celebrate the civic appointment of the Ulster Hall, Belfast Corporation commissioned a series of thirteen oil paintings by J.W. Carey. Newly refurbished, the Ulster Hall still provides entertainment and is home for the Ulster Orchestra and their world-class concerts.

PHOTOGRAPH: CARNEGIE, 2009

THE TRAM

Laying lines for the electric tramway in 1905. The elaborate junction shown here was at the corner of York Street and Donegall Street. In comparative terms, Belfast was late in electrifying its trams system.

A.R. HOGG COLLECTION, © ULSTER MUSEUM, 2008

appointment in 1906 of a new Medical Officer of Health did not at the time appear to promise much improvement, for Dr H.W. Baillie was not only less well qualified than other applicants but had been a Conservative alderman on the Council until he resigned in order to apply for the post. His appointment was derided in the medical press as well as elsewhere, but he proved to be an able administrator and, together with an active chairman of the Health Committee, tackled the typhoid problem so vigorously that by 1911 the Fever Hospital rarely saw a case.[26]

Apart from public health, with which it was not unconnected, one of the chief ways in which Belfast Corporation lagged behind other municipalities was in its reluctance to build houses for the poor. Not until 1910, by which date Liverpool, Glasgow and even Dublin had already carried out several schemes, was an Improvement Order adopted and a plan to replace 700 of the worst slums in the Millfield area drawn up. Even then little was done for many years; the first house was not completed till 1917. The delay was largely caused by objections from Nationalist councillors, who did not want those of their voters who were unfortunate enough to live in the area to be re-housed elsewhere. The Unionist majority on the Council, anxious as ever to keep down the rates, did not press the issue.[27]

PARTY POLITICS

The political balance in the Council did not change significantly during these years, despite the advance of labour and, to a lesser extent, socialist activity. Labour could never get more than the six seats they gained in 1897. The labour movement was divided both by socialism and by Nationalism. The two 'Labour Socialist' councillors elected in 1904, William Walker and John Murphy, both lost their seats in 1907. After 1911 Belfast Labour candidates stood only in Catholic wards, apart from an unsuccessful attempt in Dock Ward in 1913 by James Connolly (the future Nationalist martyr), who was the local organiser of the Irish Transport and General Workers Union from 1909 to 1914; the mixture of socialism and Nationalism he advocated was a double vote-loser in Belfast. In the Catholic wards until 1905, when it was disbanded, Bishop Henry's Catholic Association secured all the seats, despite the opposition of official Nationalist candidates and the refusal of their leader at Westminster, John Redmond, to recognise the Association on the grounds that it was sectarian. In the Smithfield Ward in 1904, however, the defeat of the Nationalist nominee was a very narrow one and the contest aroused strong feeling against clerical interference. After 1905 the Nationalist leader in Belfast, Joseph Devlin, gained control of the two wards, winning all the seats up for election in 1907 and completing the business in 1909. As we have seen, although they formed a permanent minority on the Council, the Nationalists exercised considerable influence of a mainly negative sort through their allies at Westminster. The only, serious challenge to the Conservatives, however, came from the Citizens' Association, which won five seats in 1907 and seven the following year. In 1910 one of its councillors, R.J. McMordie, was elected both lord mayor (a post he was to hold until 1914) and MP for East Belfast in succession to G.W. Wolff. Backed by the Unionist *Belfast News Letter*, the Association did not really differ much from the Conservatives; in the 1908 elections, indeed, all but one of its candidates was a joint choice. From 1911 the Association was practically absorbed by the Conservatives into a new Belfast Unionist Municipal Association, formed to make a united front against the threat of home rule, though it remained nominally independent until 1922.[28]

For much of the period it was national rather than local issues that determined the course of politics. In the early 1900s the Conservative cause in the city was weakened by the rise of an independent Protestant movement deeply dissatisfied with what its adherents regarded as complacency in the face of the Conservative government's 'Romanising' policies. In the by-election in South Belfast that followed the death of William Johnston in 1902, Thomas Sloan defeated the official Conservative, Dunbar-Buller, by 800 votes. Four years later, in the general election, he beat Lord Arthur Hill by a similar margin. Sloan's success in 1902 was achieved with the support of three Orange lodges, which were expelled from the Order. They formed an Independent Orange Order in 1903, which within a year had twenty lodges in Belfast. This weakening of Orange unity created an opening for Labour, which in 1903 formed a Labour Representation Committee and chose William Walker to contest the North Belfast seat at the next election. In a by-election in the seat in 1905 Walker was narrowly defeated by the property speculator (and former lord mayor, hence his baronetcy) Sir Daniel Dixon. Walker might well have won if – hoping to gain Protestant support – he had not lost Catholic votes by revealing his prejudices in replying to a public questionnaire, devised by the extremist Belfast Protestant Association to test his soundness on the only issue that mattered to them. In the general election of 1906, in a larger poll, Walker increased his share of the vote but failed by fewer than 300. When he contested the seat a third time in 1907, in a by-election caused by Dixon's death, the Conservatives had recovered their strength and he lost by more than 1,800. His election agent in 1905, incidentally, was the future Labour prime minister Ramsay MacDonald. Walker was undoubtedly hampered by the fact that the British labour movement with which he strongly identified was in fact, if not officially, sympathetic to home rule, though Walker himself was not.

Catholics in West Belfast were also divided in the early 1900s, between supporters of the Catholic Association and those who favoured the wider aims of Redmond's reunited Home Rule Party. The sitting Liberal Unionist member, Arnold-Foster, returned unopposed in 1900, was faced three years later (in a by-election caused by his appointment as Secretary for War) by a Nationalist, Patrick Dempsey, who came within 240 votes of him. By 1906, with the Catholic Association disbanded, the Catholic voters were united behind Joseph Devlin, who defeated a Unionist candidate, Capt. J.R. Smiley, by the narrowest of margins (16 votes). Thereafter Devlin held the seat more easily.[29]

By 1907, then, the Unionists had seen off the challenge from both Labour and their own dissidents, and the Nationalists were united behind Devlin, who could call on the powerful Home Rule Party in parliament. The landslide victory of the Liberals in 1906 brought to an end a long period of Conservative power during which home rule had ceased to be an active issue. For a time the Liberals, though committed in theory to another Home Rule Bill for Ireland, had such a large overall majority in the Commons and so many other urgent priorities that the threat to the Union remained more potential than actual. The elections of 1910 transformed this situation by reducing the Liberals' majority and making them dependent on the votes

UNIONIST BAKERY

As the Unionists prepared to take over the government of Ulster if the Home Rule Bill became law, the City Council of Belfast cooperated in allowing council property to be used in the Unionist cause. The Technical College started a bakery staffed by UVF members. This photograph shows Sir Edward Carson and Lady Carson visiting the bakery in February 1913. Carson is on the right with his hand on the table. His wife holds a large bouquet and behind Carson is James Craig, a future Prime Minister of Northern Ireland.

UNIONIST RESISTANCE

Mural on the Shankill Road commemorating the UVF gun-running operation of 1914.

PHOTOGRAPH: CARNEGIE, 2009

Anti-Home Rule propaganda in the form of a picture postcard. The Albert Memorial is being pulled down to make way for a statue of King John (Redmond), leader of the Nationalist party, with hordes of paupers, an emigrant ship at the dock, and grass growing in the street. Note also that city-buildings have been converted into a Protestant Emigration Office and an annexe to the Poor House.

of the Irish party. This immediately brought home rule to the top of the agenda and, with the passing in 1911 of the Parliament Act, which removed the veto hitherto exercised in favour of the Unionists by the House of Lords, the way was opened for Redmond at last. In 1910 the Unionists chose Sir Edward Carson as their leader and began to prepare to resist home rule. Increasingly from 1905, when the Ulster Unionist Council had been formed to bring together Unionist associations, Orange lodges, MPs and other defenders of the Union, Belfast had been at the centre of anti-home rule activity. Now it became the headquarters of the Unionist conspiracy to defy the will of parliament. The great demonstrations of September 1911 and Easter 1912, designed to show the government that home rule if it came would be resisted, were both staged in Belfast; and the Solemn League and Covenant campaign reached its dramatic climax in the Ulster Hall and the City Hall in September 1912. The organisation of the Ulster Volunteer Force in 1913, its arming with rifles smuggled from Germany in 1914 (which replaced the wooden models bought from an enterprising local firm) and the arrangements made to establish a provisional government in the event of home rule – all centred on Belfast; the old Town Hall in fact became the headquarters of the UVF. Only the outbreak of hostilities in Europe, postponed a showdown in which the city might well have become a war zone.[30]

It may indeed be true, as one historian has argued, that the very determination of Belfast Protestants to fight to keep the city British may, paradoxically, have made it 'no longer a British, but an Irish city'.[31] Certainly in Britain itself such recourse to extremes in the cause of religious conviction or prejudice was no longer fashionable.

left

ALBERT CLOCK TOWER

A lion on the Albert Memorial Clock Tower. Built on wooden piles on marshy land, the tower leans four feet off the perpendicular and is known locally as Belfast's 'Leaning Tower of Pisa'.

PHOTOGRAPH: CARNEGIE, 2009

below

SIR EDWARD CARSON

Carson was the leader of the Ulster Unionists in the struggle to prevent the passing of the Home Rule Bill. Had it not been for the outbreak of war in Europe in 1914, civil war in Ireland might have broken out then rather than later. This photograph was issued as a postcard.

CHAPTER ELEVEN

THE FIRST WORLD WAR
AND AFTER, 1914–1939

T HE First World War and the two decades that followed brought great economic and social changes to Belfast, changes which closely resembled those in other British cities despite some particular local problems. Still greater were the political changes that gave Belfast a new role as the capital of a new, semi-autonomous state, Northern Ireland, in which Protestants were a distinct – if rather insecure – majority. In these circumstances the traditional sectarian divisions in the city assumed still greater prominence and ferocity.

WAR AND PEACE

The First World War affected Belfast, as it affected the rest of Ulster and indeed Ireland, in two main ways. One was the high number of casualties suffered by those (all volunteers, for there was no conscription in Ireland) who joined the forces and most of whom ended up on the Western Front. In 1914, when war broke out, Carson and Craig offered Kitchener 35,000 UVF volunteers. In return, their request for a distinctive organisation for these men was granted and the 36th (Ulster) Division thus came into existence. The division fought heroically and suffered appalling losses in the battle of the Somme in 1916, no fewer than 5,500 being killed or wounded on the first day alone. The Twelfth of July celebrations were abandoned that year; instead, in an act of remembrance anticipating Armistice Day, everything stopped in Belfast at the stroke of noon.

As in other cities and towns where local lads joined local regiments, the effect of the casualties in Flanders was devastating. As one historian has put it: 'In house after house blinds were drawn down, until it seemed that every family in the city had been bereaved'.[1] The sacrifice was shared, for many National Volunteers, encouraged by Redmond as Carson encouraged the UVF, also joined up. By contrast, more extreme nationalists saw the war as an opportunity to overthrow British rule; the Easter Rising in Dublin in 1916 and its aftermath served to polarise opinion in the country still further. About half of the 49,000 Irishmen killed in the war came from the six counties that later became Northern Ireland, and a high proportion of that fearsome tally came from Belfast.[2]

The other main effect of the war was a prolonged economic boom that brought increased employment and prosperity to the city. The war itself created a great demand for linen for military purposes – tents, haversacks, hospital equipment, aeroplane fabric (some 90 million yards of it) – which more than made up for the loss of overseas markets. Half of all the cordage needed by the Royal Navy was produced by the Belfast Ropeworks. Munitions were produced on a comparatively small scale, though Davidson's Sirocco works made submarine parts as well as fans and heaters for war purposes, and other engineering firms were organised to produce shells, hand grenades and aeroplane parts.[3] But it was in the building of ships that Belfast made its outstanding contribution to the war effort. By 1916 German U-boats were sinking each month three times the tonnage that was being built. Ship-building became a high priority for the government, which brought all the shipyards in the country under its own control and embarked on a crash programme of building standard ships, the first of which was launched in Belfast. When the yards failed to meet their targets, Lord Pirrie was appointed to the new post of Controller General of Merchant Shipbuilding. Under his ruthless leadership the two Belfast yards broke

JAMES CONNOLLY

James Connolly played a leading part in the Easter Uprising of 1916 in Dublin. In 1911 he was appointed the Belfast organiser for the Irish Transport and General Workers Union. In 1912 he helped form the Irish Labour Party. This mural is on Rockmount Street, one of several fairly typical terraced streets off the Falls Road, near the Belfast City Cemetery.

PHOTOGRAPH: CARNEGIE, 2009

Young women engaged in war work and Labourers in the shipyard during the First World War. These paintings are by Ulster's most popular artist, William Conor RHA, RUA, ROI, 1881–1968. He received many official commissions, but his enduring achievement is his many impressions of ordinary Belfast working people and scenes of city life.

BY KIND PERMISSION OF MRS KAY DALZELL

all records. Altogether Harland & Wolff launched 400,000 tons of merchant and naval shipping, Workman Clark 260,000 tons.

The shipyards worked day and night, and by the end of the war were employing nearly 30,000 people. Because some skilled men had joined up, the labour force had to be diluted to a certain extent by less skilled replacements, and flat wage increases narrowed the differential between craftsmen and labourers. The craft unions did not like it but accepted the situation. There was no serious trouble of the kind that occurred on the Clyde, apart from a short strike by shipyard engineers in 1917. Enormous amounts of overtime had to be worked in order to reach production targets; in 1917 the Time Office at Harland & Wolff joked that H & W stood for Harassed & Worried. In the early years of the war, overtime was needed to maintain living standards, as wages lagged behind rising prices, but from 1917 wages rose faster than prices and with overtime working shipyard hands were financially well-off. In addition to ships Harland & Wolff produced aeroplanes during the latter part of the war, after Pirrie offered to open an aeroplane works. Starting with De Havilland Six machines, of which a hundred were made, the firm went on to build 300 Avros and twenty of the giant Handley Page V-1500 bombers, which were intended to reach Berlin but were finished too late in the war to be needed. It was Pirrie who acquired the land at Aldergrove, now the site of Belfast International Airport, for use with these planes.

The war boom was followed by a post-war boom which lasted till the latter part of 1920 as the losses of war were made good and a public starved of consumer goods such as linen was at last able to spend its accumulated wealth. The number of spindles and looms at work in the province reached its highest between 1918 and 1920, while the shipyards were never again to employ as many as they did in 1919, when Harland & Wolff and Workman Clark were respectively first and second among United Kingdom yards in terms of tonnage launched.[4]

The ending of the war, however, did bring to an end an era of harmonious labour relations. Unionist leaders, faced with a new wider franchise (the outcome of the 1918 Representation of the People Act), tried to maintain a united front on the constitutional question by establishing a Unionist Labour Association, three of whose nominees were accepted as official candidates and duly elected. Long hours and the suspension of normal trade union rights were tolerated while the war lasted, but with the coming of peace the shipyard workers at once demanded a significant reduction in the working week, from 54 hours to 44, three hours fewer than the unions' national leadership was prepared to accept in a negotiated settlement. The Belfast branches rejected the result of the national ballot and went on strike in January 1919, calling out not only their members in the shipyards and engineering works but also those in the city's gas and electricity stations. By the end of the first week 60,000 workers in over forty firms were affected, directly or indirectly.

WAR MEMORIAL, ST ANNE'S CATHEDRAL

All of those who joined the forces, most of whom ended up on the Western front, were volunteers as there was no conscription in Ireland. Kitchener was offered 35,000 UVF volunteers who were organised into the distinct 36th Ulster Division.

PHOTOGRAPH: CARNEGIE, 2009

There were no trams or street lights and most homes were without normal lighting and cooking facilities; newspapers were reduced in size or (in the case of the *Irish News*) closed down completely, and there was a serious threat to supplies of bread and coal. Strikers smashed the windows of shops which remained open by using whatever power the authorities managed to produce with volunteer labour. At a time when the Bolsheviks had seized power in Russia, when revolutionary socialists were trying to seize power in Germany and Italy and when a general strike was paralysing Glasgow, local extremists hoped and local moderates feared that the strike represented the rising of the workers against the capitalist system – or even a sign of disillusionment with Unionism (the *Belfast News Letter* emphasised the encouragement that was being given to Sinn Féin). In fact the strikers were mostly Protestant workers who had no interest in socialism and no intention of overthrowing the Union; they simply wanted better conditions. Unionist leaders hesitated to act against them but called in the troops after pressure from the authorities in Dublin. On 14 February soldiers occupied the gasworks and the electricity station and the strike quickly collapsed.[5]

The Representation of the People Act had replaced the four Belfast constituencies by nine, eight of which were won in the elections of the same year by Unionist candidates. The remaining one was taken by Joseph Devlin, who found himself leading a rump of only six Nationalists at Westminster when Sinn Féin, the heirs of 1916, swamped the Nationalist party at the polls yet refused to take their seats. Devlin himself easily defeated the Sinn Féiner de Valera. Lloyd George's government attempted to settle the Irish question by the Government of Ireland Act of 1920, which allowed for separate home rule regimes in Dublin and Belfast. The north reluctantly accepted this arrangement, and thus Belfast became in name what it had long been in fact, the capital of Ulster. The first Parliament of a six-county Northern Ireland was opened in Belfast City Hall by George V on 22 June 1921. George V's insistence on going to Belfast to carry out his duty in person was greatly admired by the thousands of Unionists who flocked to cheer him. The impression of a great imperial event was enhanced by the splendid open coach in which the royal party travelled and their glittering escort. The self-congratulation expressed by the government was tempered somewhat a couple of days later when the train taking the 10th Hussars and their mounts back to barracks at the Curragh in Kildare was ambushed at Adavoyle in South Armagh. Four soldiers were killed on the scene and another six were wounded; more than fifty horses were killed or had to be destroyed. The Army had been made to appear incompetent by its opponents, according to some press comment in Britain. (The Parliament later met for some years in the Presbyterian college, before moving to Stormont in 1932.) The 73 Sinn Féin MPs, however, rejected the 1920 Act, having already set up their own assembly in Dublin, Dail Eireann, which proclaimed an Irish Republic in January 1919. Their military wing, the Irish Republican Army, intensified the guerilla war against the

The war memorial
in front of the main
university building was
designed by Sir Thomas
Brock and executed by
Arnold Wright in 1923.

British begun in 1919, and in 1920 extended it to the north in order to prevent the establishment (or survival) of the Unionist regime there.[6]

The reaction of Protestant workers in Belfast was to expel all 'disloyal' elements – Catholics of course but also lukewarm Protestants and socialists – from the shipyards and engineering works. This in turn led to a period of serious rioting in east Belfast, in which seven Catholics and six Protestants were killed. As well as reflecting the extremely tense political situation, the expulsions also reflected the fact that a significant number of Catholics had been recruited into skilled trades during the war and were now seen as noncombatants occupying the jobs of ex-servicemen who could not get work. The beginning of what was to be an increasingly serious slump thus added economic rivalry to political and religious division, to bring about communal strife far more serious and prolonged than any in the nineteenth century, a local civil war in everything except name. From 1920 to the end of 1924 Belfast lived under military curfew. Despite this and severe action by the new government's police force, the Royal Ulster Constabulary, and its special constables, the Troubles became steadily worse, reaching a climax in 1922. By that time the death toll in Belfast had reached 453 of whom 257 were Catholics and 37 members of the security forces – not to mention those injured and terrified in communal warfare of extreme viciousness on both sides. Up to 10,000 Catholics lost their jobs, and more than twice that number were forced to flee from their homes. Protestants suffered death

A detail of the ornate decoration upon Church House, home to General Assembly of the Presbyterian Church. It was designed by Robert Young and opened in 1905.

PHOTOGRAPH: CARNEGIE, 2009

and displacement to a lesser extent, while many businesses on both sides were destroyed. The outbreak of the civil war in southern Ireland, which diverted the attention of the IRA, and the arrest of some of the worst Protestant thugs, brought peace at last.[7]

Municipal affairs in this post-war period were also not without excitement. At the end of the war, as at the beginning, the City Council was completely dominated by Unionists (who included the first women councillors, co-opted because there were no elections after 1916). In 1919, however, Lloyd George's government put through the Local Government (Ireland) Act, which altered the voting system in Irish boroughs to one of proportional representation. Much against its inclination, Belfast Corporation was obliged to draw up a suitable scheme for nine wards, corresponding to the new parliamentary constituencies in the city. The first election took place in January 1920. The result, if not quite the 'deathblow to the Unionist clique' that the *Irish News* thought, reduced their numbers from 52 to 29. The Nationalists and Sinn Féin each won five. Belfast Labour Party, the official labour group, won no fewer than ten, independent Labour candidates another three, while the Labour Unionists won six. This outcome significantly altered the social composition of the Council as well as its political balance. At the start of the century all but five of its sixty members had belonged to the upper-middle or middle class, in 1914 all but ten; now no fewer than nineteen were working-class. This situation did not last long. Determined to maximise their power in local as in provincial and national politics, the Unionists got an abolition bill through Westminster in 1922. The old ward boundaries were thereupon restored, and with them the old absolute majority. Without PR Labour could not capitalise on its support, which was thinly spread throughout a number of wards. In the local elections of 1923 its representation was

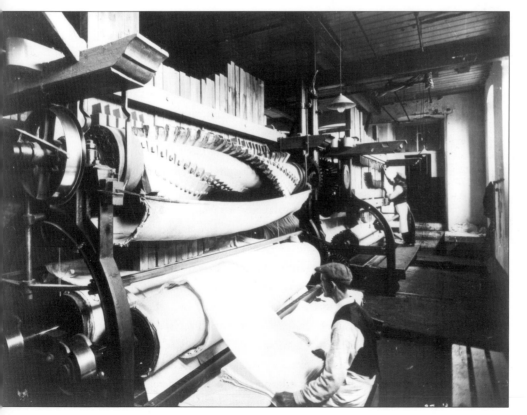

INSIDE A LINEN MILL

'Beetling' linen in an Ulster mill in the 1930s. The heavy wooden 'beetles' pounded the surface of the cloth as it went round, giving it fullness and a characteristic sheen. Deafness was almost inevitable for beetlers: in country areas the noise of the mill could be heard for miles.

A.R. HOGG COLLECTION, © ULSTER MUSEUM, 2008

cut to two. The Nationalists, on the other hand, recovered their former control of Falls and Smithfield and were thus the other group besides the Unionists to benefit. Sectarian politics was firmly reinstated.[8]

THE ECONOMY: TROUBLE AND CHANGE

CLOTHING MANUFACTURE

Tailors sewing by hand in the workroom of W.J. Marshall, 37 High Street, Belfast, in crowded conditions but with good light. This photograph was taken in 1931.

A.R. HOGG COLLECTION, © ULSTER MUSEUM, 2008

The population of Belfast continued to rise after 1911. At the next census in 1926, it was 415,151, an increase of 7.3 per cent in the fifteen years. By 1937 it had reached 438,000 – getting on for one-third of the total for the province. At about 5 per cent in each decade this rate of growth was very much less than it had been in the nineteenth century, and not much more than half of what it had been in the years before the war. The figures reflected the difficulties experienced by Belfast's staple industries, which depended almost entirely on export markets. In retrospect we can see that these were not merely temporary setbacks; in reality they marked the end of the long and virtually uninterrupted period of expansion that began in the mid-nineteenth century and the beginning of a long decline. So, just when Belfast became a capital city of a sort, changes in international trade began to undermine the industries that had made it great. If it had not been for the growth of jobs in the service sector, some of them created by the establishment of the new provincial government, things would have been even worse than they were between the wars; the number employed in such jobs in Northern Ireland rose from about 80,000 in 1926 to 100,000 in 1937, and most of them were in Belfast.[9]

Production of linen in Ulster, which had amounted to well over 200,000 million square yards in the years before the war, fell by 1924 to 161 million and by 1930 to 116. In 1935 it was up to 146 million, but the general trend was downward. The numbers employed in the industry inevitably fell sharply, from a post-war peak of 90,000 to 75,000 in 1924 and to 57,000 in 1935. In the later 1920s the United Kingdom's return to the gold standard and high tariffs on linen imports in the United States – the main export market – made things difficult for employers, but they fought back in the 1930s and in fact held their own with foreign competitors most of the time in the American market. It was not that Belfast firms failed to maintain their share of the market, but rather that the market itself shrank worldwide and for good. Cloth as expensive and durable as linen was no longer in such demand for female fashion, skirts were shorter and required less underwear, the modern fashion for polished wood tables and an increase in eating out lessened the demand for fine linen tableware, fewer domestic servants were employed

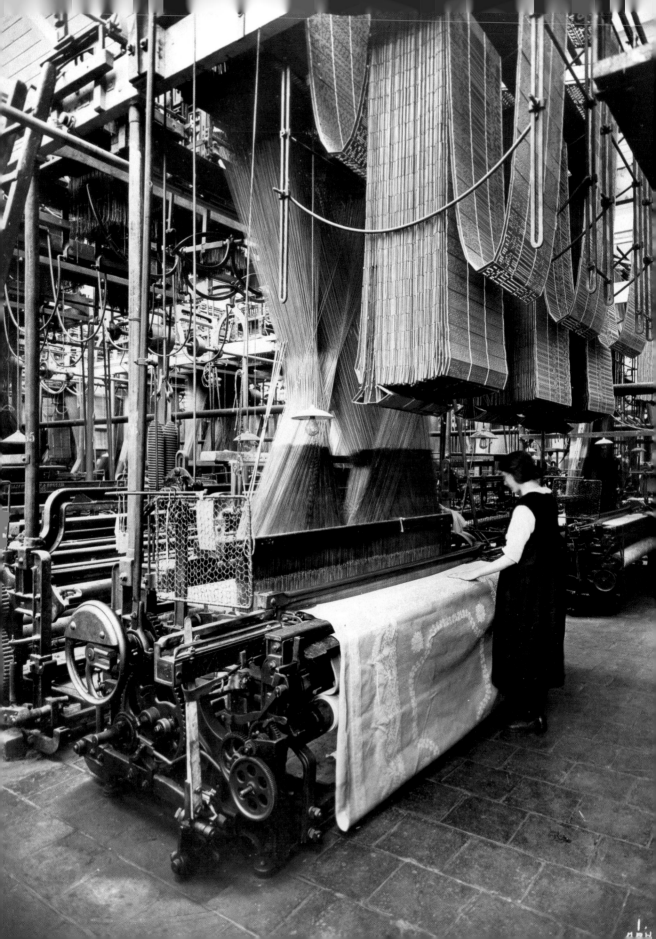

DAMASK LOOMS

Power-driven damask
looms, showing the
swags of punched cards
carrying the design
automatically to the
weaving machinery.
Each of the female
attendants would have
been responsible for
two or three of these
larger and complicated
machines.

A.R. HOGG COLLECTION. © ULSTER MUSEUM.
2008

to give it the care it needed. In these changed circumstances, cotton was a cheaper and more attractive alternative for the mass market that came into existence.[10]

In ship-building, too, it was the state of the world market rather than a failure of enterprise that accounted for the decline that took place. In general between the wars there were too many ships for the level of trade and too many of them recently constructed during the post-war boom to need replacing; in 1921 the world's shipping was much newer than before the war. During the war, too, the United States and other countries had developed their own ship-building industries, which made the market still more competitive. In fact Belfast during the 1920s suffered less than some other areas of the United Kingdom, because there was still some demand for the passenger liners and large merchant vessels in which Harland & Wolff specialised. Between 1922 and 1930 the firm launched 9.7 per cent of the merchant shipping tonnage produced by UK yards, the same proportion as before the war, and in 1929, as so often before, it launched both the largest tonnage in the world and also the biggest ship, the third *Britannic*. Pirrie's foresight (he died in 1924, appropriately at sea) in becoming involved with the firm of Burmeister & Wain in the development of the diesel engine was one advantage, cheap imported steel (not available to other British yards because of a voluntary embargo) another. Even so, Pirrie had lost most of his fortune in keeping the firm afloat. After 1930, as the slump in world trade took effect, orders ceased and more and more men had to be laid off. By the winter

CITY OF SYDNEY

This photograph
captures the moment
of the launch of
the *City of Sydney*, at
Workman Clark's yard,
2 October 1929. This
image was taken by
A.R. Hogg, at that time
official photographer
for the firm, just as R.J.
Welch was for Harland
& Wolff.

A.R. HOGG COLLECTION. © ULSTER MUSEUM.
2008

of 1932–33 employment was only a tenth of the 1929–30 level. After the launch of the *Georgic* in 1931 grass began to grow on the slipways at Harland & Wolff, and for two years running the firm did not launch a single ship. It survived, however, partly by building things other than ships – the first diesel electric train in the British Isles (made for the Belfast & County Down Railway), locomotives for companies in America and Australia, engines for an oil pipeline in the Middle East, grain silos, steelwork for shops and cinemas. There was a strong suspicion, possibly justified, that it got less than a fair share of Admiralty contracts – one cruiser out of fifteen and one aircraft carrier out of five, but no battleships or destroyers.

The other yard, Workman Clark, did not survive the slump and went out of business early in 1935, when its south yard and engineering works were taken over by Harland & Wolff, the rest sold. Its failure was in large part due not to the slump but to difficulties caused by financial sharp practice back in 1920 which left Workman and Clark themselves very rich (one left £800,000, the other £1,500,000) but saddled the firm with a huge burden of debt. After a court case for fraud in 1927 the business was financially reorganised as Workman Clark (1928) Ltd, but orders began to dry up. Its last ship, a tanker launched in January 1935, was the 536th completed since the firm had begun in 1879.[11]

Where the two great staple industries struggled to survive, other, smaller concerns fared better. Gallaher's – whose Irish sales were hard hit in the 1920s, first by a boycott of Belfast goods in the Irish Free State and then by prohibitive duties there – recovered well after becoming a public company in 1928, increasing its export of tobacco and cigarettes from 4,000 tons in 1930 to 10,000 in 1936. Employing over 3,000 people, mainly women, it was still the largest independent tobacco factory in the world. Davidson's Sirocco works continued to produce nearly three-quarters of the world's tea-drying machinery, as well as heating and ventilating equipment (also produced by Musgraves, as the market for expensive stable fittings and solid-fuel stoves contracted). The Ropeworks continued to employ more than 2,000 people. The decline of ship-building was partly compensated for by the employment of some of its skilled workers in the only important new industry to be attracted to Belfast between the wars. Short Brothers of Rochester, makers of flying boats, received a large order for Sunderlands from the RAF and needed to expand. Facilities at Belfast were ideal: skilled labour, a deep-water dock, sheltered water suitable for flying boats and an adjacent airport (on 400 acres of slobland recently reclaimed by the Harbour Commissioners). By 1939 the firm was employing 6,000, and was soon to employ many more.[12]

LIVING STANDARDS AND UNEMPLOYMENT

It is well to remember that, despite the misfortunes of some, the majority of insured workers between the wars remained in employment throughout the period and

indeed improved their position in terms of real income. The improvement was a modest one, only 10–15 per cent in Northern Ireland compared with about 25 per cent in the rest of the United Kingdom. Incomes per head in the province, though, already in 1924 only 61 per cent of those in the rest of the UK, fell to 57 per cent in 1937. In other words, the base line for Belfast workers, already low compared with that in similar British cities, fell lower still. In the worst years of the slump, 1931 and 1932, more than a quarter of the city's working population – over 50,000 people – were out of work. In these circumstances the nature and extent of public relief were a matter of vital concern.[13] Workers who were covered by national insurance were eligible for the dole, but only until their entitlement, based on the stamps gained while in work, ran out. Economy measures introduced by the British government in 1931 also applied to Northern Ireland, which since the late 1920s had the same level of insurance as the rest of the UK. Benefit was limited to a maximum of 26 weeks a year. After that, claimants had to seek 'transitional benefit', but many of the unemployed did not qualify for such help and had to fall back on outdoor relief from the Guardians (made possible by an Act of 1928). In September 1932 there were 48,000 registered unemployed in Belfast, almost half of whom were not receiving benefit. Of that number, 14,500 were not receiving transitional benefit and therefore had to seek outdoor relief.

Successful applicants had to pass a stringent means test – some 'relieving officers' obliged people to sell furniture and even the linoleum on the floor – and were subjected to insulting inquisitions; the chairman of the Guardians, a Mrs Coleman, gave great offence by remarking that if the poor worked as hard at finding a job as they did under the blankets there would be less of a problem. Even when successful, applicants were put to outdoor tasks, such as breaking stones, for which many of them were unfit. If unable to get a place on one of these schemes (of which there were never enough) they got no cash, only payment in kind. Single men who failed to get places were entitled to nothing, and single women got no assistance. To make matters worse, the relief rates in Belfast were exceptionally low, ranging from only 8s. a week for a married man with no children to a maximum of 24s. for a family with four or more; single men got only 3s. 6d. if they were lucky enough to get a place on a scheme. These rates, as local clergy pointed out, compared very unfavourably with those in other cities. In Manchester a family with one child got 21s., in Liverpool 23s., in Glasgow 25s. 3d., in Bradford 26s., and some got a rent allowance in addition. In one of those rare outbreaks of working-class solidarity that occasionally raised false hopes among socialists, an Outdoor Relief Workers' Committee in October 1932 organised a strike of workers engaged on task schemes. A protest demonstration, led by a band playing 'Yes, we have no bananas', the only non-sectarian tune in its repertoire, headed a crowd of 60,000 from the Labour Exchange in Frederick Street to a torch-lit rally at the Custom House. Next day 7,000 accompanied a delegation to the workhouse. When pleas of starvation failed to move the Guardians, rioting broke out, and when the government banned all marches there was a violent confrontation between the unemployed and the police. A curfew had little effect, and when police opened fire on looters in the York Street area one man was killed and over thirty wounded. Summoned before an alarmed cabinet at Stormont, the Guardians gave way and announced substantial increases in benefit – to 20s. for a man and wife and up to 32s. for a family with four children, all to be paid in cash; single men and women living on their own were also to receive assistance. It was a notable victory.[14]

**WORKERS IN
CONFLICT**

Loyalist workers attack
Catholic shipyard
workers travelling
via York Street on
their way to work, 2
September 1920.

SECTARIAN VIOLENCE AND MUNICIPAL GOVERNMENT

This brief period of co-operation between Catholic and Protestant workers did not
put even a temporary end to outbreaks of sectarian feeling, which had a life of its
own. Its climax in the 1930s was the York Street riots of 1935, which began with
an attack on or by (it proved difficult afterwards to establish which) a parade of
Orangemen and their supporters returning from the Twelfth of July celebrations.
For more than a month mobs on both sides vented their fury on each other and on
the armed police who tried to keep them apart. Troops and a curfew had little better
success in the maze of narrow streets, in which a mixed population lived cheek by
jowl. By the time it was all over eight Protestants and five Catholics were dead. Most
of the wounded were Catholics, however, and over five hundred Catholic families

(2,240 people) were driven out of the area to take refuge in the Ardoyne district of north Belfast, where they took over a partially completed housing estate. The fact that 95 per cent of the £21,699 later paid out in compensation was paid to Catholics illustrates the balance of damage inflicted.[15]

Belfast Corporation played little or no part in these events. In some respects the establishment of a provincial government with a permanent Unionist majority simply reinforced the undesirable attitudes of the permanent majority in the City Hall, for the prime minister, James Craig, was anxious not to stir up trouble with local authorities. In 1924, in the course of a dispute with the Corporation about public housing, he told a junior minister: 'We always have to bear in mind that the city represents in many respects one-half of Northern Ireland and therefore requires careful handling.'[16] At the same time, anxious to achieve parity in social services with the rest of the UK, the government felt obliged to put pressure on the City Council. In housing this precipitated a clash and exposed the most serious municipal scandal since 1855. Under the Irish Local Government Act of 1919 the Corporation had prepared a housing scheme and had established a Housing Committee (chairman Sir Crawford McCullagh, vice-chairman T.E. McConnell, an estate agent) and a

FALLS ROAD PUBLIC LIBRARY

The library was fortified as a base for the Special Constabulary 1923. The poster on the right advertises an Ancient Order of Hibernians' excursion to Dublin.

R.J. WELCH COLLECTION, © ULSTER MUSEUM, 2008

Housing Department. Valuers and agents were appointed. Most of the proposed houses were to be built by direct labour under the supervision of the city surveyor, the rest by outside contractors. In 1925 the auditor of the new Ministry of Local Government wrote to complain of irregularities in the accounts and extravagance in the purchase of materials. The Housing Committee was obliged to set up an inquiry, which was led by a KC appointed by the Minister of Home Affairs. The Megaw Report, published in October 1926, disclosed scandalous negligence, the purchase of inferior materials, contracts awarded without tenders, members and officials of the Committee (and even the Town Solicitor) with a financial interest in sites chosen for development – sites chosen 'for profit to the vendor and not suitability for working-class housing'. In one case thousands of missing bricks were said to have been used to build a cinema owned by a committee member. Many similar things may not have come to light, for Megaw complained that officials were unco-operative and failed to produce all the documents he asked for and that members of the Committee were unwilling to give evidence. The outcome was that both the Town Solicitor and the Surveyor resigned, and several contractors were prosecuted.[17]

These revelations led to a demand for reform and a general investigation of the city's administration, which was carried out by a London accountant named Collins. In his report in 1928 Collins said that Belfast was being run on lines more suitable for a village; that there were far too many committees, whose members encroached on work that ought to be left to officials and interfered too much in the hiring and firing of staff (five whole meetings of the Education Committee or its sub-committee were taken up with sifting through 1,460 applications for a porter's post); and that the reviewing of all decisions by the full Council, instead of delegating powers to committees, was long out of date (it had been in operation since 1842). Collins made more than thirty recommendations, all of which were accepted. Apart from those concerned with better financial control and the replacement of patronage by competition in the making of staff appointments, the greatest change was the reorganisation of the committees and their reduction from twenty-one to fourteen (Housing was among those abolished). Sir Crawford McCullagh, whose chairmanship had been criticised by Megaw, was opposed in the 1929 municipal elections by an Independent Unionist, a member of a reform group based on the Chamber of Commerce. McCullagh was defeated (and thus deprived of the lord mayorship for 1929, for which he had already been chosen), but he got back for a different ward two years later and thereafter was lord mayor for no fewer than sixteen years. This was testimony not only to his lavish style of hospitality but also to the tight discipline of the City Hall Unionist Party that developed under his leadership. One-party rule in the 1930s resulted in apathy rather than scandal. In the 1932 elections only three of a possible twenty-two seats were contested, in 1931 and 1934 only two out of fifteen, though the 45 per cent turnout of electors in the contested wards was much the same as that in other British cities.[18]

One by-product of the housing scandal was that the Corporation decided not to proceed with the building of 870 houses already approved. None at all was built after 1930, by which date only 2,562 had been completed (and 375 of those were for sale, with low-interest loans to approved buyers, rather than for rent). Instead, estate agents and developers built cheap houses for sale, with the help of housing subsidies, such as the 2,500 planned for the Glenard estate in north Belfast which cost £200 each. It was these, still uncompleted, that the refugees from York Street took over. Having got there and arranged to pay rent, they conducted a successful rent strike, which made the place so notorious that in 1937 all the street names were changed in an attempt to attract buyers. In all, 28,450 houses were built in the county borough between the wars. Excuses can be found for the Corporation's dismal record. The financial position in Northern Ireland was different from that elsewhere – per capita income was not much more than half the average for the UK as a whole, and there was no equivalent of the Wheatley Act (which had stimulated subsidised council house building in Britain) – and the city's housing stock was still better than most. Nevertheless, at the bottom end, conditions were far from satisfactory and the failure to do anything effective about them was to create even greater problems later.[19]

EDUCATION

In primary education, on the other hand, the Corporation's record was a creditable one. The Lynn Committee, which reported in 1923, estimated that at least 12,000 children of school age could not be accommodated in the city's national schools and that many of the places available were in dirty and insanitary buildings. The 1923 Education Act which resulted from the committee's recommendations proposed to increase grants and to make local authorities responsible for primary schools. There was to be no denominational religious instruction within school hours in state-funded schools. The Belfast Education Committee was set up in October 1923 under the chairmanship of Alderman James Duff. The committee found that only six of the city's elementary schools could be classed as satisfactory. Another twelve could be made satisfactory. Most of the rest 'would not be tolerated in any other part of the United Kingdom'; about forty of them were 'a direct menace to the health and physical development of the children', who might have been better off on the street. Within five years fifty schools had been closed down, many improved and sixteen large new ones either built or started.

The new schools, built entirely out of public funds and entirely under the control of the Education Committee, were described as 'provided' schools. In addition to these the 1923 Act allowed for the transfer of existing schools from the managers or trustees (in most cases churches) to the Committee; thereafter the schools would be run by management committees on which the 'transferors' would be represented.

A third category consisted of voluntary schools which did not want to transfer completely but did wish to qualify for a substantial degree of financial help by agreeing to have management committees composed of four representatives of the managers and two of the Education Committee, hence the name 'Four and Two' schools. Last, voluntary schools which preferred to remain outside the system would get no help from public funds except the salaries of teachers and half the cost of lighting, heating and cleaning. It was hoped that a large number of Catholic schools would come in as 'Four and Twos', but the Church authorities wanted to retain complete control. In any case, strongly opposed to Partition, they did not wish to recognise the new government, and thus missed an opportunity to negotiate changes to the system.[20]

As in the nineteenth century, the attempt to avoid sectarianism in the state schools by excluding denominational teaching was defeated by the churches. The Protestant churches were very unhappy with the parts of the Act that permitted the Education authority to 'afford opportunities' for religious instruction but did not permit them to provide it. Under great pressure from a joint action committee and in the absence of his Minister of Education (Lord Londonderry), who subsequently resigned, Craig agreed to make important concessions. The amending Act of 1925 enabled (but did not compel) education authorities to make provision for religious teaching and to allow management committees to appoint teachers. In practice the Belfast authority agreed that Bible instruction would be given daily by teaching staff. This persuaded many Protestant church schools to transfer. The early trickle – only five in 1924–25 and six in 1925–26 – became a flood in 1926–27, when 34 transferred. By 1929 the number had reached 73. Some Protestant clergy remained unsatisfied with anything less than 'simple Bible instruction' in all religious education lessons and places for clergy by right on the management committees of transferred schools. The Belfast Education Committee, which had an acrimonious meeting with a deputation of these clamorous divines, led by the Presbyterian Dr Corkey (manager of nine schools in the Shankill area), urged the Minister of Education not to increase clerical representation, but its stand was not supported by the City Council. The 1930 Act gave the Protestant churches all they wanted, in effect ensuring that only Protestant teachers were appointed to state schools attended by Protestant children. Bible teaching accompanied by church teaching, which was essential so far as Catholics were concerned, was forbidden in state schools by the 1930 Act. In these circumstances the transfer of Catholic schools was out of the question (it probably was in any case), but Bishop Mageean was successful in his campaign for better financial treatment. The church schools henceforth received half the cost of building and repairs, which in fact was more than similar schools got in Great Britain.[21]

Separation in education extended to the training of teachers. In 1922 a state training college for primary teachers of both sexes (later to be known as Stranmillis College) was established in Belfast. The following year it was agreed that St Mary's, the Catholic training college for women, would receive government support, while remaining entirely under church control. The small number of Catholic male students at first enrolled in the state college. Since canon law prohibited mixed education, however, the Catholic authorities refused to let this arrangement continue – despite an offer from the government to build a separate, clerically supervised hostel for the students – and argued instead for a Catholic men's training college as well as a hostel. This was refused, but the government did agree to fund male students at the Catholic college at Strawberry Hill, Middlesex. Thus from 1925 Stranmillis College inevitably became a Protestant institution. Not only that, but the joint committee of the three main Protestant churches, which had triumphed in 1925 and again in 1930 was thus enabled to put such pressure on the government that in 1932 the prime minister, now Lord Craigavon, once again ditched his Minister of Education, Lord Charlemont, and agreed to appoint three clergy to the college's management committee of nine.[22]

Expenditure on new and improved primary schools in Belfast continued even during the depressed 1930s. One of the ancillary services provided was a schools' medical service which by 1929 was carrying out more than a quarter of a million inspections a year; the Medical Officer reported in 1933 that many of the children he saw were suffering from malnutrition and anaemia. The school attendance service, taken over from the national school system, was improved and made more efficient. 'Necessitous children' were provided with free books and free meals, the latter with considerable help from Toc H, St Vincent de Paul and other volunteers. No more was done for secondary education, however, than to provide fifty scholarships (30 boys, 20 girls) each year to the city's grammar schools, a wholly inadequate response by comparison with other UK cities. At university level there was no advance on the five scholarships, each for £160, awarded since 1913.[23]

HEALTH

To turn to public health, the voluntary hospitals were expanded or rebuilt to meet a growing need. The Royal Victoria Hospital was considerably enlarged between the wars. A new Royal Maternity Hospital, with a hundred beds, was opened on the same site in 1933. A new Royal Belfast Hospital for Sick Children had been opened the year before. At the Union Infirmary the Jubilee Maternity Hospital was completed in 1935, but despite this and an extension to the children's wards and the appointment of more specialised staff, the Infirmary was overcrowded with patients and constantly short of nurses, and the food was abominable. Another, macabre shortcoming was that visiting clergy had to conduct funeral services in the mortuary, where mourners were surrounded by corpses. In 1939 the Board was dissolved and replaced by two commissioners appointed by the government. Like other places, Belfast suffered from the great post-war epidemic of influenza, which reached the city in 1920. So many staff died in the Union Infirmary that the Guardians were moved to order that nurses should be issued with an extra ounce of butter and a half-ounce of Bovril every day. The Infirmary, dealing with the poorest, also experienced epidemics of measles and scarlet fever in the early 1920s which carried off many children. A more unusual occurrence, which reached the proportions of a minor epidemic, was an outbreak of encephalitis lethargica or sleepy sickness in the years after 1922. Many who did not die of the disease were permanently afflicted. The historian of the Infirmary recalls 'a bizarre band of zombies shambling along in their workhouse clothes'. More and more, as medical costs rose, the voluntary hospitals were obliged to consider charging in-patients. In the post-war period it was notable that 'a great change had taken place in the class of patients who now attended hospitals'; they were no longer used only by charity cases. At the Infirmary, according to one recollection, any patient staying overnight had to do a day's work the next day before being discharged.[24]

Public health improved in Belfast between the wars. The general death rate declined and life expectancy at birth increased. The improvement during the same period in other large cities of the United Kingdom was much greater, however, so the relatively poor standing of Belfast was maintained and in some respects became worse. A comparison of average death rates for various diseases, per thousand of the population, between Belfast in the late 1930s and English county boroughs in 1938 shows similar figures for scarlet fever, syphilis and diphtheria but far greater mortality in Belfast from whooping cough (11 compared with 4), measles (19 to 5), influenza (24 to 11), epidemic influenza (46 to 13), pulmonary tuberculosis (88 to 66) and other tuberculosis (21 to 12). The greatest killer everywhere was pneumonia (97 to 75), which often developed as a complication of some other condition, especially in children and old people, though tuberculosis was regarded with far more terror. The malnutrition noted by the Schools Medical Officer must have increased the risk of serious disease for some children. Infant mortality, which averaged 77 per thousand births in the province as a whole in the period 1934–38, was 97 in Belfast, high by any comparison; where Belfast had a lower rate than any city in the north of England in 1901, it had the highest in 1938 (Liverpool's was 74, Manchester's 69). The risk to mothers of dying in childbirth actually increased by one-fifth between 1922 and 1938. Though poor housing and poverty itself contributed to this deplorable situation, the main reason for it was the inadequate medical services provided by the Corporation and the Guardians. The author of a detailed examination carried out in 1941, Dr Carnwath, concluded: 'In respect to personal medical services, Belfast falls far short of what might reasonably be expected in a city of its size and importance.' Midwifery services were poor, there was very little education or help for expectant mothers and few health visitors, and many infant deaths could have been avoided by the expenditure of a little more money. The Medical Officer of Health lacked specialist staff and was responsible for things other than personal medical services, such as inspecting food, milk, the abattoir and lodging houses. His advice so far as venereal disease was concerned was that 'people should get a grip of themselves'.[25]

PUBLIC WORKS AND PRIVATE PLEASURES

Aided by government grants and unemployment work schemes, the Corporation was rather more determined about other kinds of municipal improvement. The capacity of the gasworks was further increased and a new electricity generating station was built at the Harbour in 1923 to meet a growing demand. The use of electricity was promoted by the Corporation's Electricity Department, which demonstrated and sold lighting and cooking appliances of all kinds as well as providing the power supply (the first 'all-electric' house was advertised for sale in Balmoral Avenue in 1928). Petrol buses appeared in the city from 1923, at first operated by competing private companies; from 1928, however, the Corporation had a monopoly over all within the boundary. Its Transport Department acquired more land on the slopes of Cave Hill, which it developed as a park in addition to Bellevue (where the Zoo was opened in 1934). And to Hazelwood and Bellevue were added Belfast Castle and its lovely grounds, acquired from the earl of Shaftesbury in 1934. Land on the south side, given to the city by Henry Musgrave, was laid out as a park in the early 1920s using unemployed labour. The long-promised Museum and Art Gallery was begun in the Botanic Gardens in 1924 and opened five years later. Under powers obtained in 1924 a lock and weir were constructed on the Lagan below Ormeau Bridge, to control the tidal flow which at low water uncovered evil-smelling mudbanks, and embankments and roadways were built along the river. In 1924 Belfast opened the first municipal aerodrome in the British Isles, at Balmoral; the first flight conveyed the lord mayor, Sir William Turner, to Manchester.[26]

The other civic agencies responsible for maintaining and improving the city were also active. The Water Commissioners in 1933 opened the Silent Valley reservoir in the Mournes, which took ten years to build and increased the daily supply to 21 million gallons. In the same year the Harbour Commissioners opened the Herdman Channel and Pollock dock on the County Antrim side of the river. Tonnage cleared through the port rose from 3 million in 1923 to over 4.5 in 1937. The reclamation of the sloblands, which had been going on for a long time in a comparatively small way, gathered pace in the early twentieth century. The annual amount excavated in the mid-nineteenth century averaged somewhere between 100,000 and 200,000 tons a year (the formation of the second cut in 1849 produced more than 300,000); the average for the century as a whole was perhaps about 180,000. Except for particular years, notably 1902 when a million and a half tons were excavated for the Musgrave Channel, the yearly average remained similar up to 1920. Thereafter however, it rose to nearly 700,000 and in the 1930s it was over 800,000 a year. This increase reflected the purchase of Dutch equipment, namely an elevator dredger which could be used also as a suction dredger. By this means 15 to 20 acres were added to the land at the head of the Lough each year in the 1920s, 35 acres a year in the following decade. Creating land was not the least of the services the Harbour Commissioners performed for Belfast industry. The new harbour site was first used by aircraft in 1933 though Belfast Harbour Airport did not open until 1938.[27]

The replacement of horse transport by cars and lorries was one of the major social changes of these years in Belfast as everywhere else. The number of motor vehicles on the roads of Northern Ireland almost quadrupled, and the number of private cars rose tenfold. By 1937 one family in seven had a car, compared with one in sixty at the end of the First World War. Naturally, much of the increase took place in and around Belfast. The number of motor car agents and hirers listed in the Belfast directory rose from 38 in 1920 to 170 in 1939. In 1928 the flood of imported Fords, Morrises and other makes finally proved too much for the one successful native firm of car manufacturers, Chambers Bros, the first of whose beautiful hand-built machines had been produced in 1903. The arrival of branches of Woolworth's, Burton the tailors, Austin Reed and other cross-channel shops added to the choice for shoppers in the city centre. Leisure activities too became more varied, for people of all classes. Drinking and drunkenness declined as the first milk bars made their appearance and cinema-going increased. By 1935 Belfast had 31 cinemas capable of seating more than 28,000 people, one seat for every fifteen of the population (the London figure was fourteen). Listening to the wireless became another popular thing after the BBC opened a studio in Belfast in 1924 (Tyrone Guthrie's first post on coming down from Oxford was assistant producer in Belfast). Greyhound racing started in Belfast in 1927, at Celtic Park, the second track to be established in the UK; another was opened in the 1930s at Dunmore Park on the Antrim Road. Sport of all kinds, and for all levels of society, became more widespread. Association football attracted capacity crowds to Linfield's Windsor Park and the ground of their great rivals Belfast Celtic, the 'Catholic' team – the most successful club between the wars. For the middle classes, the Ravenhill ground with its new reinforced concrete grandstand accommodated 30,000 at international rugby matches, and several new golf courses were opened on the outskirts of the city.[28]

In short, despite desperate sectarian tensions and serious economic difficulties, the living standards and social life of the majority of Belfast citizens showed signs of improvement between the wars, in much the same ways as in other British cities.

CHAPTER TWELVE

The Second World War and After, 1939–1972

I N T H E P E R I O D of thirty years or so that began with the outbreak of war in 1939, Belfast adapted successfully to many economic and social changes – changes which were similar to those experienced by other British industrial cities and which brought similar problems and benefits.

WARTIME

The Second World War, like the First, was good for Belfast business. Pre-war rearmament had already brought to the city an aircraft industry which by 1939 was employing 10,000 people. The demands of war work, especially in ship-building and all kinds of engineering, were to reduce the unemployment of the 1930s to low levels. The shipyard, which employed 9,000 in 1939, had a workforce of more than 21,000 by 1944. Aircraft manufacture in 1943 employed 32,600. Other engineering, which accounted for 14,000 or so before the war, employed over 29,000 in 1943–44. In all, 80,000 or more found work in ship-building and engineering, an increase during the period 1939–45 of no less than 138 per cent (the figure for Great Britain was 65.6 per cent). The wartime output of Short & Harland and their sub-contractors (among whom were Harland & Wolff and Mackie's) included 2,381 Stirling bombers and 133 Sunderland flying boats. Harland & Wolff built 170 warships, mostly corvettes, minesweepers and similar small craft but including the aircraft carrier *Formidable*. In addition the firm carried out a large amount of repair and conversion work for the Admiralty, especially the conversion of cargo vessels to aircraft carriers; it also produced large quantities of propelling and auxiliary machinery for ships, not to mention 550 tanks (assembled at Carrickfergus), 10,000 pieces of ordnance, ball bearings, gun mountings and parts for Stirlings and Sunderlands. Lastly, more than sixty merchant ships, with a total tonnage of 421,500, were launched during the period 1941–45. Mackie's and the Falls Foundry made lathes for the production of munitions and Mackie's organised the manufacture of armour-piercing shells and aircraft parts in redundant linen mills. Sirocco and Musgrave's produced heating and ventilation equipment for war purposes, while smaller firms made motors and generators. The output of the Ropeworks included parachutes and camouflage netting as well as its usual products, for which there was no less demand than in peacetime.[1]

The same could not be said for linen. In the early stages of the hostilities every effort was made to keep the American market supplied and thus earn vital dollars for the war machine, but the German occupation of Belgium cut off the main source of both flax and seed (five-sixths of the former and all of the latter were imported). Ulster farmers were encouraged to grow more, with such success that the acreage rose from 21,000 in 1939 to 124,000 in 1944. The flax that was available was rigidly controlled and directed entirely to approved uses, some for immediate war needs (the Ministries of Supply and Aircraft Production took half of all the cloth made in Northern Ireland), the rest for civilian use such as 'utility' clothing. The military uses included aeroplane fabric – each Wellington bomber took well over a thousand yards of linen – flying suit canvas, parachute harness, gun covers, nurses uniforms, uniform linings, ground sheets, kit bags, awnings and sail cloth. Most military uses of linen, however, were better met by the coarse dry-spun yarns of Dundee than the fine wet-spun yarns of Belfast. Mills closed or were adapted to produce munitions. Employment fell drastically; the number of insured linen workers out of work in the province, 12,000 in April 1940, was 23,000 by September. Some found work again in textiles as the production of rayons and mixtures was developed, but most had to learn a different trade. The autobiography of William Topping, an overseer in a damask weaving factory, tells how he went to England to be trained to inspect ball-bearings.[2]

The earnings of engineering workers, which had fallen behind those in Britain in the late 1920s and were 10 to 20 per cent lower in the 1930s, caught up with the national average in the early 1940s, largely because of the long hours of overtime worked. Voluntary enlistment in the forces, after an initial rush, was low throughout the war, even after the Belfast Blitz of 1941. Conscription was seriously considered by the British government but – despite the advocacy of some leading Unionists – was in the end rejected, partly because any suggestion of it was vehemently opposed by the Nationalist population. In practice if not so openly, many Unionists were not enthusiastic about it either, fearing that the jobs of those who went would be filled by immigrants from the south. One strong practical argument against it was that if imposed it might cut off the flow of recruits from Eire, which between 1941 and the end of the war amounted to 18,600, as compared with only 11,500 volunteers from Northern Ireland. Nor was there much compulsion on workers to go wherever they were most needed, though some thousands volunteered to work in England.[3]

Industrial relations were not particularly good in Belfast during the war. Between 1941 and 1945 there were 57 disputes in the shipyard, twenty of which led to stoppages affecting 35,000 workers and losing more than 320,000 working days. In other

SUNDERLAND
SEAPLANE

A Shorts Sunderland
seaplane, c.1944. These
splendid machines, all
25 of which were built
in Belfast, played a vital
role in spotting German
submarines in the
North Atlantic during
the Second World War.
© CORBIS

engineering works stoppages cost 52,000 days, on the docks a further 30,000. The poor performance of Belfast's war industries reflected what English observers saw as a general laxity in Northern Ireland. The strike record of the workers at Short & Harland was described by one official as 'by far the worst of any major military services supplier in Northern Ireland'. In 1943, when it was suddenly taken over by the government, the firm was reckoned to be no more than 65 per cent efficient, and the Ministry of Aircraft Production official who made that assessment also remarked that 'any amount of people are drawing pay for loafing about'. Absenteeism in the shipyard was said to be twice as bad as in the worst British yards, and productivity was low.[4] Mackie's were an honourable exception. Much was later made of the importance of Northern Ireland's contribution to the defeat of Nazi Germany. In truth its greatest contribution was to be still part of the United Kingdom and therefore available – as neutral Eire was not – as a base for the aeroplanes and ships that kept the North Atlantic open, and as a safe training ground for American troops preparing for the invasion of Europe. The presence of a German embassy in Dublin throughout the war, and de Valera's official message of regret to the ambassador at the news of Hitler's death, appeared to underline the difference between north and south. In practice Eire's neutrality was exercised benevolently towards the allies. Aircrew who came down south of the border were usually handed back, while de Valera's ruthless suppression of the IRA in the south made it much easier for the Stormont government to deal with a renewed campaign in Belfast. Six IRA men captured after a policeman was killed in the city in 1942 were sentenced to death; one was executed. Further republican attacks led to a curfew, armoured police patrols and the addition of yet more suspects to those already imprisoned or interned.[5]

Though Belfast did not pay the heavy price in dead and wounded service personnel that it had paid in the First World War, its civilian population this time shared with other British cities the suffering and destruction caused by aerial bombardment. No city was less well prepared for the Blitz when it came in 1941, either militarily or psychologically. Few people thought that it would be a target at all, despite the presence of important war industries. In 1941 it had no night fighter cover, no searchlights, no effective balloon barrage and very few heavy anti-aircraft guns. This was scarcely the fault of the Northern Ireland government, which relied on British advice in such matters. The lack of serious planning, on

THE BELFAST BLITZ

The lower end of High Street on the morning of 16 April 1941, showing the devastating effects of the Easter Tuesday blitz on a city that was virtually defenceless because of the complacency of the government.

BELFAST TELEGRAPH

the other hand, and the failure to take adequate precautions in the event of an air attack, were largely due to the government's complacency in the early stages of the war. The fall of France and the Battle of Britain in 1940 led to some action, notably the establishment of a Ministry of Public Security which encouraged the building of air raid shelters and the recruitment of civil defence volunteers and firemen, but by that time other priorities made materials hard to find. When the Blitz came in April 1941 most of the people in Belfast had no physical protection. There were no shelters even for 30,000 workers engaged in vital war work, let alone for ten times that number of ordinary citizens who had been promised them at the start of the war. It was no wonder that the Unionists lost a by-election seat to the Labour firebrand Harry Midgley in 1941.[6]

Most of all, perhaps, Belfast Corporation was to blame for a lack of practical preparation that made the effects of the bombing much greater than they need have been. The Fire Brigade in April 1941 consisted of only 230 full-time men, though the Corporation had powers to recruit far more, and the 1,600 auxiliary firemen were scarcely trained at all and were disregarded by the chief fire officer. An official report a month before the Blitz indeed recommended that this man should be retired at once. When the bombers came he never left his office and was reported to have hidden under his desk in tears. The sheer incompetence of many Corporation officials, men promoted well beyond their ability, was cruelly revealed. Preparations to deal with dead bodies turned out to be very inadequate. The city's mortuary service could cope with no more than 200, less than a quarter of the number on the worst night. The facilities that might be needed for the homeless were similarly underestimated: the seventy schools and church halls designated as rest centres and equipped with food and bedding could cope with only a tenth of those actually made homeless.[7]

The first raid, on the night of 7–8 April, started before the sirens could be sounded. Considerable damage was inflicted on the shipyard and docks, but only thirteen people were killed and 81 injured. Apart from installing smokescreen equipment at the docks and getting some searchlights, little could be done to meet the shortcomings revealed that night before the enemy returned in much greater force a week later. The Easter Tuesday raid was a much more serious affair, a five-hour bombardment by over a hundred planes which rained more than 200 tons of high explosive, 76 land mines and some 29,000 incendiary bombs on the almost defenceless city. The peculiar tragedy was that most of the bombs fell not on strategic targets but on densely populated residential streets from which very few people had been evacuated. The very success of the smoke screen over the Queen's Island may have contributed to this by confusing the German bomb-aimers. At any rate the result was a great many civilian casualties. Estimates vary, but a recent authoritative history of the Belfast Blitz puts the number at not fewer than 900 dead.[8] The official historian of Northern Ireland's part in the war wrote: 'No other city in the United Kingdom, except London, had lost so many of her citizens in a single night's raid. No other, except possibly Liverpool, ever did'.[9] Fearing worse to come, the authorities now set about building more shelters and trying to ensure that fire-watching was taken seriously; they also had all the dangerous wild animals in the Zoo destroyed, lest they escape next time. The bombers returned on the night of 4–5 May, another major raid, when they caused severe damage to the shipyard and aircraft factory, and in smaller force the following night. Only thereafter were defence and civilian services adequately organised to cope with such an emergency, which never came again. One extraordinary feature of the Blitz was the appearance on the streets of Belfast of fire crews from neutral Eire, volunteers from Dublin, Drogheda and Dundalk who had come to offer their help.[10]

For several weeks during and after the raids, in the absence of shelters, thousands of people left the city every night by any means they could and slept in the fields and ditches. As many as 10,000 'ditchers' shared a common fear and a rare sense of togetherness. Fortunately the weather stayed fine. Shared suffering in some instances brought Catholics and Protestants together. It did not entirely alter their suspicion of each other, however. Even the fact that Catholic districts of the city suffered much less than Protestant ones, and that large numbers of Protestant churches were destroyed while Catholic ones escaped, could be made to support the belief that the bombers had been guided by Catholic signals, that 'the Pope was in the first aeroplane'. A more likely explanation was that most of the bombers' industrial targets, such as the shipyard, were in Protestant areas. The republican activities and attitudes of some Catholics seemed to give substance to Protestant fears. Quite apart from the antics of the IRA (which included war sabotage), they evinced a lack of enthusiasm for the war effort, a reluctance to undertake civil defence work, and dislike, even hostility, towards the American troops who arrived in 1942. Catholic opposition to any suggestion of conscription was vehemently expressed even before the war began, in a statement by the Ulster bishops read out from the pulpits in April 1939. Their opposition was reiterated, in very much the same words, in 1941 by Cardinal MacRory, to whom at this time of crisis for European civilisation the essence of the question was that 'an ancient land, made one by God, has been partitioned by a foreign power, against the vehement protests of its people,' and that conscription would 'seek to compel those who writhe under this grievous wrong to fight on the side of its perpetrators.'[11]

The Blitz, especially the Easter Tuesday raid, destroyed or damaged an enormous number of houses. The official estimate was 3,500 totally destroyed and 53,000 damaged, 18,000 of them severely. An existing shortage was thus made much worse. The first comprehensive survey, in 1944, estimated that more than 23,500 new homes were needed. The mass evacuation that followed the Blitz revealed to some middle-class people the dreadful condition of the poorest in Belfast – 'the submerged one-tenth of the population' – unhealthy, filthy, verminous, 'inhuman in their habits'. The Moderator of the Presbyterian Church told his congregation:

After the big Blitz of a few weeks ago I was inexpressibly shocked by the sight of people I saw walking in the streets. I have been working 19 years in Belfast and I never saw the like of them before – wretched people, very undersized and underfed down-and-out-looking men and women ... Is it creditable to us that there should be such people in a Christian country? [12]

In the midst of all this another Corporation scandal was revealed. It began with a dispute between the medical superintendent and some of his staff at the sanatorium in Whiteabbey. The Corporation asked the Minister of Home Affairs for an inquiry into the running of the hospital and two inspectors were appointed. The Council declined to give evidence, however, apart from that furnished by its officials. The inquiry lasted thirty-four days and reported on 15 June 1941. On the immediate point at issue the medical superintendent was censured, but the report went far beyond that to investigate the management of the accounts and the purchasing decisions of the Corporation's TB Committee. The City Treasurer's department was condemned for 'complete laxity' and 'gross neglect' in the management of the accounts, and the Committee was found to have made many 'improvident bargains', including the purchase of totally unsuitable blackout material. The inspectors recommended that the Committee should be dissolved and the Corporation relieved of its powers under the Tuberculosis Prevention Acts. The Corporation immediately set up a special committee of six councillors consisting of the Lord Mayor (Sir Crawford McCullagh), three Unionists, one Labour and one Nationalist to investigate the affairs of the Council. The six recommended that they should control future appointments. The dud blackout material was traced to a firm in which an interest was held by four councillors, who were asked to resign. At the same time the Town Clerk and Town Solicitor, John Archer, conveniently retired on reaching the age limit. When the Council next met, on 7 August, it voted to dissolve the special committee, a decision rescinded a week later after Sir Crawford had used his considerable personal influence. The committee then appointed a new Town Clerk and got on with preparing its report, which appeared in March 1942. It recommended a special appointments committee, a return to direct employment of unskilled and semi-skilled labour, a stricter definition of what constituted an 'interest', and a requirement that anyone tendering for a Corporation contract should disclose the names of helpful councillors. On 2 April the City Council rejected all these recommendations. When it failed to put its house in order within two months the Council was then replaced by three administrators appointed by the Ministry of Home Affairs for a period of three and a half years to make all appointments, purchases and contracts and to fix rates and taxes. A senior civil servant, C.W. Grant, was appointed along with two part-time commissioners, both of them well-known businessmen and former presidents of the Chamber of Commerce. John Dunlop, author of the original report, was brought in as Town Clerk in 1943. Sir Crawford McCullagh, in this instance on the side of the reformers, had given way as lord mayor to one of the opposition, but when this man retired at the end of 1942 Sir Crawford returned and remained in the post until 1946. Ten of the 21 councillors who had voted to dismiss the Big Six sued the *Northern Whig* for libel after it had made derogatory references to them. They won the case but were awarded only nominal damages of £50 each; three of them had already resigned from the Council. The war could scarcely have been less glorious for the Corporation.[13]

INDUSTRY: CHALLENGE AND CHANGE

The high level of employment in manufacturing industry which had made Belfast prosperous during the war continued for some years after it. Even linen had a period of revival, which lasted until 1952, as the demand for consumer goods after years of austerity gave textile producers a seller's market. Thereafter the decline that had started between the wars resumed and gathered pace. In 1951 the number of Belfast workers employed in linen was 31,000. By July of the following year, however one-third of them were out of work, by the mid-1960s one-half, and in 1971 only 8,000 or so jobs remained. In Northern Ireland as a whole in the years 1958–64 almost one-third of the linen plants closed and over 45 per cent of the workers lost their jobs. Fortunately the economy was in general buoyant and most of them were able to find other work.[14]

The other great staple industry, ship-building and marine engineering, fared much better in the post-war period. Not only was there a great demand for ships but two major competitor countries, Germany and Japan, were for a time in no position to compete. The end of the war, of course, meant an end to new orders for warships, so the workforce had to be reduced to some extent, but the continuing work on three aircraft carriers already started – *Eagle*, *Centaur* and *Bulwark* – provided employment for several years. Indeed *Eagle*, the Navy's largest warship, was called the 'iron lung' of the Queen's Island, as the Admiralty kept on modifying its requirements; some of her compartments were said to have been refitted twenty times. Work on all three ships was resumed in earnest in 1950, after the Korean War had broken out. Payments from the Admiralty enabled Harland & Wolff to repay a £2.5 million government loan and a large bank overdraft; by the middle of 1946 the firm was £1.6 million in the black. Apart from naval work there was a stream of orders for new passenger and cargo vessels – twenty contracts were signed in 1946 alone – and numerous pre-war passenger liners such as Union-Castle's *Capetown Castle*, *Warwick Castle* and *Athlone Castle*, which had been used as troopships, were reconverted. New ships ordered in 1947 included several oil tankers, for which there was an increasing world demand, and two more Union-Castle liners were reconverted. The chairman, Sir Frederick Rebbeck, began a programme of improvements at the yard which included a welding shop (costing over £300,000) for prefabricating sections of ships – the development that was soon to supersede riveting. The engine works also thrived in the immediate post-war period, producing not only marine engines but also stationary diesel generating and pumping engines for use in Africa, Malaya and the Middle East; the engine works was in fact extended.

The Korean War raised freight rates and created a demand for more cargo ships. In 1950 Harland & Wolff received orders for eighteen cargo/passenger vessels. Among the launches that year was the whale factory ship *Juan Peron*, ordered by an Argentine firm and named after the dictator. The ceremony was to have been carried out by his wife Eva, but she was prevented from coming to Belfast by the outbreak of the Troubles that were to lead to Peron's downfall. Instead, a secretary from the Queen's Island office, chosen for her Latin American looks, went through the motions. The development of the Cold War in the 1950s brought more orders from the Admiralty. Despite this, in 1952 the shipyard's profits fell by more than half, and those from the engine works by 40 per cent. Such fluctuations could still be seen as normal, however, rather than as symptoms of long-term decline, and in fact the year 1953 was the best since 1946. More orders came in 1954 and results were

THE *CANBERRA*

The building of the *Canberra*, the last of the great passenger liners built by Harland & Wolff, at the Queen's Island in 1960. The year 1957 was the last good year for orders.

pretty good for a couple of years. By 1955, however, when the Queen launched Shaw Savill Line's *Southern Cross*, Rebbeck's reluctance to introduce modern methods was resulting in dangerously low levels of productivity compared with those achieved by foreign competitors. Then the Suez crisis and the closure of the canal in 1956 led to the cancellation or postponement of a number of orders. In the yard itself a prolonged wage dispute with riveters, untypical of the good relations between employees and management that usually prevailed, delayed several launches.

The last good year for orders was 1957. The *Canberra*, built for P&O and launched in 1960, was the last great liner to be built by Harland & Wolff. By 1958 all UK ship-builders were facing changed circumstances with which they were not well equipped to deal. Successive Conservative governments took the view that ship-building and marine engineering were old, declining industries and preferred to offer incentives instead to new enterprises in light engineering. In these circumstances Rebbeck's conservative style of management was almost fatal for the Belfast yard. Only after he retired in 1961 were essential changes embarked upon. As the historians of the firm have put it, his retirement not only marked the end of the prosperous post-war years, it also symbolised the demise of a whole shipyard culture, the disintegration of a social and technical system based on high standards of personal skill and judgement, and its replacement by an organisation in which skill was built into machines, and judgement passed from the craftsman to the manager.[15]

Much of the social cohesion of the workforce, as reflected in social clubs sports clubs and choirs, survived for a time, but as the number of employees declined this too would largely disappear.

Canberra was the first post-war contract on which Harland & Wolff lost money. From 1964 onward, however, it made a loss every year, the Belfast yard itself losing £887,000 in 1964, £381,000 the following year, over £2 million in 1966 and 1967, and more than £3 million in 1970. Its engine works lost money every year except 1964 and 1968. By 1966 overall losses totalled more than £4 million, by 1969 more than twice that sum. The deepening financial crisis was in contrast to the technical achievement represented by the successful launch in January 1966 of the huge oil rig *Sea Quest*, the first time indeed that such a contraption was launched in one piece (each of its three legs rested on a separate slipway). Unfortunately it did not lead to repeat orders. Another notable achievement was the completion in 1969 of the 190,000 ton oil tanker *Myrina*, the largest launched in Europe that year. The next year, work began on the construction of a great new building dock, 1,825 feet long and 305 feet wide, which would allow even larger ships (up to a million tons deadweight) to be built and floated off instead of launched down a slipway in traditional fashion. The Goliath crane with which the dock was equipped was to become the city's most prominent landmark. The workforce fell from its post-war peak of around 20,000 in 1960 to 9,000 in 1968. The whole period since 1945 was a story of relative decline while maintaining absolute levels of output. Harland &

Wolff in fact raised their share of the UK's output, from an average 9.8 per cent in the years 1946–61 to 17.4 per cent in the years 1962–79. The trouble was that the UK share of the world's output, 24 per cent in 1946–61, fell to only 5 per cent in 1962–79. The great days were gone for good.[16]

Aeronautical engineering was a different story, though it too had a chequered history. Short & Harland, which became Short Bros & Harland in 1947 when the works at Rochester were closed down and all activity concentrated in Belfast, reduced its workforce at the end of the war, when production of Stirling bombers ceased. The firm's most successful venture during the next few years was the Sealand flying boat, of which twenty-five were built for sale overseas. There was no long-term future for such craft however, and by 1950 both the RAF and the airlines had given them up. The firm failed to win production contracts for other aeroplanes it developed, such as the SA-4 Sperrin, a turbo-jet four-engined bomber. The Korean War led to a major rearmament, in which Shorts got useful subcontract work from other companies, notably for Canberra bombers, of which it produced more than 130 for English Electric. A contract for Bristol Britannias in the later 1950s followed the Bristol Aeroplane Co.'s acquisition of a share in the Belfast firm. The fluctuations in demand, partly caused by frequent changes in government defence policy, led to labour trouble throughout the 1950s. In the following decade the firm's most successful products were anti-aircraft missiles – the Seacat and Tigercat systems and the shoulder-launched Blowpipe – which were sold in large numbers all over the world. The aeroplane success of the decade was the SC-7 Skyvan. This versatile aircraft, with its ability to take off and land in very little space, was produced in both military and civilian versions and sold particularly well in developing countries where normal landing facilities were in short supply. The firm's research and development work on VTOL (vertical takeoff and landing) aircraft, begun in the 1950s with a 'flying bedstead', was an important aspect of its work, if not immediately profitable. More and more in the late 1960s its bread and butter came from 'aerostructures', work undertaken for other companies, such as building the wings for the Dutch Fokker Friendship and the 1968 contract for 'pods' for the Lockheed Tristar's Rolls Royce engines. Finance was a constant problem, however. By August 1966 the accumulated deficit was up to £10.4 million and 550 workers had to be laid off. This still left about 8,000, almost as many as the shipyard employed. The survival of Shorts was all the more important to the local economy as ship-building declined, hence the substantial support the company received from the Northern Ireland government.[17]

The engineering firms of Mackie's (textile machinery) and Sirocco (ventilation equipment) not only survived but prospered during the decades after the war, adapting their products to suit a changing market. In the case of Mackie's this meant producing not only machinery for processing flax but also for the new artificial fibres that were replacing it. The old engineering firm of Musgrave's, however, went out of business in 1965, and the famous Ropeworks, which was still employing 2,000 workers in 1951 was forced to reduce to 700 by 1971 (and did not survive the decade). 'Other engineering' (including vehicles) in the census employment returns fell from 13,325 in 1951 to just under 10,000 in 1971, while 'Other manufacturing' fell from 30,189 to 22,828.[18]

Yet the total employed in manufacturing jobs in the Belfast urban area in 1967 – about 100,000 – was only slightly lower than it had been in 1950 (or indeed at the start of the century). This was because, as traditional industries declined, new ones were attracted to greenfield sites outside the city boundary. By the late 1960s these were employing more than 20,000 people. Most of the new firms were engaged in light engineering of some sort, producing such things as oil-drilling equipment (Hughes Tool at Castlereagh), computers (ICL, also at Castlereagh) and tape recorders (Grundig at Dunmurry). Other new products included tyres (Michelin at Mallusk). Not only was manufacturing employment maintained, if given a different emphasis and location, but so too was employment in general. By the late 1960s well over a quarter of a million people in the Belfast area had jobs of some kind. This was the result of continuing growth in service trades, distribution, professional services and public administration – which in turn reflected greater prosperity, improved standards in state services such as health and education (there was one teacher to every 34 children in 1961, compared with one to every 58 in 1901) and many more civil service and local government jobs. Unemployment in the Belfast area in the mid-1960s was only about 3 per cent, in retrospect a golden age. As an economist writing in 1967 put it:

> The years since the Second World War have witnessed the transformation of the industrial structure and the emergence of Belfast as a modern administrative and commercial centre with widely diversified industrial interests.[19]

TRADE AND TRANSPORT

The Harbour Commissioners continued to improve and modernise the facilities of the port after the war, to keep pace with an ever-rising volume of trade. New wharves for foreign trade were completed in 1958, a new deep-water wharf was constructed on the west side of the Victoria Channel, and the channel itself was widened and deepened between 1958 and 1963. A 200-ton cantilever crane was installed in 1959. These and other improvements had by 1966 cost £9 million. By that time work had started on a new dry dock on East Twin. Finished in 1968, it cost over £5 million and was 1,100 feet in length and 165 feet wide at the entrance. Its construction involved the demolition of an earlier harbour improvement – the Inner Lighthouse, erected in 1851. The Musgrave Channel was also widened and deepened in the late 1960s, spoil from the dredging being used to reclaim further areas on both sides of

FERRY TERMINAL

Cross-channel passenger
ships at Donegall
Quay, c.1960, soon
to be transformed
as more and more
travellers found going
by air convenient and
affordable.

TOURIST BOARD COLLECTION. © ULSTER
MUSEUM, 2008

the river mouth. In 1964 BP opened an oil refinery on the Harbour Estate, beyond the shipyard. The changing nature of port business can be seen in the growth of container traffic, which started in the late 1950s; Link Line's service to Liverpool began in 1959, a service to Heysham soon followed, then a weekly service to Preston. Within ten years container tonnage handled by the port amounted to 1.35 million a year, with a hundred sailings a week taking 5,000 containers to Great Britain and the Continent. Roll-on, roll-off facilities were provided to cope with this change in the traditional pattern, which of course had knock-on, knock-off effects on employment at the docks. The bustle of Belfast harbour in the 1960s can be gauged from the fact that as well as daily passenger and cargo sailings to Glasgow, Liverpool and Heysham and container services to Heysham, Liverpool and Preston there were freight services to and from Preston every day, twice a week with Ardrossan, Bristol, Greenock and Manchester, and weekly with Aberdeen, Cardiff, Dundee, London, Leith, Middlesbrough, Newcastle, Stornoway and Swansea. The tonnage of imports and exports handled, a little under 5 million in 1956, had risen to 7 million by 1970. By the 1960s a large proportion of the import tonnage was accounted for by oil, which increasingly replaced coal as the fuel used to produce power (the electricity generating stations used it from 1962, and when the BP refinery was opened two years later the Corporation gasworks started using its byproducts instead of coal). By 1970 imports of crude petroleum and petroleum products amounted to nearly 2 million tons, coal to 954,000; total imports were 5,826,000. Twenty years earlier, the figure for oil and motor spirit was 1.15 million, for coal and coke 1.36. To look at it another way, in terms of value 1968 imports of oil were worth nearly £16.5 million, of coal just over £22 million; twenty years earlier the figures were respectively £2.57 million and £8.4 million.[20]

More and more passengers preferred to travel by air rather than by sea, however. In 1949 only 56,000 did so, but by 1955 the number had risen to 227,000 and it passed the one-million mark in 1966. The Nutt's Corner airport, new in 1948, was replaced by a much larger one at Aldergrove in 1963.[21] On the ground, too, public transport underwent a great transformation. In the 1930s the Corporation's Tramways Committee had operated a mixed fleet of trams and motor buses. Early in 1938 it introduced an experimental trolleybus service on the Falls Road route which was so successful that the decision was taken to replace all the trams with trolleybuses, starting with east Belfast. The cost for the whole city was estimated at £1.25 million, and it was aimed to complete the operation by 1944. The war delayed the process of conversion but after 1945 the trams disappeared rapidly; the last service, on the 'Island' route, ran in February 1954. The trolleybuses were quiet and pollution-free, but they got in the way of the ever-increasing numbers of cars and lorries on the streets, so it was not long before they too began to be superseded. Buses, which had been rejected in 1939 in favour of trolleybuses, had completely replaced them by 1968. These changes not only altered the appearance of the traffic in the streets but the streets themselves, as tramlines and square setts were removed or covered over with asphalt and overhead power lines taken down. Railway lines as well as tramlines were abandoned in favour of road transport, especially after the creation in 1948 of the Ulster Transport Authority, which amalgamated road and rail services outside Belfast. With the closure of many lines the three rail termini in the city became much less important. There was to be no revival until the 1970s, after the break-up of the UTA and the establishment of Northern Ireland Railways, when a new Central Station was built at Maysfield. Underlying all the problems of public transport was the phenomenal growth in the ownership of private cars, from one to every 33 people in 1951 to one to every 8 in 1965.[22] No wonder it was felt that the city's traffic was a problem best tackled by long-term planning.

CHAPTER THIRTEEN

SOCIETY AND POLITICS, 1945–1972

NORTHERN IRELAND's contribution to the survival and victory of the United Kingdom was rewarded after the end of the war, when new financial arrangements with Westminster enabled the Stormont government to establish the same kind of welfare state as in Britain. The social history of Belfast in the generation after 1945 was therefore, more closely than ever before, similar to that of urban centres elsewhere in the UK. Social changes, in particular the transformation of secondary and higher education, were not without their effect on politics, but here hopes of a new departure were in the end overwhelmed by the strength of traditional attitudes and enmities.

HOUSING AND URBAN DEVELOPMENT

By the later 1940s the population of Belfast had reached its greatest extent. The 1951 census figure was 443,671, which represented 32 per cent of the entire population of the province; a further 7 per cent lived in the Belfast urban area outside the boundary. Ten years later, in 1961, the total had actually fallen to 415,856, and by 1971 it was down to 362,082, little more than it had been at the start of the century. This reversal of a trend which had continued without interruption for a century and a half came about through a combination of factors. The most important was the refusal of the government in 1947 to agree to the Corporation's request for another extension of the city boundary. This refusal was followed by extensive building of new dwellings for Belfast people (and for numbers of new immigrants to the Belfast area) outside the boundary. The process of dispersal was encouraged by the fact that new industries attracted to the region in the post-war period were deliberately established in greenfield sites outside the boundary rather than in the city itself, where traditional employment in manufacturing was beginning to decline. The population of the fringe, many of whom enjoyed Corporation bus and other services and looked to Belfast for employment, major shopping facilities and recreation, grew steadily. The built-up areas beyond the boundary – Andersonstown, Dunmurry and

Lisburn to the west and south, the towns and villages that became Newtownabbey to the north, Castlereagh and Holywood to the east – had a population of 120,000 in 1951, half as much again ten years later, and 220,000 by the mid-1960s. The fall in Belfast's population was therefore up to a point not so much a decline as a redistribution. At any rate the result was that more and more Belfast city and the Belfast urban area ceased to coincide. By the late 1960s, indeed, geographers could distinguish not one Belfast but three: the Inner City, within the county borough; Greater Belfast, consisting of the inner city and its fringe; and a Regional City, covering an area within a 25-mile radius of the city centre and tied together by road, rail and telephone communications and the ability of its inhabitants to travel to work within it.[1]

The idea of restricting future development went back to a Planning Commission established by the government in the latter part of the war. 'With the unfortunate development of English cities in mind', the Commission in 1945 stressed the importance of 'regulating and limiting the outward growth of Belfast' and strongly recommended that a 'Green Belt' should be established. In 1951 it reiterated the need to distribute population more evenly and to preserve the Green Belt, estimating that some 22,000 houses were needed immediately, with the long-term aim of reducing the population of the Inner City to about 300,000.[2] Nothing much was done in a positive way, however, before the 1960s, by which time the need for a plan was much more obvious. Then in 1962 Sir Robert Matthew produced his Urban Area Plan, which took as its premise the view that Belfast and its fringe were too big and concluded that they should be confined for the future within a Stop Line. The Corporation, faced with the problem of finding houses for large numbers of people from inner-city areas which were in need of redevelopment, accepted the Stop Line with great reluctance, by no means convinced that the municipal impulse towards bigness was such a bad thing as the planners thought. The fact that the Corporation had no planning department of its own until 1965 put it at a disadvantage in the argument. The immediate effect was to stop most of the building already taking place in suburban areas and to slow down the Corporation's not very impressive redevelopment programme.[3]

Most of the 53,000 houses damaged in the 1941 Blitz had been repaired by the autumn of 1943. That is not to say that the position at the end of the war was satisfactory; far from it. The Planning Commission's estimated need for 22,000 new homes was, if anything, a conservative one. What was needed was not only better houses but much less dense housing in many parts of the inner city. Even in 1961 Belfast had the highest density of population per square mile of any city in the United Kingdom with the exception of Glasgow and Liverpool – 16,846 (Glasgow 17,465, Liverpool 17,184), compared with Manchester's 15,517, Birmingham's 13,838, Hull's 13,479, Greater London's 11,323; all the rest were 10,000 or less. The City Council's post-war housing record in fact was not much better than its record between the

NEW HOUSING

Post-war housing at
Annadale Embankment.
This council scheme
was successful, unlike
some of the high-rise
developments within
the city boundary.

TOURIST BOARD COLLECTION, © ULSTER
MUSEUM, 2008

wars. Between 1945 and 1972 the yearly average of council houses built was only 470, far short of the numbers which the city surveyor had in 1959 estimated were needed: 2,600 a year for twenty years. A special Housing Committee was set up and modest development plans were made. According to the official handbook for 1950, sites amounting to 525 acres had been acquired at Highfield, Ballymurphy, Clara Park, Mount Vernon and Inverary, upon which 4,850 houses and flats were to be built, and 800 aluminium bungalows were about to be erected at Glendhu, Inverary, Taughmonagh, Whiterock and Ashfield. By April 1950 over 1,100 houses, 18 flats and 1,000 Arcon prefabs had been erected and occupied. It was noted that the Corporation had been approached by the government to 'try out' blocks of flats in the Parkmount and Skegoniel area on the Shore Road. 'This will be a new departure for Belfast,' the handbook noted, 'and since there is a feeling that blocks of flats may not appeal to Belfast people the result of this experiment is awaited with interest.'[4]

The Corporation built on whatever land was available within the boundary – blitzed sites or undeveloped, usually undesirable, areas. The resulting estates were laid out solely with an eye to accommodating as many people as possible, with densities far too high for families with children, in small houses well below the preferred standards for public housing (the Parker-Morris standards). The 1956

Housing Act made the Corporation responsible for slum clearance, and thus enabled it to start planning for a programme of inner-city redevelopment, but progress was held up by the discovery that large amounts of land, or ground rents from it, were owned by churches and could not therefore be purchased by compulsory order without first amending the relevant provisions of the 1920 Government of Ireland Act, which had been designed to prevent religious discrimination. In 1965 a joint working party of city and government officials produced a report on redevelopment; three years later the City Council at last adopted a scheme prepared by its planning consultants, Building Design Partnership, for work in three phases. Since its foundation in 1945 the Northern Ireland Housing Trust, funded by the government to supplement the efforts of local authorities, had helped to ease the housing problem in Belfast by building estates outside the boundary. Now its help was enlisted to redevelop the Divis Street and Cullingtree Road areas. As the chairman (and historian) of the Trust's successor, the Housing Executive, puts it, 'The authors of these schemes failed to learn from the bitter experiences of redevelopment in Britain; and it is arguable that the widespread demolition which preceded these sweeping and ill-thought-out schemes contributed largely to the violence of the sectarian strife which marked the Troubles.'[5]

In January 1972, when the Corporation ceased to have any further responsibility for housing, it handed over to the Executive a total of 22,129 dwellings, of which 5,000 were slums acquired for redevelopment and another 1,446 were new ones contracted for. The answer to the question raised in 1950 as to whether the citizens of Belfast would like flats was in most cases an emphatic negative. The Turf Lodge flats on the Falls Road, built in 1966, were detested by people who had known the community life of the little streets of kitchen houses. So, too, were the 'Weetabix' flats on the Shankill, so called because they looked like cereal packets. Both had to be demolished within a few years. The outbreak of the Troubles in 1969 and especially the massive movements of population and destruction of property that occurred in 1971, made an existing problem much worse. (Whatever else might be said about the Corporation, it made a genuine attempt to have its estates mixed in religion, and most of them stayed so until 1969.) By 1970 the fact remained that there was still a first-class housing crisis in Belfast, not much diminished since 1945. According to the calculations of the Housing Executive no fewer than 29,750 houses in the Belfast Council area in 1974 (24 per cent of the total) were unfit for occupation. The criteria used were more exacting than those used earlier, but it was nevertheless a sad indictment.[6]

EDUCATION

The attempts made to bring education in the city up to standard were much more successful. The 1947 Education Act for Northern Ireland followed similar lines to those laid down by the Butler Act in Britain, with some local variations. The Act was notable, not only because it laid the foundations of a vastly improved service, but also because for once the Unionist government defied pressure from its more extreme supporters by insisting that teachers in transferred schools should not be obliged to teach Bible instruction and that the capital grant to voluntary (in effect Catholic) schools should be raised from 50 per cent to 65 per cent. The Blitz had destroyed eighteen schools in Belfast and damaged another thirty-four, so there was much to be done in any case. Now, on top of this, the 1947 Act completely recast the education system, requiring education authorities to produce plans for a structure of primary (to age 11), secondary and technical schools (to a new leaving age of 15), as well as facilities for further education and ancillary services. The Corporation's Education Committee had in fact decided in 1939 to raise the leaving age to 15, but had been obliged to postpone action because of the war, and during the war it had started providing milk for needy children as well as a general meals service. The first grammar school under its control, Grosvenor High School, had opened in part of an existing primary school in January 1945, while the number of scholarships offered to the voluntary grammar schools had been increased from 50 to 200.[7]

The committee took two years to produce a scheme for the county schools, as those under public control were now called. Most existing public elementary schools became 5–11 primary schools, but a few were converted into secondary intermediates, the new category for the 80 per cent of pupils who would not transfer to the grammar schools at the age of 11. New purpose-built intermediates were planned, the first of which opened in 1950. By the end of the decade there were sixteen in all, as well as two more county grammar schools. The 1949 development plan was followed by two others, in 1953 and 1957, as population changes and a steadily declining birth rate made revisions necessary. The raising of the leaving age was only achieved finally in 1957.[8]

In the 1960s the main advances were in further education. The Colleges of Domestic Science and Art, both of which had been housed in the College of Technology, got separate new premises in 1962 and 1968; the Rupert Stanley College of Further Education (named after the city's first director of education) was opened in east Belfast in 1965, replacing an earlier institute, and the College of Business Studies opened in its new building in 1971. A School of Music and Youth Orchestra was started in 1965. The committee also played a part in the establishment of the new Ulster College at Jordanstown, the Northern Ireland Polytechnic, which opened in 1968; the more advanced diploma courses were transferred to it from the Technical College, while degree-level teaching was transferred to Queen's University.

By 1960 the proportion of the Belfast rate spent on education was 35 per cent, and ten years later it had risen to nearly 43 per cent (health and welfare, the next greatest accounted for 12 per cent). Another Education Act, in 1968, gave the voluntary schools, which had hitherto remained entirely outside the county system, full grants provided they set up management committees consisting of at least six people, of whom one-third must be nominees of the education authority. Most of the Catholic schools accepted this and became what were known as 'maintained' schools. The grievance felt by Catholics, rightly or wrongly, that the 1947 Act had in effect endowed Protestant control of the county schools while refusing to do the same for the Catholic system thus came to an end. The outcome, a triumph for sectarianism, was two separate state-funded systems. The Education Committee was faced with increasing financial difficulty in the 1960s. In order to make ends meet it postponed capital projects such as the building of new schools. The result was to lay up trouble for the future. When the Corporation's consultants produced their plans for the city's development at the end of the decade they forecast that by 1986 nearly a hundred new schools would be needed in the Greater Belfast area, 35 of them within the boundary.[9]

Welfare services

The welfare state created in Great Britain after 1945 was reproduced by similar legislation in Northern Ireland. This was only possible because it was agreed that, provided its citizens paid tax at the same rates as elsewhere in the United Kingdom, the province would get the necessary funds from Westminster. The necessity for a transformation in public health, first demonstrated in Dr Carnwath's report of 1941 and reinforced by the evidence uncovered by the Blitz, was further confirmed by a government inquiry in 1944. The figures for deaths from tuberculosis, in fact, were so horrifying that the Stormont government anticipated one of the aims of the national health service by setting up a Tuberculosis Authority as early as 1941. This determination, and the fortunate discovery of effective drugs, brought about a transformation within a few years. By 1954 the death rate had been reduced to the same level as that in Britain, and by 1959 the Authority had worked itself out of a job and was disbanded; the chest hospitals at Whiteabbey and Galwally were converted to other uses. So far as the citizens of Belfast were concerned the elimination of TB was one of the most significant medical advances ever made. The national health service in general, indeed, which came into operation in Northern Ireland in 1948, made a great impact on the lives of Belfast people precisely because things had been so much worse than elsewhere. In medical services the dispensary system and voluntary control of separate hospitals were swept away, to be replaced by a centralised General Health Services Board and a Hospitals Authority. Centralised services for laboratory work, radiotherapy and blood transfusion were set up, along with an Institute of Clinical Science to serve the teaching hospitals and additional chairs of medicine and dentistry at the university. The number of outpatients departments in the city was increased from 46 in 1948 to 85 in 1959. A new 200-bed geriatric unit was opened at the City Hospital (as the old Union Infirmary was renamed when it was made into a general hospital), and work started in 1959 on another, completely new general institution, the Ulster Hospital at Dundonald. By 1954 deaths in childhood, which had been a particular scandal between the wars, had fallen to the same level as in Britain.[10]

The Poor Law system was abolished at last in 1948, when the unlamented Guardians and the two commissioners who had exercised their functions since 1939 were stripped of their powers. First the Infirmary, then the entire premises of the Workhouse, were handed over to the City Hospital. The memory lingered on, however, and it took some time for the hospital to rise in public esteem. The only discordant note in this tale of improvement was a well-publicised and long-lasting

RUC CONCERT

The band of the Royal Ulster Constabulary giving a concert in the grounds of the City Hall in the early 1960s, a time of apparent peace and hope.

dispute over the Mater Hospital. One of the few differences between the British National Health Act and the Stormont version was the omission in the latter of a clause allowing hospitals such as the Mater to retain their denominational character. Without such a clause the hospital management refused to enter the national health service. The government then refused to allow the hospital to claim payment for the treatment it offered to the public at large. It was left to finance itself, which it did largely by the proceeds of a football pools scheme – YP Pools, so called because it was devised by the Young Philanthropists' Association, a group of supporters. Not until 1968 was the Mater able to claim for the services it provided free, and the matter was not finally resolved until three years later, when it gained access to government grants and became part of the health service. Not unnaturally, Catholics felt a strong sense of grievance, more clearly justifiable in this case than in the matter of their schools since the hospital's services were truly open to all without distinction of creed. In fact Unionists themselves were somewhat divided on the question, both at Stormont and in the City Council.[11]

SOCIAL TRENDS

Social change in Belfast in the post-war years followed much the same lines as in other cities of the United Kingdom. Until the mid-1950s radio and the cinema remained extremely popular. As measured by the number of wireless licences issued – no doubt an underestimate of the true figure – radio indeed went on growing: the total for the whole province, 150,000 at the end of the war, was nearly 220,000 ten years later. Thereafter the figure fell steadily as the number of television licences rose. When first noticed in the official statistics in 1953 these numbered only 558. A year later the figure was well over 10,000; ten years later it was 215,700. As television waxed the cinema waned. In the mid-1950s there were three dozen cinemas operating in Belfast. One after another they closed, starting in 1956; by 1972 only seven remained open. In a city as addicted as Belfast had been to the silver screen this was a minor social revolution.[12]

While the cinemas emptied, Belfast retained what was by British standards a very high level of church attendance. Reliable statistics, indeed statistics of any sort, are hard to come by, though the impression recorded by visitors was invariably the same, whether approving or dismayed. One frequently quoted source is a survey conducted among undergraduates of Queen's University in 1959, when the church attendance figures were 94 per cent for Catholics, 64 per cent for Methodists, 59 per cent for Presbyterians and 46 per cent for members of the Church of Ireland. Undergraduates at that date were probably too middle-class a group to constitute a valid sample of the population at large, an objection which would have had less force in the case of the Catholics. The Protestant average of 50–55 per cent would have been less representative; church attendance in many working-class areas was likely to have been rather lower than that.[13] Many of the new churches built by the Protestant denominations after the war were replacements for buildings destroyed or badly damaged in the Blitz. In most cases, however, they were designed for smaller congregations than the original ones. Nevertheless, religion remained a potent force in the lives of most Belfast people and, because it mattered to them, a continuing source of division. One of the more obvious cultural differences between Catholics and most Protestants was their contrasting attitudes towards Sunday activities. Sabbatarianism of a strict kind was deeply engrained among respectable Protestants, especially those of an evangelical persuasion; unlike Catholics, they did not play or attend organised games on a Sunday. The more extreme disapproved of any use of public facilities on the Sabbath, other than for religious purposes, equating such activities with Catholic practice or the 'Continental Sunday'. Even a proposal, made in wartime, to allow one cinema to open on Sunday for uniformed members of the armed forces met with determined opposition in the City Council; after being turned down several times between 1940 and 1942 it was eventually approved, but only by a small majority. Twenty years later a similar issue – that of 'Sunday swings' – caused a much greater furore, which perhaps showed that public opinion had moved somewhat in the meantime. The question was whether Corporation play centres for children and the swings in the parks should be opened for use on Sundays. A narrow vote in the Education Committee in October 1964 in favour of opening was reversed in the City Council the following month after a campaign by the churches (notably the Rev. Ian Paisley's new church, the Free Presbyterians), backed by the Orange Order. Unionist and Labour councillors were divided among themselves on the matter. Some conscientious Labour representatives were greatly embarrassed by having to choose between private belief and public principle. The Council later agreed to open the swings in the parks but not the play centres. Eventually in 1968 all except four of them were opened, after local residents had voted in favour, and the same device of a local referendum was adopted in respect of the swings. The still considerable power of the sabbatarians in local politics was demonstrated in the municipal elections of 1967, when three liberal Unionist councillors who had voted in favour of Sunday opening were not re-adopted by their local committees and all the Labour councillors who stood were defeated, regardless of how they had voted on the crucial issue.[14]

Belfast politics

In local politics, throughout this period as before, Unionists retained a huge majority on the City Council. This simple electoral fact conceals a more complex story of three phases – the late 1940s, when Northern Ireland Labour briefly challenged Unionism, only to founder on the constitutional question; a torpid period in the 1950s when little challenge was offered by stricken Labour or feuding Catholic parties to the complacent Unionists; and a restless period in the 1960s which saw a recovery by Northern Ireland Labour, the rise of Republican Labour and the appearance of sharp divisions between liberal and traditional Unionists (to say nothing of municipal scandals over housing and a controversy caused by flying the City Hall flag at half-mast on the death of Pope John XXIII). In the end, despite some hopeful signs of changing attitudes, the basis of local politics for most voters was to remain a matter of religion rather than class.

In the first post-war election, when housing was the main issue, the Northern Ireland Labour Party doubled its representation from four seats to eight and Harry Midgley (ex-NILP under his own banner of Commonwealth Labour) was elected alderman for Ormeau Ward, though Minister of Labour in the Stormont government at the time. Four Nationalists were successful in Smithfield, but three of the seats in the other Catholic ward, Falls, went to Independent Labour ('Labour with a republican tinge') – a sign that Catholic voters too were changing. Although Labour representatives of various kinds therefore formed a significant section of the Council, the Unionists still dominated it with 43 of the 60 seats.[15]

One of the changes demanded by the vociferous marchers who thronged the streets of Belfast in the 1960s was the reform of the Local Government Franchise Act of 1946 under which councillors had to stand for re-election every third year and aldermen every sixth year; half of the aldermen were elected every third year. Unlike Great Britain, however, where the franchise was widened in 1948 to correspond to the parliamentary one, Northern Ireland continued to restrict the vote to householders and their spouses (thus excluding large numbers of lodgers and adult children), while occupiers of property with an annual valuation of £10 or more got an additional vote and could nominate a voter for each extra £10 of valuation, up to a limit of six. The result was that whereas before 1948 the local government franchise in Belfast had compared favourably with that in other British cities, it became in UK terms an anomaly. Furthermore, though the retention of the old link between ownership of property and the right to vote was arguably motivated as much by conservatism as anything else – the system discriminated equally against poorer Protestants and poorer Catholics – the fact that most high-valuation property was owned by Protestants meant that it was the Unionist Party that benefited most from making no change. This departure from the usual post-war policy of keeping in step with Britain was later to provide the civil rights movement of the 1960s with the convenient, if rather misleading, rallying cry of 'One man, one vote' – misleading because the impression was created that large numbers of Catholics were deprived of general political rights. In fact the franchise in Northern Ireland for elections to Westminster was exactly the same as elsewhere in the United Kingdom; for Stormont elections there was also universal adult suffrage, but additional votes for owners of businesses and university graduates – abolished in Britain in 1948 – were retained until 1968. The four MPs elected by Queen's University were chosen by proportional representation.[16]

Both the Stormont and the municipal elections of 1949 were inevitably dominated by the constitutional issue. Early in that year the government of Eire declared the country a republic and left the British Commonwealth. The effect on the Unionists, and on their opponents in Belfast, was profound. The constitution of the southern state, drawn up by de Valera in 1937, claimed the whole island of Ireland as its national territory; and while the claim may in reality never have amounted to anything more than a pious hope of eventual unity, its retention in the constitution of a state now completely separate gave the northern prime minister, Sir Basil Brooke, the chance to go to the polls on the only issue that really mattered to Unionists. Moreover, an Anti-Partition League, supported by funds from the south collected at the gates of Catholic churches, ensured that the same issue dominated the minds of their Nationalist opponents. Incidentally the Northern Ireland Labour Party, which up to this point had managed to accommodate both partitionists and anti-partitionists within its ranks by concentrating on economic issues, was now forced to choose and came down in favour of the constitutional status quo; it promptly split in two and was demolished at the polls, losing all three of the Stormont seats it had won in Belfast in 1945. The party suffered a similar fate in the municipal elections, when six wards went to Unionists without a contest and Labour were reduced to one seat. Most of the Catholic vote went to an anti-partitionist splinter group from the NILP calling itself Irish Labour, which got seven seats; the Nationalists retained only one, that of alderman in Smithfield. The triumphant Unionists increased their numbers from 43 to 48. The constitutional issue – the maintenance or abolition of partition – was to continue thereafter to weaken all attempts to create a united front to the dominant Unionists.

In the 1950s there was little sign of Labour groups recovering to challenge the Unionist control of the Council. The last Nationalist was defeated in 1952 by an Irish Labour candidate, but a renewed effort by the NILP in 1955, when it put forward nineteen candidates, brought only one success. Three years later it had an unexpected gain in Court Ward, when a former lord mayor was defeated for the alderman's seat. Among Catholic voters, Irish Labour gave way to Independent Labour, which took all seven seats in Falls and Smithfield.[17]

There were minor manoeuvrings among the various Labour councillors elected in the early 1960s; Gerry Fitt's success in Dock Ward was a step in a political career that was to take him eventually to the House of Lords. One of the periodic scandals that one-party local government made inevitable now rose to the surface. Sir Cecil McKee, one of the four knights suspected of sharp practice, was refused the usual nomination from his ward committee. Furious, he stood as an independent Unionist and was elected, displacing Mrs Florence Breakie, who had already been chosen as next lord mayor. The NILP also gained two seats in Court Ward in this election. The Labour revival reached its height three years later in 1964 when the party won two more seats in Clifton Ward and polled well everywhere – a sign of increasing anxiety among skilled Protestant workers about the decline of traditional industries, and of the willingness of some Catholic voters to vote NILP instead of some republican splinter group. Among Catholics in general, however, Fitt's Republican Labour Party, founded in 1962, soon ousted Independent Labour, taking three seats in Dock and two in Falls. At Stormont the Unionist government, led since 1963 by Terence O'Neill, blunted the Labour advance (the NILP had gained four seats in 1958 and kept them with increased majorities in 1962) by giving more prominence to economic issues and state planning. In the 1965 general election two Labour MPs in Belfast were unseated; both had lost credibility with voters for their part in the Sunday Swings controversy a year earlier.

Labour's advance was then further frustrated at the 1967 municipal elections, the last before the present Troubles erupted, when the results reflected an increasing instability in politics and a sharpening of traditional tensions. The NILP lost four seats and was left with only two (one of them a new seat in Falls). Fitt's Republican Labour Party won eight, reducing its Independent Labour rivals to two. But even the main Unionist Party had problems, when the Protestant Unionists improved their support. By the time the next local contest was due, in 1970, the situation in the city had changed dramatically and the future of the Corporation itself was under review.[18]

SECTARIAN CONFLICT

Compared with earlier periods in the city's history, the post-war years were pretty quiet so far as sectarian strife was concerned, after the 1949 general election at least. High employment, improving social conditions and changing attitudes created hopes that the outbreaks seen in the past might not be repeated. Belfast was scarcely affected, for example, by the IRA campaign of 1956–62, which was almost entirely a rural affair, though events in the border counties of course encouraged Unionists to go on playing the constitutional card. The failure of the IRA, the lack of support for it among Catholics generally, the emergence of a more confident and forward-looking spirit in the Catholic community combined with the appointment of Terence O'Neill as Unionist leader to usher in a brief era of rapprochement after 1963. In January 1965 O'Neill astonished everyone (including, significantly, most of his own cabinet colleagues) by receiving the prime minister of the Irish Republic, Sean Lemass, for economic talks at Stormont. O'Neill's liberal approach, however, only raised hopes among Catholics which he proved unable to fulfil, since many of his own followers became uneasy about the direction in which he was leading them. In the end, he split the Unionists without gaining the loyalty of nationalists. Inside parliament his position was undermined by ambitious rivals, outside it by a strident, and very effective, 'O'Neill must go' campaign led by the Reverend Ian Paisley. Disappointed Catholics, and some radical Protestants who made common cause with them, turned to campaigning aggressively for civil rights, in the manner of the blacks in the southern states of the USA. By the end of the decade two opposing protest movements were on the streets.[19] The leading Ulster historian shortly afterwards summarised the 1960s as follows:

> Among Ulster Protestants there was a growing body who felt that the union could be maintained without reliance on the old sectarian warcries. Among Roman Catholics there was a new readiness to accept Northern Ireland as, for all practical purposes, a permanent fact … It seemed not impossible to believe that at last Northern Ireland was approaching a condition in which all its citizens could feel a common interest in promoting a common prosperity.

Two factors, not unusual in such a situation, brought about the reversal of this hopeful trend – impatience on one side and fear on the other.[20]

In these circumstances the 1960s in Belfast were both a time of hope and a time of rising tension. In September 1964, during a Westminster election campaign, a

PROTESTANT HOMES DESERTED

Farringdon Gardens in the Ardoyne area of north Belfast, 10 August 1969. The Protestant inhabitants of the street, who had been forced out by intimidation, had set fire to their homes as they departed the night before. A few are shown here salvaging whatever belongings they could find.

BELFAST TELEGRAPH

serious riot directed against the police followed the removal of an Irish tricolour flag from the headquarters of the Republican Party in Divis Street in the Falls; thirty people, including several police, were injured. A loyalist march, organised by Paisley, to protest at the flying of the flag (which was illegal under an act of 1952) and the failure of the authorities to remove it sooner, had been turned away from the area to avoid trouble. Two years later in 1966, the fiftieth anniversary of both the Easter Rising and the battle of the Somme, there was more serious trouble. The fire-bombing of the Unionist Party's headquarters in Glengall Street in February was followed by a similar attack two days later on a Catholic primary school on the Crumlin Road. Celebrations in west Belfast of the Rising caused great indignation among Unionists. A woman died when a public house was petrol-bombed early in May, and at the end of that month a Catholic man (the wrong one, in mistake for a known or suspected IRA member) was shot and killed in Clonard Street. There was a short sharp riot early in June, when Paisley led a loyalist march through Cromac Square in the predominantly Catholic Markets area; arrested later in the same day for creating a disturbance outside the Presbyterian General Assembly, he refused to be bound over and was sent to jail for three months. At the end of June the Ulster Volunteer Force, a recently formed secret organisation of Protestants calling itself by the name originally used by Carson's followers, shot three Catholics in Malvern Street off the Shankill Road; one of the victims died of his wounds. The year 1967 was comparatively quiet, however, apart from a minor incident in July during a royal visit when a piece of concrete struck the bonnet of the Queen's car.[21]

The present Troubles, then, did not erupt without warning. They were, however, immediately more serious in character than anything experienced since the 1930s, beginning with a Protestant invasion of the lower Falls area and Ardoyne on the night of 14–15 August 1969 in which five Catholics and one Protestant were killed and 200 homes burnt, most of them Catholic ones. According to official estimates based on hospital records (certainly a conservative figure), some 450 people were injured, 178 of them Catholic civilians, 199 Protestant civilians, the rest policemen. Over 3,500 families moved house as a direct result of the rioting, to seek safety in areas controlled by their co-religionists. The Stormont government called in the Army to separate the two sides, a move at first welcomed by the beleaguered Catholics. The IRA, which had proved unable to defend them, split in two. The breakaway portion, calling itself the Provisional IRA, was at first organised to defend Catholic areas, but soon developed into a militantly republican guerrilla force with the Army as its main target (its first victim among the troops was shot in February 1971). By that time Belfast was in a state approaching civil war. The introduction of internment without trial in August 1971, which was meant to scotch the threat from the IRA, backfired badly and in fact strengthened it; 85 per cent of the 172 people who died violently in 1971 did so after the start of internment. Serious rioting in response to the arrests caused a number of deaths; on 10 August alone eleven people were

killed, one of them a priest administering the last rites. There was massive support thereafter in Catholic areas for a rent and rates strike. More frightened families, over 2,000 of them this time, migrated to safety. It has been estimated that in the first four years of the Troubles somewhere between 30,000 and 60,000 people in the Greater Belfast area were driven to leave their homes, at that date possibly the largest enforced movement of population in Europe since the Second World War. In addition to all this, an enormous amount of property was destroyed. By June 1971 criminal injuries claims in the city totalled nearly £9.5 million, a sum that increased rapidly as things became even worse. Early the following year, in March 1972, the Stormont government was suspended and Northern Ireland came under direct rule from Westminster.[22]

LOCAL GOVERNMENT REFORM

That was by no means the end of the Troubles, but 1972 did see the end of Belfast Corporation as citizens had known it. Among the changes put in train by O'Neill's administration was the reform of local government. Following the publication of aims and proposals in 1967 and 1969, the Macrory Committee was appointed in January 1970. Its report, published five months later, was even more radical in its

recommendations than the Redcliffe-Maud and Wheatley reports for Britain and
Scotland. Pointing out that Northern Ireland was smaller than Yorkshire and had a
total rateable valuation of only £14 million, compared with nearly £22 million for
Leeds alone, Macrory proposed to set up twenty-six district councils to deal with
minor services; major services or functions such as education and libraries, planning,
roads, water, main sewerage, gas, electricity, motor taxation, public transport and
fire brigades should be transferred to regional authorities. The report did note that
Belfast fire brigade was the only one in the United Kingdom to receive no assistance
from central government and that Belfast Gas was 'efficient, well-run and up-to-
date' and likewise made no call upon the public purse, but such remarks were little
consolation. Macrory's proposals were accepted in their entirety and came into effect
on 1 October 1973.[23]

The shock of diminution was all the greater because, as one leading civil servant
put it, City Hall had always resented interference from 'a parvenu Parliament and
Government dating only from 1921', whereas Belfast could trace its origins to the
seventeenth century.[24] It was even more galling to be equated with other, much
smaller, local authorities. Though retaining its ceremonial dignities and functions,
the Corporation would henceforth be directly responsible only for such relatively
minor and uncontroversial services as environmental health, cleansing, parks and
cemeteries and civic improvement schemes – in crude local parlance 'bins, bogs and
burials'. The decision had already been taken to transfer all responsibility for public
housing to the Northern Ireland Housing Trust, which was reorganised in 1972 as
the Housing Executive. One hundred and thirty years of uninterrupted municipal
advance thus came to an abrupt and unhappy end.

In many important respects the history of Belfast during the generation after the
Second World War was similar to that of other major cities of the United Kingdom.
As elsewhere, traditional heavy industry declined and the jobs thus lost were for
the most part replaced by others in light industry and in a growing service sector.
Socially, public services such as education, housing and welfare expanded, bringing
about a significant improvement in living standards particularly for sections of the
population hitherto disadvantaged. In the planning of urban development too, and
in such things as entertainment and recreation, the Belfast experience followed
national UK trends. It is important to stress these similarities, because in other
respects – arising from its deeply ingrained sectarian divisions and its position in
a province whose very existence as part of the United Kingdom was a bone of
contention between the main political groupings – the history of post-war Belfast
was notoriously different and produced by 1970 a very different result. The reform
of local government was to the city what the imposition of direct rule was to the
province – a judgement that a system which produced the endless rule of one party
could no longer be allowed to continue.

CHAPTER FOURTEEN

SOCIAL CHANGE, 1973–1993

For most of the past forty years, in this respect a microcosm of the province as a whole, Belfast has been overshadowed by the continuing Troubles. As by far the largest urban area, the city has provided the most favourable ground for urban guerilla activity by paramilitary forces and has therefore suffered a high proportion of the damage inflicted on life, property and prospects. Between 1969 and 1977 over a thousand people were killed in Belfast and 2,280 explosions occurred, not to mention thousands of injuries, forced migrations, lives ruined or disrupted and livelihoods lost. Though the cost in human life never again reached the level of the worst years in the 1970s, by the late 1980s the number killed had risen to around 1,500. The cost of the damage to property and business life from car bombs, incendiary devices and disruption of trade ran to hundreds of millions of pounds.[1] By no means everything that occurred during this period was due to the Troubles, however. Life was not normal, but so far as they were able people behaved if not normally then at least with an appearance of normality and much of what happened in the way of economic and social change would have happened in any case for in its de-industrialisation, as in its industrialisation, Belfast shared the experience of other British cities.

The Troubles did, however, make common problems worse or gave them a peculiar local slant in Belfast. Population changes are a good example. The decline in the population of the inner city was greatly accelerated in the 1970s and 1980s by the flight of Protestants in particular to safer areas outside the boundary. The total population of the city, just over 400,000 in 1971, was down to 330,000 ten years later and the figure by 1991 was only 281,000. Not only the inner city but the whole urban area declined, losing 73,000 inhabitants between 1971 and 1981, by which date – at 510,000 – it was 90,000 below the limit regarded as desirable even by the self-confident planners of the early 1960s. The number of households in the inner city fell dramatically, in some wards by more than half between 1971 and 1978 (in Central Ward by 57 per cent, in Crumlin Ward by 64 per cent). The number of people in the average household fell too, from 3.2 in 1971 to 2.8 in 1981, because the Protestants who remained included a disproportionate number of elderly residents;

the effect on the enrolment of many state (i.e. Protestant) primary schools in the city was quickly apparent. The simultaneous redevelopment of densely crowded areas of working-class housing contributed to these changes; many of the scenes of urban desolation which formed the backdrop to television reports of the violence in the 1970s were caused by slum clearance rather than Semtex, while the availability of accommodation in new Housing Executive estates, outside the boundary and well away from the worst of the violence encouraged some households to move voluntarily.[2]

The Troubles clearly had some effect also on the city's economic problems, most obviously on its ability to attract outside investment, though it is difficult to say how much was due to the Troubles in the 1970s and 1980s and how much to other, underlying factors. One estimate, made in 1987, is that 2,000 to 3,000 jobs in manufacturing industry were lost each year in the 1970s. This was all the more

PEACE LINES

The establishment of 'peace lines' separating Protestant and Catholic communities. Both sides felt safer.

© BELFAST TELEGRAPH

serious because, as elsewhere, industry was adversely affected by the oil crisis of 1973. The severe recession in the early 1980s made things worse. The shipyard, which was still employing 9,500 people in 1975, had less than a third of that number by the late 1980s; later, privatised and its debts written off, it employed 2,800. The only area of substantial growth in employment in the 1970s was in the service sector, where successive Westminster governments made increased funds available for social improvements. Manufacturing continued to decline, and, though governments were less generous in the 1980s, it was the case that by 1985 Belfast had, like the province as a whole, become dependent to an extraordinary degree on employment in the public sector – jobs in the civil service, government agencies, local government and so on. In Northern Ireland in 1985 there were 346,000 service jobs (nearly 65 per cent of the total); of which no fewer than 207,000, or 60 per cent, were in the public sector. Not surprisingly, perhaps, commentators took to referring to the development of a 'workhouse economy', dependent on public expenditure, in which those not unemployed were chiefly engaged in servicing or controlling each other, few of them in producing tradeable goods.[3]

Paradoxically, whilst unemployment rose to very high levels, average incomes and living standards also rose considerably. Personal income per head, always the lowest of any region in the United Kingdom rose from 68 per cent of the UK level in 1960 to 79 per cent in 1979 and to 84 per cent in 1984. Average weekly earnings rose from 81 per cent in 1960 to almost 93 per cent in 1979.[4] Those in work had more money to spend, and they did indeed spend it, as the 1980s boom in retailing showed. The Belfast branch of Marks & Spencer, which opened a short time before the Troubles began, became one of the firm's most lucrative outlets despite the attempted destruction of the city centre by the bombers in the 1970s. Following the introduction of urban development grants in 1982, the central business district was further revitalised by major investments such as the Castle Court shopping complex, while the decayed docks and riverside area began to be transformed by the Laganside Corporation, a joint development enterprise by the public and private sectors. Port traffic statistics reflected this remarkable upturn: in 1973 the amount of cargo handled was 7.5 million tons. By 1982 it had sunk to 5.5 million. Five years later, however, it had risen to 7.8 million; and the figure for 1990 was 8.9 million. It is essential to point out however that most of the increase (about 85 per cent) was accounted for by imports rather than exports.[5]

The most successful social enterprise in Belfast in this period was the public housing programme carried out by the Northern Ireland Housing Executive. The estimated number of 'unfit' houses in the city in 1974 was reckoned to be nearly 30,000, or 24 per cent of the total housing stock. The Troubles created both exceptional needs and exceptional difficulties, which upset all the calculations of the planners and delayed the action that was so urgently needed. An authoritative survey of housing conditions in Belfast as compared with other British cities, the work of the Executive's chairman, Charles Brett, in 1980, was startling in its revelations. In Belfast, 3.7 per cent of households were two or more rooms below the bedroom standard (that is, they were severely overcrowded), compared with 1.4 per cent in Liverpool and 0.4 per cent in Leeds. In Belfast 24.2 per cent had no inside flushing WC, more than twice as bad as the next worst, Liverpool (11.1 per cent). Those without their own bath or shower were 23 per cent in Belfast, compared with Liverpool's 10.1 per cent, Manchester's 8.4 per cent and Birmingham's 5.7 per cent. By 1985, however, the 1974 proportion of unfit houses had been halved to 12 per cent and by 1987 the estimated target figure was down to 7.4 per cent. Not only was the long-standing housing problem in Belfast thus substantially solved, but also the quality of the houses built and the planning of the estates in which they were laid out were of a very high standard, and far more acceptable to the people who occupied them than anything earlier. This time, lessons were learned from the mistakes made elsewhere.[6] The same is true of the transport plans drawn up in the 1960s which by the time they came to be constructed had been changed by community pressures, notably when the intention to build an elevated road joining the M1 and M2 motorways was abandoned in favour of the present West Link.

Meanwhile the City Council, elected since 1973 by proportional representation, continued to be dominated by Unionists, though they were soon to become sharply divided between Official Unionists and Democratic Unionists (Paisleyites). Ranged against them, and representing almost exclusively Catholics of a moderate sort, were the Social and Democratic Labour Party (SDLP), founded and led by Gerry Fitt. He was later ousted by the other political heavyweight in the party, John Hume from Derry. Among a mixed group of Republicans who would not take part in any political body in the north were Sinn Féin (extreme republicans, who supported the Provisional IRA's 'armed struggle') and the Workers' Party, a rival republican group with socialist priorities. The diminishing middle ground between the Unionists and their opponents was occupied by the Alliance Party, which drew support from both Catholic and Protestant voters in the middle classes. Compared with the great days of the municipality, the doings of the Council were of relatively minor interest, though Council meetings were just as vociferous as before. It made the most of its limited role by adding to the amenities of the city by developing municipal parks and leisure centres and by visibly improving the appearance of the city by planting trees and flowers. Unfortunately more important matters which were to have been transferred to the City Council

CASTLE COURT

The IRA bombing campaign in the 1970s caused enormous disruption and damage to premises, but following the introduction of urban development grants in 1982, the central business district began to be revitalised by major developments such as the Castle Court shopping complex.

BELFAST TELEGRAPH

continued to be run by civil servants in the Northern Ireland Office; locally elected politicians were far from happy about this.[7]

In one respect at least the experience of the Troubles was not altogether a negative thing: contact and cooperation between the clergy of the main Protestant denominations and the Catholic church grew more frequent and positive. The Peace People movement of the mid-1970s, attracted an extraordinary outburst of goodwill and its two leading figures subsequently shared a Nobel peace prize. It could not sustain its dynamism indefinitely however. In education the existence of two parallel systems was widely believed in liberal circles to be one of the causes of sectarianism. Criticised by both of the main stream systems the new integrated schools (the first of which was Lagan College, opened in 1981),[8] however small their beginnings were, and whatever may have been the motives of the pioneers, the experiment became a third system. In politics, however, there was remarkably little real change. The names of some of the parties were different, but despite numerous initiatives to bring the protagonists to the conference table the main question in dispute remained the same. Attitudes had been hardened by the horrors experienced on both sides. The segregation in working-class areas which had long marked Belfast as different from other cities had been made still nearer complete by continuing vexatious movements of population – to the extent that the so-called 'peace line', literally separating the Protestant and Catholic communities at points where they met and contended went on being added to.

After all that had happened in the years since 1968, the situation in the 1990s could still be summarised in 1993 by the concluding words of an earlier version of this history of Belfast, namely 'Divided we stand'.

QUEEN MOTHER MURAL

This is a Unionist/loyalist mural in West Belfast commemorating the death of the Queen Mother in 2002. There is a Union flag above the portrait surrounded by the flags of the union and the royal coat of arms.

PHOTOGRAPH: CARNEGIE, 2009

The long war: a short history

N O O N E who was active in Irish or British politics in the 1960s could have foretold that the Troubles just then beginning to disturb the Unionist regime in Belfast would quickly escalate into the Troubles, let alone that they would go on for a whole generation and bring down Stormont. In the process (the word 'process' was to become very familiar) of restoring order, and negotiating an acceptable solution of some kind to a seemingly intractable problem, much had to be learned and the courage, ingenuity and stamina of many of the people involved were to be tested to the limit.

It is scarcely possible at this stage to offer the reader a satisfactory account of the so-called 'long war' – 'so-called' because calling it that was seen in some quarters as a gain or a loss in the ceaseless propaganda war that was the background to the dramatic events reported by the various media.

Faced with large amounts of partly processed historical material the best that can be done here is to choose a selection of what appears to be the most significant 'facts' and summarise the emerging plot from time to time. The first stages were much concerned with the growing discontent that brought reformers and agitators on to the streets not only in Belfast but notably also Derry, until the reforming prime minister O'Neill found himself caught between the marchers and his own party stalwarts – not quick enough with reforms to satisfy the first, yet much too liberal for upholders of the status quo.

A particular trial to O'Neill from the right wing of Unionism was the Reverend Ian Paisley, whose campaign against O'Neill's policy was strident but effective. O'Neill resigned in April 1969.[1] The growing violence in the city stretched the resources of the police, and serious rioting both against the police and between the two communities led to the deployment of additional British troops in Belfast in August of the same year. The IRA, ill-prepared for this turn of events, failed to protect its own community but did not welcome any move that might acknowledge, let alone strengthen, the British presence in the six counties. Some Catholics welcomed the troops at first, nevertheless. The violence increased and hardline Unionist politicians

right

STORMONT

In 1920 Home Rule was established in Northern Ireland, and plans were launched to construct separate parliament buildings in the Stormont region of Belfast. The new government wanted to build a massive domed structure similar to the US Capitol building in Washington, DC. However the Stock Market crash of 1929 brought economic hardships and the idea of a dome was abandoned. Architect Sir Arnold Thornley designed a classical building with six round columns and a central triangular pediment. Fronted in Portland stone and ornamented with statues and bas relief carvings, Stormont shares many similarities with neo-classical government buildings found in many parts of the world.

PHOTOGRAPH: CARNEGIE, 2009

such as Brian Faulkner (Minister of Commerce) and William Craig (Minister of Home Affairs) favoured internment, which had been used successfully to quell an earlier IRA campaign. The effect this time, however, was to increase the trouble on the streets and to provide volunteers for the republican cause. The organisation presently divided into two parts, one of which called itself the Provisional IRA. It was not long before the Provisional (or PROVOs) became dominant and, aided by blunders on the part of the British security forces and favourable circumstances in Europe and elsewhere.

On 30 January 1972 ('Bloody Sunday') riots in Londonderry involving a civil rights rally, an Orange parade and the police led to the British troops opening fire killing fourteen men and wounding another seventeen, none of whom appeared to have had guns.[2] The inquest returned an open verdict and the inquiry into the deaths has been going on ever since. The widespread condemnation that followed led to the closure of Stormont, the burning down of the British Embassy in Dublin and even more mayhem in Belfast. A period of 'Direct Rule'[3] replaced the government at Stormont on 25 March 1972. Violence continued, the worst outrage to date in

EVERYONE.
REPUBLICAN
OR OTHERWISE
HAD THEIR OWN
PARTICULAR
ROLE TO PLAY

...OUR
REVENGE
WILL BE THE
LAUGHTER
OF OUR
CHILDREN

Bobby Sands MP
POET, GAEILGEOIR, REVOLUTIONARY, IRA VOLUNTEER

BOBBY SANDS MURAL.

This mural, celebrating the former MP and hunger striker Bobby Sands, is on the side of the Sinn Féin office on Belfast's Falls Road.

PHOTOGRAPH: CARNEGIE, 2009

Belfast being the setting off of twenty-six bombs by the IRA – 'Bloody Friday' for 'Bloody Sunday'. Both the British and the Irish governments were preoccupied at this time by their entry to the EEC. Prime Minister Heath was therefore anxious to sort out the problem in Northern Ireland. Towards the end of 1973 he convened a meeting at Sunningdale in Berkshire which set the scene for a programme of reform which included power-sharing between the unionists and the SDLP and a Council of Ireland recognising the interest of the Republic.[4] A power-sharing executive was appointed and took office, but the Unionist majority in the province were horrified. Brian Faulkner was appointed to carry out the programme but it proved impossible to implement against united Unionist resistance, resistance which culminated in the Ulster Workers Strike. The Ulster Workers Council (UWC) consisted of prominent unionists backed by thousands of workers from the Harland & Wolff shipyard and other industrial enterprises. The idea of power-sharing was bad enough, but the Council of Ireland was the last straw.[5] After a long period of political resistance and yet more horrendous violence, the net result by 1976 was that 'an acceptable solution to the problems of Northern Ireland was further away than at any time since the violence began'.[6]

It was becoming apparent, however, that neither the British army nor the IRA would be able to achieve its stated aim by military means alone. Both of them reviewed their tactics and prepared for a long engagement.

The early 1980s were full of dramatic developments, most notably the death of ten hunger strikers, the emergence of Sinn Féin into open politics, and the attempted destruction of the whole British Cabinet at Brighton.

The upshot of all the activity was the Anglo-Irish Agreement, signed in 1985 by Mrs Thatcher and the then Taoiseach, Garret FitzGerald.[7] To the unionists the Agreement was a betrayal, made worse by the secrecy in which the negotiations took place. Their reaction was a huge campaign of opposition which went on for five years and at first enjoyed much public support. Unionist politicians refused even to talk to British ministers until 1991. A new Anglo-Irish Intergovernmental Council, meeting near Holywood, County Down and chaired jointly by the Irish Minister for Foreign Affairs and the British Secretary of State, was staffed day and night by British and Irish officials so that if necessary the SDLP could make complaints on behalf of nationalists to Irish officials and have these complaints instantly passed on to a higher level.[8] An enormous demonstration, possibly as many as 100,000 people it was reckoned, took over the centre of Belfast to hear Molyneaux (UU leader) and Paisley (DUP). The latter's rousing speech ended with the words 'Ulster says NO!' We say 'Never, Never, Never!'[9] As it turned out, the unionists did not find the Agreement quite so bad in practice as they had feared.

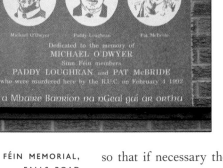

SINN FÉIN MEMORIAL, FALLS ROAD

Memorial to the memory of Michael O'Dwyer, Paddy Loughran and Patrick McBride who were shot dead by an RUC member at the Sinn Féin office on the Falls Road in 1992.

PHOTOGRAPH: CARNEGIE, 2009

SINN FÉIN/IRA

One of the most interesting developments of the period 1986–1992 was the growing sophistication and influence of Sinn Féin, the IRA's political wing led by Gerry Adams. If splits among his followers were to be avoided Adams had to progress very carefully and slowly to bring about changes in policy. The strategy was apparently two-fold – attracting as many electoral votes as possible while continuing the military campaign. The policy described in 1981 as an armalite in one hand and a ballot box in the other, though not entirely successful, on the whole succeeded in turning movement in a more political direction. The more votes for Sinn Féin the more support republicans could claim for their policy. The hard men approved of the bombings and the improved weaponry and explosives which were used to devastating effect in town centres. By 1986 however, the republican leaders had come to believe that force alone was unlikely to persuade the British to leave Ireland but that only force would bring them to the negotiating table. Secretly, Adams made contact with the British, at the same time reminding them of the IRA's strength by stepping up the bombing campaign. A new Secretary of State, Peter Brooke, in effect replied to the changing situation in two key statements, namely that he thought talks with Sinn Féin were inevitable sooner or later, and secondly that if they came about Great Britain had 'no selfish, strategic or economic interest' in Northern Ireland in the long run. Brooke's attempts to set up talks in 1990 did not prosper, however.[10]

1992–1997

Margaret Thatcher's successor in Downing Street, John Major, in his understated way helped the process along. Bill Clinton, not yet US president, visited Ireland and promised if elected to give Adams a US visa, vital for fund-raising and support from the Irish-American lobby. Brooke's successor, Sir Patrick Mayhew, re-started political talks. The UDA (Ulster Defence Association, an extreme loyalist organisation) was banned however. All the while the bombs continued. It was one of 2,000 lbs that destroyed the forensic science laboratory in Belfast and damaged 1,000 homes, not to mention other outrages in London. Mayhew's talks collapsed in November 1992. A year later, secret contacts between the IRA and British officials were revealed – a rare glimpse of the murky depths below the murky surface. It is perhaps worth noting that for the first time loyalists were killing more people than republicans were.

In December 1993 the Downing Street declaration was signed by Major and the Taoiseach, Albert Reynolds. Though deliberately vague in parts, it provided a basis for negotiations. But first the IRA would have to call a cease-fire. Adams stalled for time, asking for clarification. The process dragged on for months. Enter President Clinton, who talked of appointing a 'peace envoy'.[11] Downing Street did not welcome his intervention. It took to 31 August 1994 for the IRA to announce 'complete cessation of military action'.[12] Six weeks later the loyalist terrorist groups also announced a cease-fire. In talks between Sinn Féin and British officials the decommissioning of weapons was identified as a major obstacle to progress. In November 1995 George Mitchell, a former majority leader in the US Senate, accepted an invitation to head an international body to try to resolve the decommissioning issue. He was to play an important role in the latter stages of the peace process.

President Clinton visited Belfast in November 1995 to a great welcome in front of Belfast City Hall. He endorsed George Mitchell, visited east Belfast, west Belfast and

Derry and shook hands with Gerry Adams.[13] In February 1996, the IRA cease-fire
ended with a huge bomb at Canary Wharf in London.

1997–2004

Four years of frustration ended in 1997 when Tony Blair's New Labour Party won
the general election in Britain with a landslide (179 majority). Following a general
election in the Republic, Bertie Ahern became Taoiseach. Both men were determined
to push on.

LEST WE FORGET

Unionist memorial
on the Shankill Road,
commemorating the
deaths of UVF leader
Trevor King and
others in the 1980s
and 1990s. The style
and symbolism of the
memorial consciously
and clearly echo that of
British war memorials
from the Great War.

PHOTOGRAPH: CARNEGIE, 2009

In July 1997 the IRA called another cease-fire and the following month an independent commission was set up to supervise the decommissioning of weapons. A new Secretary of State, Dr Mo Mowlam, announced that Sinn Féin could now join the talks and the Ulster Unionist Party joined in September though five of its members expressed their concern about what the direction the talks were taking. In 1998 a paper from the two governments entitled *Heads of Agreement* was rejected by the IRA. The Good Friday Agreement, one of the most important signs of progress was signed and in simultaneous referenda both in the North and the South was endorsed by large majorities, 94 per cent in the south and 71 per cent in the north.

The Assembly stalled over decommissioning and was suspended in February 2000 by the current Secretary of State, Peter Mandelson, because of IRA/Sinn Féin's current failure to put its weapons beyond use. In May Unionists agreed to return to Stormont. Another crucial matter was the future of policing. The Patten Report

**BELFAST NEWS
VENDOR, 16 MARCH
2009**

News of US financial
support came at a
welcome time amid
a brief but worrying
renewal of inter-
community violence in
the spring of 2009.

PHOTOGRAPH: CARNEGIE, 2009

on the subject was published. An executive was formed from the Assembly and ten ministers were appointed. In December the North/South Ministerial Council met. The arms dumps were eventually inspected in June 2000 by representatives of the independent commission, chaired by a Canadian, General John de Chastelain. All the latest elections only confirmed what had been expected, that support for the traditional Unionist party and the moderate SDLP was waning. In July 2001 David Trimble, leader of the Unionists and First Minister of the Stormont Executive, resigned, but was re-elected and continued to serve until 2005, the UUP lost all but one seat in Westminster elections, including Trimble's own. Shortly afterwards he resigned completely and in 2006 was elevated to the House of Lords.

In 2002 devolution was again suspended, this time over allegations of an IRA spy at Stormont, which ended in farce. In another election, in 2003, the DUP emerged as the largest single party and Sinn Féin displaced the SDLP as the major voice of Nationalism. Yet another incident disturbed the public mind when in December 2004 more than £22 million in banknotes was stolen from the headquarters of the Northern Bank in Belfast. Everyone assumed that this spectacular heist could only be the work of the IRA or at the very least, that it could not have been carried out without the Army Council's approval. In 2006, on July 28, a formal end to the armed campaign was announced. Yet another election was summoned; as before, the DUP and Sinn Féin improved their results at the expense of the moderate centre parties. Difficult negotiations over the new police body led to the endorsement of the Police Service of Northern Ireland, in outline at least. Even then there were last-minute delays, but finally the new power-sharing government met at Stormont in 2007, with Ian Paisley (DUP) as First Minister and Martin McGuinness (SF) as Deputy First Minister. The long war, it seemed, was really over at last – and, wonderful to relate, both sides appeared to have won.

The agenda in consideration of the one vital remaining matter which had so far resisted all attempts to reach agreement was drawn from the personal experience of Christopher Patten, last Governor of Hong Kong. The Patten Commission produced its report entitled *A New Beginning to Policing in Northern Ireland* in September 1999. It agreed that it was absolutely essential to have a force that would be both effective and efficient, would be fair and impartial and would be free from partisan control. As a result of the recommendations, a new name, badge and uniform came into being. In November 2001, The RUC became the Police Service of Northern Ireland (PSNI).

CHAPTER SIXTEEN

POSTSCRIPT: RENAISSANCE, REVIVAL, RECONCILIATION

T HE Good Friday Agreement (the Belfast Agreement) of 1998 was widely regarded as a turning point in the long period of decline, made worse by decades of violence and dereliction which had left the city in a pretty demoralised state. Nevertheless, as soon as people came to believe that the war was nearly over, Belfast began to revive.[1] A sustained period of investment produced new buildings and new jobs. In a comparatively short time, unemployment fell from 14 per cent to 4.6 per cent (2006 figure). A fine new concert hall and conference centre transformed part of the waterfront, and behind the high brick wall of the old Gasworks – which had been in continuous use for that purpose from the early 1820s until its closure in the 1960s – a Business Park took shape. Amazingly, tourists began to turn up in droves – the 1.3 million visitors in 1998 had become 5.3 million in 2003.

Regeneration got off to a good start in the period 1998–2005. Many historical geographers and town planners, however, reckoned that Belfast had a long way to

NEW USES FOR OLD BUILDINGS

Old seed warehouse buildings, built in the 1850s for two rival seed merchants, Lyttle and McCausland. The buildings stood empty for nearly forty years, but could not be pulled down because of their magnificent frontage. Now converted into a 'top boutique' hotel, the Malmaison, it combines period features with contemporary style.

PHOTOGRAPH: CARNEGIE, 2009

go to match really successful cities in Britain and parts of Europe. One important deficiency they pinpointed was a lack of leadership; another was the comparatively small population. Belfast would not fulfil its potential unless the population could be increased (over a period of years) from 277,000 to something like 400,000 by 2025. Nor was there one overall authority to direct and energise what needed to be done, since City Hall no longer had such powers. Instead, Belfast was subject in such matters to no fewer than eleven government departments, as well as numerous quangos. The sheer number of these arrangements was a hindrance rather than a help.

A report produced for the City Council by Professor Michael Parkinson of Liverpool Moores University in January 2004 concluded that the prospect for Belfast, if not good, was not entirely bleak. One positive aspect was that Belfast's performance was better than that of many large English cities. It had a well-qualified workforce, with no fewer than 24 per cent of its working-age population qualified to degree level. The problem was that at the other end of the educational spectrum 26 per cent of its working population had no qualifications at all. This was higher than that of any of the English cities. Perhaps most critical of all was Belfast's record on innovation, worse than the worst of the British cities used as comparators, yet the capacity to innovate is an absolute necessity for ongoing success.

The creation of a new core city, larger than the present one, has become a major 'task area', one of five requiring special attention. This new centre would run from the docklands and Titanic Quarter, east and north of the city through the retail centre, to Queen's University and the City Hospital in the south. A new approach to developing the environment of the city (river, parks etc.), in fact a complete transformation in the way the city is presented, has been adopted: 'The challenge is a big one but the history of Belfast is a story of practicality, straight talking, courage and tenacity. Whether it succeeds in the twenty-first century will depend on its ability to harness these same qualities.'

GASWORKS PILLAR

The distinctive funnel and clock tower mark the site where the city's first gas-making industry began production in the early nineteenth century. The area has now been re-landscaped with a business park, hotel shops and enterprise workshops.

PHOTOGRAPH: CARNEGIE, 2009

CULTURE WARS?

A city and its people cannot escape their history. In recent years another type of concern has been expressed about the city's future. Professor Longley has argued that, with the war appearing to be over, and the 'peace process' having produced positive results politically, economically and socially, more attention should be paid

REDEVELOPMENT

Over the past decade the city has seen expansive redevelopment – the Waterfront Hall, the BT Tower, the Odyssey Complex and the Hilton Hotel. The Victoria Square project (*left*) opened in 2008, a commercial, residential and leisure development. Meanwhile the Titanic Quarter (*above*) begins to take shape among the redeveloped shipyards, with the Titanic Dock (*right*) now a tourist attraction.

to its cultural dimension.[2] An ongoing cultural war amounting to a desire to suppress or wipe out the cultural presence and cultural memory of the 'other side', is part of an organised continuing struggle. One aspect of that struggle, difficult to trace exactly though often using religious labels for political purposes can lead to attacks on the revered possessions (and processions) of the other side – war memorials, churches, schools, Orange Halls or GAA sports facilities. In other words for true peace to be achieved cultures as well as armaments will need to be 'decommissioned'.

Professor Longley cites Dr Gillian McIntosh's work on Unionist propaganda after 1921 (*The Force of Culture*, Cork University Press, 1999). McIntosh's analysis concludes that the Unionist attitude was focused on their unique identity in Ulster, their historic separateness form the rest of Ireland, and a bond with Britain which was firmly rooted in the seventeenth-century Plantations and recently reinforced by participation in the Great War. The underlying problem according to the author was this: officially, Northern Ireland was a united and homogeneous Protestant state; unofficially it was a diverse state, made up of Catholics as well as a variety of Protestant sects and full of tension and disharmony.[3] When Stormont fell it left a cultural as well as a political vacuum. Left to themselves most Ulster Protestants were unaccustomed to explaining their outlook and attitudes when challenged.

Meanwhile the Britain to which they looked for strength and reassurance had changed considerably, becoming more secular and more cynical about the traditional values which the Ulster Protestants had been taught to admire.

WHAT OF THE FUTURE?

Peter Hain was Secretary of State for Northern Ireland on 8 May 2007, the day Ian Paisley and Martin McGuinness agreed to form a government together. When asked if he thought this incredible breakthrough would last, Mr Hain said that devolution would last, but that the one outstanding issue which could cloud the future was how to deal with 'The Past'. Nearly 4,000 people had lost their lives and more than 30,000 had been jailed for terrorist offences. This would have been the equivalent of 129,000 killed in Britain or one million involved in paramilitary activity.

Given the remarkable progress in Northern Ireland the context had changed, and we really had to ask whether reliving the Troubles in the courtroom, the public

ODYSSEY ARENA

The Odyssey is a large sports and entertainment centre, situated on Queen's Island on reclaimed land in the city harbour. It is part of the new Titanic Quarter. This building has a seating capacity of 14,000 and has hosted many high-profile sporting and music events since its opening in 2001.

PHOTOGRAPH: CARNEGIE, 2009

enquiry or police investigation would be the best way forward. He said he had therefore decided to set up a small independent group to consult widely and suggest ways of building a shared future, rather than looking constantly over shoulders to a divided past. It would not be easy.[4]

Lack of trust on all sides characterised the intermittent negotiations which went on to move the peace process to its conclusion. Equally clear among the general public was the wave of optimism that greeted the prospect of peace at last when the paramilitaries announced their ceasefires and which, when ratified overwhelmingly by referenda north and south, confirmed the approaching rediscovery of this new-found land.

In reality, it took another eleven years for Sinn Féin/IRA to decommission their weapons and during that period of peace-building (as it was expected to be), rioting, petrol bombing, and all manner of mayhem broke out again. Were all the hopes to disappear? After all, real progress had been made in relations between the British and Irish governments and some of the local politicians had shown signs of being prepared to share power. Yet at a different level, it appeared, the capacity to demonstrate naked sectarianism had actually increased. What students of sociology call the reproduction of violence subverts healthier attitudes and beliefs. It can be argued that Belfast does not entirely conform with the ideal of the post-conflict city which planners, investors and British and Irish politicians imagined it might become.

Many concerned with the achievement of peace – not least the citizens who had undergone the worst of the Troubles in their own persons and those of their friends and colleagues – were relieved that the worst might be over. Their relief was still tinged with acute anxiety from time to time, for all might yet break down again as so often in the past. Disaffected elements ('Real' or 'Continuing' IRA) among the extreme republicans repudiated any settlement except what had proved impossible in 1916. Almost everything in Paisley's political record, from the foundation of his Democratic Unionist Party in the early 1950s to the most recent elections in which he improved the DUP's standing, mainly at the expense of the UUP, was consistent with his language which was no less tough than before. Nevertheless at the time of writing (May 2008) the power-sharing regime of Paisley and McGuinness has survived better than expected: with occasional awkward periods, but no complete collapse. The two principals in the process appear to have set aside or at least moderated their personal feelings. More than that, they have even appeared to enjoy each other's company and laughed at each other's jokes.

Here it is worth remembering that power-sharing at a practical level had been going on in a number of district councils for some time. The Unionist boycotting campaign had been abandoned along with its dismal 'Ulster says No' or 'Belfast says No' posters. In some districts the work of the councils could only be done by giving Sinn Féin councillors a share of power. It was a defining moment when in Belfast

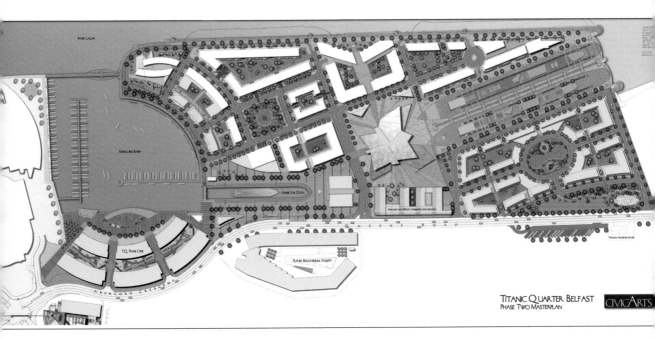

TITANIC QUARTER BELFAST
PHASE TWO MASTERPLAN

CIVICARTS

TITANIC QUARTER

This signature project for Belfast is an extensive urban regeneration on the banks of the river Lagan. Titanic Quarter is transforming 185 acres of former shipyard lands on the fringe of the city centre into a new focal point for Belfast. The development will celebrate the significant maritime industrial heritage of the area. Titanic Dock, which, it is hoped, will attract 400,000 visitors a year, will be constructed and operational in 2012, in time to celebrate 100 years of the legacy of the most famous shipwreck the world had ever known.

COURTESY OF TITANIC QUARTER LTD.

Councillor Alex Maskey got sufficient support to become Lord Mayor for the year 2002-03, the first member of Sinn Féin to hold the post. Remarkably, he not only accepted the annual invitation to the opening ceremony of the General Assembly of the Presbyterian Church but attended in person to welcome the delegates on behalf of the city. A second, more controversial move was to lay a wreath at the city's war memorial, in memory of Irish soldiers who had died in British service in the First World War. He successfully broke new ground.

Paisley, too, moved on to new territory when, contrary to all expectations, he led his MPs to a meeting with the Taoiseach at the Irish Embassy in London in January 2004. Ahern called it 'historic', and Paisley called it 'a good beginning'. This meeting opened the way for the eventual power-sharing administration. Not everyone in the Free Presbyterian Church was entirely happy with Dr Paisley's performance when he seemed to have turned all his previous policies on their heads. He persisted, however, and in time negotiated a settlement which was accepted by Sinn Féin and most of his own party. This was a formidable achievement. Some of his followers began to detect feet of clay under the Geneva gown. At the age of 82, Paisley's active career was approaching its end, but nevertheless it was a surprise when he suddenly announced his resignation as First Minister to take effect from May 2008, just one year after the establishment of the new government. The new leader of the DUP, Peter Robinson, would have a different relationship with Martin McGuinness and Sinn Féin. Both have spoken of approaching the work in a businesslike way.

What form their relationship may take is, of course, a story yet to unfold. Success in running a new system of governance capable of encompassing so many interests of various kinds, from the national and international to the local and parochial, is a tall order. Can it succeed? So far at least, the optimism of the young has given fresh impetus to new initiatives. The ending of most paramilitary activity, the decommissioning of weapons and the acceptance of the new police force by Sinn Féin has given substance to this optimism.

Paisley's last engagement before his retirement was to welcome a high-powered three-day conference of American political and business leaders to push for increased investment. Also present were the British Prime Minister Gordon Brown, the Taoiseach Brian Cowen and more than 100 potential corporate investors. The conference had its origin in a power-sharing plan as far back as 1998. The main speaker among the visitors was Michael Bloomberg, Mayor of New York, who praised Belfast's efforts to create in the derelict docklands its own financial district. The 'peace lines', however, would have to go: 'The best and brightest people do not want to live behind walls in a place where they are judged by their faith or their family name.'

After forty years of conflict, disruption and destruction, Belfast is adapting to a new future. People have become more secure and self-confident and are taking the opportunities offered to them; not only local people, but the many migrants, particularly from eastern Europe, whose arrival in great numbers after the expansion of the European Union in 2004, was an unforeseen phenomenon that brought a new multi-cultural dimension to early twenty-first-century Belfast.

The year 2009 saw the unveiling of projects worth around £500 million; at the same time, a number of landmark buildings opened their doors to the public again following extensive refurbishment. From architecture and planning to arts and cultural policy, education, urban renewal, tourism and marketing, there is an evident ambition to re-invent post-conflict Belfast as a modern, economically viable city. This heightened sense of ambition was perhaps illustrated by Belfast's success in being chosen as the destination for the final leg of the Tall Ships 2009 Atlantic Challenge. An estimated 750,000 people, including perhaps 100,000 visitors, watched the ships and attended the accompanying four-day festival. Such numbers would have been unthinkable a few years ago.

Despite these signs of progress, however, Belfast remains a divided city: 98% of public housing is still segregated along religious lines. Sectarian tensions persist, and inter-communal violence continues to be an ongoing problem in many 'interface' areas that have not shared in the investment and development enjoyed elsewhere in the city. To make matters worse, the poorer areas have been hit hardest by the current slump in employment. The future challenge for Belfast will be not only to tackle what has been described as 'self-imposed apartheid' (Mary O'Hara, *The Guardian*, 14 April 2004) – the social and political division that continue to characterise the city – but also to sustain and maintain the recent positive developments.

Notes and references

Notes to Chapter 1: Site for a city

1. E. Estyn Evans, 'The geographical setting', in J. C. Beckett and R. E. Glasscock (eds), *Belfast: The Origin and Growth of an Industrial City* (BBC: London, 1967), pp. 1–13.

2. *Oxford Dictionary of National Biography*, entries for George Benn by Raymond Gillespie.

3. P.C. Woodman, *The Mesolithic in Ireland* (1978); *Excavations at Mount Sandel, 1973–77* (HMSO: Belfast, 1987)

4. J.P. Mallory and T.E. McNeill, *The Archaeology of Ulster: From Colonization to Plantation* (Belfast, 1991), p. 17.

5. Ibid., p. 46.

6. Ibid., p. 47.

7. A.E.P. Collins, in *An Archaeological Survey of County Down* (HMSO: Belfast, 1966), pp. 89–91. See also *Historic Monuments of Northern Ireland* (HMSO: Belfast, 1983), pp. 9–89.

8. Mallory and McNeill, *Archaeology of Ulster*, pp. 75–7.

9. Ibid., pp. 136–9.

10. Ibid., pp. 140–1.

11. Ibid., pp. 143–5.

12. Edmund Curtis, *A History of Ireland*, sixth edition (1950), p. 18. See also Jonathan J. Bardon, *A History of Ulster* (Belfast, 1992), pp. 15–30.

13. Mallory and McNeill, *Archaeology of Ulster*, pp. 203–13.

14. Curtis, *A History of Ireland*, p. 20.

15. The process of conversion appears to have involved a good deal of accommodation between the old and the new. 'Much that was frankly pagan passed into Celtic Christendom and was given a Christian façade', according to Professor Evans. Some old pagan gods reappeared as new Christian saints. So well did some monastic foundations adjust themselves to the warrior culture of the Celts that lay abbots in particular had few qualms about claiming a share of the spoils from successful cattleraids by the local kings who were their patrons and kinsmen. See

E. Estyn Evans, 'Prehistoric Ireland', in Brian de Breffny (ed.), *The Irish World* (London, 1977), p. 46.

16. See Patrick McKay, *A Dictionary of Ulster Place-Names* (Belfast, 1999), pp. 39, 130.

17. Mallory and McNeill, *Archaeology of Ulster*, p. 184.

18. Deirdre Flanagan's article (in Irish) on place-names in the Belfast area has been translated by A. J. Hughes and published under the title 'Belfast and the place-names therein' in *Ulster Folklife*', vol. 38 (1992), pp. 79–97.

19. Bardon, *History of Ulster*, pp. 34–7.

20. *ODNB*, under Courci, John de.

21. G.O. Sayles, 'The siege of Carrickfergus Castle, 1315–16', *Irish Historical Studies*, vol. 10, no. 37 (1956), pp. 94–100; Robin Frame, 'The Bruces in Ireland, 1315–18', *I.H.S.*, vol. 19, no. 73 (1974), pp. 3–37. The garrison, it was said, were reduced to eating some Scottish prisoners they had taken.

22. Bardon, *History of Ulster*, pp. 53–4.

23. Curtis, *History of Ireland*, p. 110; Sean Duffy, *The Concise History of Ireland* (Dublin, 2000). p. 86; Roger Stalley, 'The Long Middle Ages', in De Breffny (ed.), *Irish World*, p. 92.

24. Benn, *Belfast*, vol. 1, p. 56, 'Skeleton genealogy of Brian MacFelin O'Neill, chief of Clannaboy …', from *Annals of the Four Masters*, ed. John O'Donovan, second edition, 7 vols (Dublin, 1857), vol. 5, p. 1678. See also *Dublin Penny Journal*, vol. 1 (1832), p. 208.

25. Edmund Curtis, *A History of Ireland*, sixth edition (1950), pp. 148–59; Séan Duffy, *The Concise History of Ireland* (Dublin, 2000), pp. 92–100.

26. B.C.S. Wilson, 'The birth of Belfast', in Beckett and Glasscock (eds), *Belfast*, pp. 18–19.

27. Curtis, *A History of Ireland*, pp. 168–74; Duffy, *Concise History*, p. 100.

28. Wilson, 'Birth of Belfast', in Beckett and Glasscock (eds), *Belfast*, pp. 18–19.

29. Benn, *Belfast*, vol.1, pp. 272–5.

30. Ibid., p. 56. Writing to Elizabeth's chief adviser, Lord Burleigh, Sir Thomas admitted 'The little book my son sent out was evil done …' But excuses it on the ground that 'no other way appeared of making the enterprise publicly known …'

31. There are several differing accounts of how the younger Smith died, all of them gruesome. All reports agree in blaming members of his Irish entourage; the savagery of the fighting appears to have surprised no one, however.

32. Benn, *Belfast*, vol. 1, pp. 39–40.

33. Ibid., p. 61.

34. Ibid., pp. 52–61.

35. Ibid., pp. 52–3.

36. *Annals of the Four Masters*, ed. John O'Donovan, second edition, 7 vols (Dublin, 1857), vol. 4, p. 1101.

Notes to Chapter 2: Founding fathers

1. The chief reason for Mountjoy's success in Ireland, according to his first biographer, was that unlike other deputies – who had campaigned only in the summer season – 'this lord prosecuted them [the rebels] most in the winter, being commonly five daies at least in the week on horsebacke, all Winter long …', which 'brake their hearts'. Fynes Moryson, *An History of Ireland, From the Year 1599 to 1603*, 2 vols (London, 1617; reprinted Dublin, 1735), vol. 2.

2. After submitting to Mountjoy, O'Neill and O'Donnell travelled to London in his retinue in order to make their peace with the new monarch. Though pelted by war widows along the route from Wales, they were well received by James I (O'Donnell was created earl of Tyrconnell) and the generous terms negotiated by Mountjoy were confirmed, to the fury of the 'servitors' who had fought against them. One of these military leaders, Harrington, bitterly observed.

> I have lived to see that damnable rebel Tyrone brought to England, honoured, and well liked … I adventured perils by sea and land, was near starving, ate horse flesh in Munster, and all to quell that man, who now smileth in peace at those who did hazard their lives to destroy him.

Quoted by Philip S. Robinson, *The Plantation of Ulster: British Settlement in an Irish Landscape, 1600–1670* (Dublin, 1984), p. 38, citing Hill, *Plantation in Ulster*.

3. John McCavitt, *Sir Arthur Chichester: Lord Deputy of Ireland, 1605–1616* (Belfast, 1998), p. 7.

4. Ibid., pp. 8–10. 'Wood kerne' were outlaw ex-soldiers of O'Neill and his allies who hid out in the woods of the north when official hostilities ceased; the term 'kerne' in Ireland and Scotland signified a lightly armed and highly mobile foot-soldier.

5. Cited by Wilson, 'Birth of Belfast', in Beckett and Glasscock (eds), *Belfast*, p. 23; Benn, *Belfast*, vol.1, p. 87.

6. George Hill, *An Historical Account of the Plantation in Ulster, 1608–20* (Belfast, 1877).

7. The report of the commissioners is printed in Hill, *Plantation in Ulster*.

8. Impressive use of some of the new material has already been made by Raymond Gillespie in *Early Belfast: The origins and growth of an Ulster town to 1750* (Belfast 2007). See also *Ulster Journal of Archaeology*, third series, vol. 65 (2006), which is largely given over to this scheme.

9. J. C. Beckett, 'The seventeenth century', in Beckett and Glasscock (eds), *Belfast*, pp. 26–7.

10. Ibid., pp. 28–9.

11. Jean Agnew, *Belfast Merchant Families* (Dublin, 1996), p. 1. Raymond Gillespie, 'The origins and development of an Ulster urban network, 1600–41', *Irish Historical Studies*, vol. 24, no. 93 (May 1984), pp. 20–5.

12. Peter Roebuck, 'The making of an Ulster great estate: the Chichesters, barons of Belfast and Viscounts of Carrickfergus', in *Royal Irish Academy Proceedings*, lxxix (1979), sect. C, pp. 1–27.

13. Ibid., pp. 19–20.

14. See Benn, *Belfast*, vol.1, pp. 86–7.

15. J.C. Beckett, *The Making of Modern Ireland, 1603–1923* (London, 1966), p. 75; Raymond Gillespie, 'The End of an Era: Ulster and the outbreak of the 1641 rising', in Ciaran Brady and Raymond Gillespie (eds), *Natives and Newcomers: Essays on the Making of Irish Colonial Society, 1534–1641* (Dublin, 1986), p. 198.

16. Quoted by Raymond Gillespie in 'Destabilizing Ulster, 1641–42', in Brian MacCuarta (ed.), *Ulster 1641: Aspects of the Rising* (Belfast, 1993), p. 111.

17. See Benn, *Belfast*, vol. 1, p. 97–8 for a full transcript of Chichester's letters of 24 October 1641 to Charles I.

18. *A true Relation of several Acts, Passages, done, undertaken, &c. by Captain Robert Lawson, now one of the Sheriffs of the City and County of Londonderry, upon and since the first beginning of the great and general Rebellion in Ireland, &c.* (London, 1643).

19. Ibid., See [H. Joy], *Historical Collections relative to the Town of Belfast …* (Belfast, 1817), pp. 16–20, for a digest of Lawson's pamphlet. The author's mercantile background is clearly evident from the meticulous care with which he lists the losses of his father-in-law, brother-in-law and himself in the iron works.

20. Ibid., pp. 19–20.

21. Ibid. The source is given by Joy in his *Historical Collections*

as A true copy of *a Letter sent from from Doe Castle in Ireland, from an Irish Rebel [Donnell O'Cane] to [Donoty O'Cane] in Dunkirk* [bearing date 1st August 1642] *printed for W. Hope, London 1643*. Though listed in the catalogue of the British Library, London, this pamphlet could not be found in a recent search.

Notes to Chapter 3: War, peace and survival, 1642–1706

1. David Stevenson, *Scottish Covenanters and Irish Confederates: Scottish–Irish Relations in the Mid-Seventeenth Century* (Belfast, 1981), p. 53; quotation from J. Hogan (ed.), *Letters and Papers relating to the Irish Rebellion, 1642–46* (I.M.C., 1936), pp. 3–4.

2. Ibid., pp. 65–83.

3. Ibid., pp. 103–10.

4. Ibid., pp. 120–7. O'Neill brought only 200–300 soldiers with him. As instructors for untrained raw recruits, however, these veterans made a real difference.

5. Ibid., p. 121: 'It seems likely that Monro had specific orders, either from Leven or the Scots privy council … certainly … some such limitation was in force in 1643'.

6. Ibid., pp. 139–49.

7. See J.C. Beckett, *The Cavalier Duke, 1610–1688* (Belfast, 1990), pp. 29–43.

8. Stevenson, *Scottish Convenanters and Irish Confederates*, pp. 161–2; [H. Joy ed.] *Historical Collections relative to the Town of Belfast* (Belfast, 1817), pp. 20–1; Benn, *Belfast*, vol. 1, pp. 102–19.

9. Benn, *Belfast*, vol. 1. p. 110. Theaker's deposition includes a transcript of the 'humble Request' of the 'whole free Comoners of the Burrough of Belfast …'

10. The seizure of Belfast by Monro provoked repeated demands from the English Parliament for its restoration – repeated because Monro and his masters in Scotland met all such demands with delay and prevarication. See Benn, *Belfast*, vol. 1, pp. 110–22.

11. Ibid., p. 112.

12. Beckett, *Making of Modern Ireland*, p. 99.

13. Stevenson, *Scottish Covenanters and Irish Confederates*, pp. 227–36; G.A. Hayes-McCoy, *The Irish at War* (Cork, 1964), pp. 47–58; T. O'Mellan, 'A Narrative of the Wars of 1641'; R.M. Young (ed.), *Historical Notices of Old Belfast* (Belfast, 1896), pp. 199–247.

14. Stevenson, *Scottish Covenanters and Irish Confederates*, p. 233.

15. Monck engineered the restoration of the monarchy in 1660 and was loaded with honours by Charles II, who created him duke of Albemarle.

16. Robert Monro (died *c*.1680) was one of the few Scottish officers who stayed in Ireland after the war was over, having married the widow of the second Lord Montgomery.

17. Stevenson, *Scottish Covenanters and Irish Confederates*, p. 275; quotation from J.T. Gilbert (ed.), *Contemporary History*, vol. 3, p. 159.

18. R.F.G. Holmes, *The Presbyterian Church in Ireland* (Dublin, 2000), pp. 28–40.

19. Gabbarts were small ships of anything from 5 to 50 tons. In 1635 Sir William Brereton, a seasoned traveller, recorded in his diary an uncomfortable crossing from Scotland in 'a bark of about fifteen tons', a 'good sailing vessel' but overcrowded with horses and passengers. The latter arrived cold, wet and exhausted. Donald Woodward, 'Irish Sea Trade and Shipping from the Later Middle Ages to *c*.1660', in Michael McCaughan and John Appleby (eds), *The Irish Sea: Aspects of Maritime History* (Belfast, 1989).

20. Benn, *Belfast*, vol.1, pp. 295–300.

21. Jean Agnew, *Belfast Merchant Families in the Seventeenth Century* (Dublin, 1996), pp. 14–16.

22. Agnew, *Belfast Merchant Families*, p. 21. Records of the general synod *of Ulster from 1691–1820, vol. 1; 1691–1720* (Belfast, 1890), p. 146.

23. Agnew, ibid. passim.

24. See Beckett, *Making of Modern Ireland*, pp. 136–41.

25. Benn, *Belfast*, vol. 1, pp. 154, 730, 733–5.

26. Ibid., pp. 737–8 ('List of the Refugees from Down and Antrim at the Revolution').

27. Ibid., p. 174.

28. [H. Joy], *Historical Collections* (1817), p .83.

29. Agnew, *Belfast Merchant Families*, p. 242.

30. Ibid., Appendix A, pp. 235–8, 233–5.

31. Ibid., p. 21.

32. Ibid., p. 131.

33. Ibid., pp. 42–4.

34. Ibid., pp. 44–7.

35. Ibid., p. 227.

36. Ibid., pp. 233–5.

37. Ibid., pp. 235–7.

38. Ibid., p. 234.

39. Ibid., p. 236.

40. Ibid., pp. 18–25 and passim.

Notes to Chapter 4: A long minority, 1706–1760

1. Peter Roebuck, 'Landlord indebtedness in Ulster in the seventeenth and eighteenth centuries', in J.M. Goldstrom and L.A. Clarkson (eds), *Irish Population, Economy and Society: Essays in Honour of the late K.H. Connell* (Oxford, 1981), pp. 141–2.

2. The 1704 religious test for all holders of public office was

part of the 'Act to prevent the further growth of Popery' (3 Anne, c.7), It was applied to Protestant Dissenters as well as Catholics at a late stage of its passage into law.

3. See Jean Agnew, *Belfast Merchant Families*, pp. 94–5.

4. Ibid., pp. 97–9.

5. Ibid., p. 104.

6. Ibid., p. 72.

7. Benn, *Belfast*, vol.1, pp. 478–84.

8. Ibid. See also Agnew, *Belfast Merchant Families*, pp. 34–9, 107, 127–8.

9. Minority accounts of fourth earl of Donegall (PRONI, transcript T. 1455). The vexatious dispute about 'ship money' became mixed with attempts by the Church of Ireland vicar to collect money from householders to augment his modest salary. Some of his own flock – as well as the Presbyterians – objected to this.

10. Edith Mary Johnston-Lijk, *History of the Irish Parliament, 1692–1800*, 6 vols (Belfast, 2002), vol. 3, pp. 115–16 (Anthony Atkinson).

11. McBride was evidently given warning by anonymous well-wishers. The First Congregation still treasures an oil painting of him with the rent made by the sword of a frustrated bounty-hunter. See [A. Gordon], *Historical Memorials of the First Presbyterian Church, Belfast* (Belfast, 1887).

12. PRONI, transcript T 2970/12, where the nightgown episode is described as an anecdote told to Isaac Macartney's descendants. But see *Historical Memorials of the First Presbyterian Church*, p. 55, for corroboration.

13. The sovereign reported that the Catholic priest had been put in jail and prominent citizens had offered 'the best Bail the Protestants of this County affords' for his release.

14. Donegall minority accounts, PRONI, transcript T 455/2, pages 13–14 (1707), voucher 48.

15. Phillips had recommended letting the Norman fortress at Carrickfergus run down, to be replaced when funds became available by a state-of-the-art citadel at Belfast. See Agnew, *Belfast Merchant Families*, p. 66; also Benn, *Belfast*, vol. 1, pp. 320–21.

16. R.M. Young (ed.), *Historical Notices of Old Belfast*, pp. 127–38, lists the possessions renewed to the Chichester family by new patents in 1669. The first item in the Carrickfergus section begins: 'The Castle or Mansion – House of his Lordship, now called Joymount, and lately called the Pallace *alias* the Storehouse, with all the Buildings, Gardens, Orchards &c.'

17. Donegall minority accounts, Part 2, p. 21 etc.

18. Ibid., Part 1, p. 28.

19. PRONI, transcript T 2873/2, 'The Case of William Macartney ...'

20. PRONI, D509/45 (1718).

21. PRONI, transcript T/2873/1, deed of 17 May 1720 between Thomas Vigors (first part) and James earl of Barrymore and Richard Rooth (second part).

22. Printed pleadings in Donegall and Barry *v.* Knapton, 1769, appellant's case, pp. 1–3 (National Library of Ireland, Dublin, Microfilm).

23. 'The Case of William Macartney' is the main source (though a far from impartial one) for what follows. At Broomfield the Donegalls were looked after by Hannah Glasse [née Allgood, 1708–70], author of one of the earliest popular cookery books. See *ODNB*, new edition, for an account of her chequered career.

24. 'The Case of William Macartney'.

25. Ibid. The symptoms exhibited by the fourth earl of Donegall in the Lord Chancellor's examination of him as described by Macartney, sound remarkably like those of dyscalculia, the numerical equivalent of dyslexia. This condition, thought to affect about 5 per cent of the population, has been identified only recently and is not still fully understood. (*The Times*, 4 December 2006.)

26. Ibid.

27. See Benn, *Belfast*, vol. 1, pp. 534–6.

28. Ibid., Masserene to Ludford, 26 March 1752.

29. Green to Barrymore, 28 Jan. 1725, printed in Young (ed.), *Town Book of Belfast*, p. 329.

30. Ibid., Green to Barrymore, 20 Feb. 1725.

31. Ibid.

32. Benn, *Belfast*, vol. 1, p. 536, Preamble to Donegall Estate Bill, 1752.

33. Raymond Gillespie and Stephen A. Royle, *Belfast, part 1, to 1840*; Irish Historic Towns Atlas no. 12 (2000), pp. 4–6.

34. Whole Presbyterian congregations, led by their ministers, emigrated to the North American colonies. An estimated one-third of the voyages that took them there set out from Belfast.

35. Ibid.

36. Benn, *Belfast*, vol. 1, pp. 578–9 (footnote).

37. Ibid., pp. 594–6.

38. Quotation from a letter of George Macartney, M.P. cited by Bardon, *Belfast*, p. 33.

39. R.W.M.Strain, 'The history and associations of The Belfast Charitable Society', offprint from *Ulster Medical Journal*, May 1933, pp. 22, 31–60; R.W.M. Strain, *Belfast and its Charitable Society* (Oxford, 1961).

40. 'Plan of the Town of Belfast, anno 1757' (Linen Hall Library, Belfast).

Notes to Chapter 5: Architects and agitators: Belfast, 1760–1800

1. G. E. Cokayne. Hon. Vicary Gibbs (ed.), *The Complete Peerage* (13 vols, 1910) vol. 4, pp. 391, 392 (footnote). 'Abstract of title of the manor of Fisherwick …', William Salt Library, Stafford County Record Office, Stafford, M761/8/6. See W. A. Maguire, 'Absentees, architects and agitators', *Belfast Natural History and Philosophical Society, Proceedings*, second series, vol.10. See also R. Stebbing Shaw, *The History and Antiquities of Staffordshire*, 2 vols (1798), vol. 1, p. 368.

2. 'Abstract of title of the manor of Fisherwick …', Staffs. CRO, M761/8/6; Maguire, 'Absentees, architects and agitators'. See Shaw, *Staffordshire*, vol 2, p. 368.

3. Haliday to Marchmont, June 1788, quoted in *Complete Peerage*, vol. 4, p. 392; Dorothy Stroud, *Capability Brown*, 1975 edition, pp. 151–3.

4. Maguire, 'Absentees, architects and agitators', pp. 7–8; 'Abstract of title to the manor of Fisherwick'; 'An Account of In cumbrances at the Marquis of Donegall's Death on 5th January 1799', Staffs. CRO, M761/1/6.

5. Crow and his assistants surveyed the entire estate, townland by townland, including the 'townparks' of Belfast. The maps in PRONI do not include any of the town itself, apart from small sketch plans of the holdings leased. See J.H. Andrews, *Plantation Acres: An Historical Study of the Irish Land Surveyors* (Belfast, 1985), p. 229.

6. PRONI, D 811/5–17, 43–9, 78–80, 97–8, 156–390. For detailed analysis see Raymond Gillespie and Steven A. Royle, *Belfast; Part 1 to 1840*, Irish Historic Towns Atlas no. 12, pp. 5–6; Brett, Gillespie and Maguire, *Georgian Belfast, 1750–80: Maps, Buildings and Trades*: Brett, *Buildings of Belfast, 1700–1914* (revised edition, 1985).

7. [T. Prior], *A List of Absentees of Ireland and the Yearly Value of their Income Spent Abroad* (Dublin, 1729). The Donegall estate was valued at £4,000 at that time; the sixth edition (1783) estimated the fifth earl's income at £31,000.

8. W.A. Maguire, 'Lord Donegall and the Hearts of Steel', *Irish Historical Studies*, vol. 21, no. 84 (Sept. 1979), pp. 351–76.

9. Writing to his kinsman Lord Hardwicke in April 1772, Sir Joseph Yorke gave it as his opinion that Donegall – then MP for Malmesbury – ought to be expelled if he did not 'go and do justice to his Tenants'; quoted by Edith M. Johnston, in *Great Britain and Ireland, 1760–1800* (1968), p. 181 (footnote).

10. [J.R. Scott], *The Parliamentary Representation of Ireland* (Dublin, 1790), p. 3.

11. Gillespie and Royle, *Belfast, part 1: to 1840*, pp. 6–7, 10.

12. The townland of Ballymacarrett was sold by the Pottinger family to Barry Yelverton (later chief baron of the Exchequer) for £18,000. Yelverton was MP for the borough of Carrickfergus, 1776–83, by the influence of Donegall, so when he began to lay out his property for development his patron was displeased. Donegall bought his rival neighbour out in the end, but the purchase was costly, at £25,000, most of which had to be borrowed from Hoare's bank.

13. A.P.W. Malcomson, 'The Newtown Act of 1748: revision and reconstruction', *I.H.S.*, vol. 18, no. 31 (March 1973).

14. A.T.Q. Stewart, *Belfast Royal Academy: The First Century* (1985)

15. Thomas M. Truxes (ed.), *The Greg-Cunningham Letterbook, 1756–1757* (1999), Introduction, pp. 1–90. I am grateful to Professor Truxes for his help.

16. The dry dock was constructed for the Ballast Board by William Ritchie, a Scotsman who, along with his brother, established a successful ship-building yard nearby in the 1790s.

17. D.J. Owen, *A Short History of the Port of Belfast* (1917), pp. 19–20; R. Sweetnam, 'The development of the port', in Beckett and Glasscock (eds), *Belfast*, pp. 57–9.

18. R.W.M. Strain, *Belfast and its Charitable Society* (1971), pp. 130–47.

19. Along with Robert Joy (proprietor of the *Belfast News Letter*) and a watchmaker named Thomas McCabe, Grimshaw persuaded the Charitable Society to experiment for a trial period of six months with the production of cotton on their premises, using some of the child inmates as the labour force. The experiment was a great success.

20. Emily Boyle, 'Linenopolis: the rise of the textile industry', in *Belfast: The Making of the City*, pp. 42–3; E.R.R. Green, 'Early industrial Belfast', in *Belfast: The Making of the City*, pp. 79–83.

21. Half of the total cost of building St Mary's was subscribed by liberal Protestants, and the opening ceremony was accompanied by a parade of Volunteers, led by Waddell Cunningham.

22. See A.T.Q. Stewart, *The Shape of Irish History* (2001), pp. 120ff, and the same author's *A Deeper Silence: The Hidden Roots of the United Irish Movement* (1993).

23. See also [J.R. Scott], *Parliamentary Representation of Ireland*, pp. 4–5 and Benn (vol. 2, pp. 93–4). Benn described the political condition of the town in the early 1800s as 'utterly dead'. The contempt in which it was held was illustrated by the story of a person calling one day at the Castle office asking to see the Marquis. When told that he was engaged, the visitor turned to go but was advised to wait by the sergeant on duty because his lordship would be down in a few minutes, being 'only upstairs making a member of parliament'.

24. Cunningham had played a very active role in Volunteer

politics in the events leading to the triumph of 1782. Keenly interested in parliamentary reform, he found his way blocked by the Ascendancy he despised. Like most liberals, he welcomed the overthrow of the feudal monarchy in France and was one of the chief organisers of Bastille Day celebrations in Belfast. He was entirely opposed to violent social revolution, however, and in 1797 joined the Belfast Yeomanry to thwart the United Irishmen. See T. M. Truxes, *New Dictionary of National Biography*, pp. 175–98; also S.S. Millin, *Sidelights on Belfast History* (1932), pp. 35–40.

25. *The Northern Star* made its appearance in 1792 when its rival, the *News Letter*, was losing money and needed a sponsor. There were in fact too few subscribers to support two newspapers without subsidy of some kind. The circulation war that followed is analysed in some detail in John Gray, 'A tale of two newspapers', in John Gray and Wesley McCann (eds), *An Uncommon Bookman: Essays in Memory of J.R.R. Adams* (Belfast, 1996), pp. 75–198.

26. [H. Joy], *Historical Collections Pertaining to the Town of Belfast* (1817), Preface, p. x.

27. Ibid, p. 21.

28. The origin of the reference to ancient Athens, it appears, was part of a prologue specially composed for the occasion of the play performed in the Belfast theatre on 25 February 1793. The author was a young lawyer named Hugh George Macklin:

And have not here our souls with Freedom
   glow'd;
Has she not here long fix'd her lov'd abode?
Yes – and old time shall yet with glad surprize,
View in Belfast a second Athens rise.

Quoted by J.C. Beckett, 'Belfast to the end of the eighteenth century', in *Belfast: The Making of the City*, p. 26.

29. For a detailed account of the second marquess's extraordinary career see W.A. Maguire, *Living Like a Lord: The Second Marquis of Donegall, 1769–1844* (Appletree Press: Belfast, 1994); new edition by Ulster Historical Foundation (2002).

30. [Pierce Egan], *Real Life in Ireland … By a Real Paddy* (first edition, London, 1821). The mock hero of this tale – Brian Boru esq. – visits Belfast and is introduced to Lord Done'em-all. The author was extremely well informed about the family's misfortunes and also about the town's reputation for sectarian mob violence; when about to set out for Dublin, he witnessed 'A downright fling-down betwixt two mobs of nearly a hundred people. It was

Up with the Orange and down with the Green,
Lather the dirty boys decent and clean.'

31. Mrs Martha McTier to Dr William Drennan, December 1806, letter no. 1328, in Jean Agnew (ed.), *The Drennan-McTier Letters*, 3 vols (1998–99), vol. 3, p. 547.

32. Maguire, *Living Like a Lord*, chapter 5, pp. 55–67.

33. George Chambers, *Faces of Change* (bicentenary volume of the foundation of Belfast Chamber of Commerce, 1983), pp. 98–102 re: William Tennent.

34. For a useful discussion and some fresh thoughts on the subject, see Catherine Hirst, *Religion, Politics and Violence in Nineteenth-Century Belfast: The Pound and Sandy Row* (Dublin, 2002), pp. 14–34.

35. Ibid. pp. 26–7.

36. Budge and O'Leary, *Belfast: Approach to Crisis*, p. 37 (note 58).

37. See W.A. Maguire, 'The Verner Rape Trial, 1813: Jane Barnes *v* the Belfast establishment', in *Ulster Local Studies*, vol. 15, no. 1 (1993).

Notes to Chapter 6: Industry, trade and politics, 1800–1860

1. Emily Boyle, 'Linenopolis': the rise of the textile industry', in Beckett and Glasscock (eds), *Belfast*, pp. 43–4.

2. F. Geary, 'The rise and fall of the Belfast cotton industry: some problems', *Irish Economic and Social History*, 8 (1981), pp. 30–9; and F. Geary, 'The Belfast cotton industry revisited', *Irish Historical Studies*, 26, no. 103 (1989), pp. 250–67.

3. J.L. McCracken, 'Early Victorian Belfast', in Beckett and Glasscock (eds), *Belfast*, pp. 88–9.

4. Boyle, 'Linenopolis', in Beckett and Glasscock (eds), *Belfast*, pp. 46–7.

5. G.N. Wright, *Scenes in Ireland* (London, 1834), p. 220.

6. Mr and Mrs S.C. Hall, *Ireland: Its Scenery, Character etc.*, 3 vols (London, 1841–43), vol.3, pp. 53, 56.

7. *Parliamentary Gazetteer of Ireland*, 3 vols (Dublin, 1844–46), vol.1, p. 234.

8. See M. Moss and J.R. Hume, *Shipbuilders to the World: 125 Years of Harland and Wolff, Belfast, 1861–1986* (Blackstaff Press: Belfast, 1986), pp. 11–21.

9. See W. E. Coe, *The Engineering Industry of the North of Ireland* (Newton Abbot, 1969), pp. 22–32, 46–76.

10. P. Ollerenshaw, *Banking in Nineteenth-Century Ireland: The Belfast Banks*, 1825–1914 (Manchester University Press, 1987), pp. 5–30; N. Simpson, *The Belfast Bank, 1827–1970* (Blackstaff Press: Belfast, 1975), chs 1 and 2.

11. Simpson, *Belfast Bank*, p. 49.

12. R.E. Glasscock, 'The growth of the port', in Beckett and Glasscock (eds), *Belfast*, pp. 98–101; Sweetnam, 'Development of the port', in Beckett and Glasscock (eds), *Belfast*, pp. 57–8.

13. T. Gaffikin, *Belfast Fifty Years Ago* (Belfast, 1875), p. 12.
14. Sweetnam, 'Development of the port' in Beckett and Glasscock (eds), *Belfast*, pp. 60–2.
15. Owen, *Port of Belfast*, pp. 38, 48.
16. McCracken, 'Early Victorian Belfast', in Beckett and Glasscock (eds), *Belfast*, pp. 96–7.
17. Gaffikin, *Belfast Fifty Years Ago*, p. 12.
18. Budge and C. O'Leary, *Belfast Approach to Crisis: A Study of Belfast Politics, 1613–1970* (Macmillan: London, 1973), pp. 27–33, appendix to ch. 1.
19. The statistics quoted here come from two pamphlets: *Report on the Sanitary State of Belfast* (Belfast, 1848) and A.G. Malcolm, *The Sanitary State of Belfast, with Suggestions for its Improvement* (Greer: Belfast, 1852).
20. W.M. O'Hanlon, *Walks Among the Poor of Belfast and Suggestions for their Improvement* (Greer: Belfast, 1853); reprinted by S.R. Publishers: Wakefield, 1971), pp. 5–6, 13, 16, 44.
21. P. D. Hardy, *The Northern Tourist* (Dublin, 1830), p. 137.
22. *Report from the Select Committee on the Municipal Corporations* (1833), pp. v–vi.
23. Budge and O'Leary, *Belfast*, p. 53.
24. W.A. Maguire, *Living Like a Lord: The Second Marquis of Donegall, 1769–1844* (Appletree Press: Belfast, 1983); 'The 1822 settlement of the Donegall estates', *Irish Economic and Social History*, 3 (1976), pp. 17–32.
25. W.A.Maguire 'Lord Donegall and the sale of Belfast: a case history from the Encumbered Estates Court', *Economic History Review*, second series, 29, no. 4 (1976), pp 570–84.

Notes to Chapter 7: 'Fit and proper persons', 1800–1860

1. R.B. McDowell, 'Dublin and Belfast – a comparison', in R. B. McDowell (ed.), *Social Life in Ireland, 1800–5* (Mercier Press: Cork, 1957), p. 23.
2. G. J. Slater, 'Belfast politics, 1798–1868', D.Phil. thesis, New University of Ulster, Coleraine (1982), 2 vols, 2, pp. 333–8.
3. R.F.G. Holmes, *Henry Cooke* (Christian Journals Ltd: Belfast, 1981), pp. 113–17.
4. Slater, 'Belfast politics', vol. 2, pp. 248–52.
5. Ibid., vol. 2, p. 254.
6. Ibid., vol. 2, pp. 264–5.
7. Ibid., vol. 2, pp. 264–5.
8. Slater, 'Belfast politics', vol. 2, pp. 255, 258; Budge and O'Leary, *Belfast*, pp. 60–2.
9. Slater, 'Belfast politics', vol. 2, pp. 256–71; Budge and O'Leary, *Belfast*, p. 63.
10. Budge and O'Leary, *Belfast*, p. 65.
11. Ibid., p. 32.
12. F.F. Moore, *The Truth about Ulster* (Eveleigh Nash: London, 1914), p. 24.
13. McCracken, 'Early Victorian Belfast', in Beckett and Glasscock (eds), *Belfast*, p. 96.
14. See A.T.Q. Stewart, *The Narrow Ground: Aspects of Ulster, 1609–1969* (Faber & Faber: London, 1977), pp. 145–54; A. Boyd, *Holy War in Belfast* (Anvil Books: Tralee, 1969; reprinted by Pretani Press: Belfast, 1988).
15. M. Finnane, *Insanity and the Insane in Post-Famine Ireland* (Croom Helm: London, 1981), p. 200.
16. *Report of the Commissioners of Inquiry into the … Riots in Belfast in … 1857* (HMSO: Dublin, 1858). Drew's sermon to the Orangemen, Hanna's public letters to the 'Protestants of Belfast' and McIlwaine's advertisements of his Lent Lectures on Popery – on the theme 'Is Popery Christianity?' – were printed as appendices to the report.
17. Slater, 'Belfast politics', 2, p. 339.
18. W.M. Thackeray, *The Irish Sketch Book, 1842* (reprinted by Blackstaff Press: Belfast, 1985), p. 304.
19. Budge and O'Leary, *Belfast*, p. 97, n.35.
20. When St Patrick's in Donegall Street opened in 1815, pews were sold to the more affluent parishioners, as in some Protestant churches. The practice ceased from the middle of the century.
21. P. Gibbon, *The Origins of Ulster Unionism* (Manchester University Press: Manchester, 1975), p. 48.
22. A. Macaulay, 'William Crolly', Archbishop of Armagh, 1835–49. passim.
23. Holmes, *Cooke*, pp. 346, 39–43, 47–76.
24. See T.W. Moody and J.C. Beckett, *Queen's, Belfast, 1845–1949*, 2 vols (Faber & Faber: London, 1959), vol. 1, Introduction and pp. 84–115.
25. A. Deane (ed.), *The Belfast Natural History and Philosophical Society: Centenary Volume, 1821–1921* (Belfast, 1924).
26. M. Anglesea, 'A Pre-Raphaelite enigma in Belfast', *Irish Arts Review*, vol. 1, no. 2 (1984), pp. 40–5.
27. J. Gray, 'Popular entertainment', in Beckett and Glasscock (eds), *Belfast*, pp. 106–7; E. Black *The People's Park: The Queen's Island, 1849–1879* (Linen Hall Library: Belfast, 1988).

Notes to Chapter 8: Industry, trade and society, 1861–1901

1. E. Boyle, 'Linenopolis': the rise of the textile industry', in Beckett and Glasscock (eds), *Belfast*, pp. 47–50; and 'The economic development of the Irish linen industry, 1825–1913' (unpublished Ph.D. thesis, Queen's University, Belfast, 1979), pp. 96, 100–1. See also P. Ollerenshaw, 'Industry, 1820–1914', in L. Kennedy and P. Ollerenshaw (eds), *An Economic History of Ulster: 1820–1940* (Manchester University Press, Manchester, 1985), pp. 74–84.

2. Owen, *Belfast*, p. 301.

3. Brett, *Buildings of Belfast*, pp. 53–4.

4. Moss and Hume, *Shipbuilders*, pp. 21–44.

5. Quoted in Chambers, *Faces of Change*, p. 189.

6. D.J. Jeremy (ed.), *Dictionary of Business Biography*, 5 vols (Butterworths: London, 1984–86), vol. 5, pp. 891–3 (Workman) and 1, pp. 683–5 (Clark); also Ollerenshaw, 'Industry', in Kennedy and Ollerenshaw (eds), *Economic History of Ulster*, pp. 94–5.

7. F. Geary and W. Johnson, 'Shipbuilding in Belfast, 1861–1986', *Irish Economic and Social History*, 16 (1989), pp. 43, 45–52. See also Moss and Hume, *Shipbuilders*, pp. 46–92.

8. *Dictionary of Business Biography*, 4, pp. 702–8 (Pirrie); Ollerenshaw, 'Industry' in Kennedy and Ollerenshaw (eds), *Economic History of Ulster*, pp. 89–94.

9. Coe, *Engineering*, pp. 64–7; *Dictionary of Business Biography*, 4, pp. 38–40 (Mackie).

10. Coe, *Engineering*, pp. 114, 120.

11. *Dictionary of Business Biography*, 2, pp. 18–20 (Davidson).

12. *Dictionary of Business Biography*, 5, pp. 194–7 (Smiles).

13. Owen, Belfast, *Belfast*, p. 311; A. Bernard, 'The whisky distillers of the United Kingdom', *Harpers's Weekly Gazette* (London, 1887; reprinted by David & Charles: Newton Abbot, 1969), pp. 426–7, 428–9; also J. Vinycomb, *Historical and Descriptive Guide to the City of Belfast* (Marcus Ward & Co.: Belfast, [1895]), p. 38.

14. *Dictionary of Business Biography*, 1, pp. 720–1 (Cochrane).

15. *Dictionary of Business Biography*, 2, pp. 461–3 (Gallaher); *The Industries of Ireland: Part 1, Belfast and the Towns of the North* (Historical Publishing Co.: London, 1891), p. 96.

16. Extracts from *The Pictorial World*, 1889–90, in *Industries of the North* (Friar's Bush Press: Belfast, 1986), pp. 10–14; *Industries of Ireland*, pp. 98–9.

17. PRONI Microfilm.

18. Owen, *Port of Belfast*, pp. 41–6.

19. Census reports; Budge and O'Leary, Belfast, ch. 1., appendix.

20. L. Hyman, *The Jews of Ireland, from Earliest Times to the Year 1910* (Irish Universities Press: Shannon, 1972), pp. 203–9.

21. Clarkson, 'The city and the country', in Beckett and Glasscock (eds), *Belfast*, p. 156.

22. Housebuilding in Belfast between 1861 and 1900 is analysed in detail in P.G. Cleary, 'Spatial expansion and urban ecological change in Belfast, with special reference to the role of local transportation, 1861–1917' (unpublished Ph.D. thesis, Queen's University, Belfast, 1979), ch. 6, pp. 285–339. For a useful summary of this material see J. Bardon, *Belfast: An Illustrated History* (Blackstaff Press: Belfast, 1982), pp. 137–141.

23. Cleary, 'Spatial expansion', pp. 308–28.

24. Cleary, 'Spatial expansion', pp. 333–4; A.C. Davies, 'Roofing Belfast and Dublin, 1896–98', *Irish Economic and Social History*, 6 (1977), pp. 26–35.

25. B. Collins, 'The Edwardian city', in Beckett and Glasscock (eds), *Belfast*, pp. 172–3.

26. Cleary, 'Spatial expansion', ch. 5, pp. 180–207.

27. C.E.B. Brett, *Housing a Divided Community*, Institute of Public Administration (Dublin, 1986), pp. 19–20 and caption to pl. 10.

28. Quoted in R. Blaney, *Belfast: 100 Years of Public Health* (Belfast City Council and Eastern Health and Social Services Board: Belfast (188), p. 21.

29. Quoted in Blaney, *Belfast: 100 Years*, p. 11.

30. J. Loudan, *In Search of Water, Being a History of the Belfast Water Supply* (Wm Mullan: Belfast, 1940), pp. 52–95.

31. *Belfast Corporation Act*, 1899 (62 & 63 Vict., ch. ccxlvi), para. 43.

32. Blaney, *Belfast: 100 Years*, pp. 21–4.

33. Ibid., p. 12.

34. Ibid., pp. 25–9; Budge and O'Leary, *Belfast*, pp. 109–11.

35. D.L. Armstrong, 'Social and economic conditions in the Belfast linen industry, 1850–1900', *Irish Historical Studies*, 7 (1951), pp. 235–8.

36. *Belfast News Letter*, 1 July 1874, quoted in Armstrong, 'Social and economic conditions', p. 243.

37. Armstrong, 'Social and economic conditions', pp. 245–53, 258–60.

38. Quoted in A. McEwen, 'Half-timing in Belfast', *The Northern Teacher*, vol. 14, no. 1 (1983), pp. 1–5; see also Armstrong, 'Social and economic conditions', pp. 260–2.

39. Macaulay, *Dorrian*, pp. 271–4, 270.

40. R. Marshall, *Methodist College, Belfast: The First Hundred Years* (Belfast, [1968]), pp. 1–11, 44; Macaulay, *Dorrian*, p. 280.

41. Census reports and Belfast street directories; Eric Gallagher, *At Points of Need: The Story of the Belfast Central Mission, Grosvenor Hall, 1889–1989* (Blackstaff Press: Belfast, 1989), pp. 10, 33.

42. A. Jordan, 'Voluntary societies in Victorian and Edwardian

Belfast', Ph.D. thesis, Queen's University, Belfast (1989), 2 vols, vol. 2, p. 582; and *Who Cared?: Charity in Victorian and Edwardian Belfast* (Institute of Irish Studies, Queen's Unversity, Belfast, 1992), pp. 191–8, 222–8.

43. R.S. Casement, 'History of the Mater Infirmorum Hospital', *Ulster Medical Journal*, 38 and 39 (1970).

44. R.S. Allinson, *The Seeds of Time, Being a Short History of the Belfast General and Royal Hospital, 1850–1903* (Brough, Cox and Dunn: Belfast, 1972); H.F. Calwell, *The Life and Times of a Voluntary Hospital: The Royal Belfast Hospital*

for Sick Children, 1873–1948 (Brough, Cox and Dunn: Belfast, 1973); R.S. Allison, *The Very Faculties: A Short History of the Development of Ophthalmological and Otorhinolaryngological Services in Belfast (1801–1964)* (W. & G. Baird: Belfast, 1969); R. Marshall and K.N.M. Kelly, *The Story of the Ulster Hospital* (Brough, Cox and Dunn: Belfast, 1973).

45. D.S. Johnson, 'Prostitution and venereal disease in Ireland during the second half of the nineteenth century', unpublished paper.

Notes to Chapter 9: Party politics and local government, 1861–1901

1. See Stewart, *Narrow Ground*, p. 148.

2. See Boyd, *Holy War*, pp. 44–89, for a detailed and racy account of the 1864 riots; for a sociological analysis of Belfast rioting in the nineteenth century see Gibbon, *Origins of Ulster Unionism*, pp. 67–86.

3. *Northern Whig*, 16 August 1864.

4. *Report of the Commissioners of Inquiry into the Riots in 1864*, Parliamentary Papers, 1865, xxviii (HMSO: Dublin, 1865), p. 22. The report in fact acknowledges that the local constables were too few in number to do much.

5. Slater, 'Belfast politics', vol. 2, p. 259.

6. D. Dunlop, *Brief Historical Sketch of Parliamentary Elections in Belfast* (Belfast, 1865), p. 11, quoted in Budge and O'Leary, *Belfast*, p. 98, n. 55; *Belfast News Letter*, 15 July, 1865.

7. The property qualification for the parliamentary franchise had been reduced in 1850 from £10 to £8. The Irish Act of 1868 was less democratic than the English Act of 1867, which established household suffrage in boroughs. The property qualification for the municipal vote in Belfast remained £10.

8. For an account of Johnston's chequered career, see A. McClelland, *William Johnston of Ballykilbeg* (Ulster Society Publications: Lurgan, 1990). His first attempt to repeal the Party Processions Act, in 1869, was seconded by The O'Donoghue of the Glens, a great-nephew of Daniel O'Connell and Liberal MP for Tralee. Johnston, incidentally, was a son-in-law of the Rev. Dr Thomas Drew, the Orange cleric.

9. Budge and O'Leary, *Belfast*, pp. 102–3.

10. *Northern Whig*, 6 Feb. 1874; Gibbon, *Origins of Ulster Unionism*, p. 102.

11. Gibbon, *Origins of Ulster Unionism*, pp. 1047.

12. Budge and O'Leary, *Belfast*, p. 103.

13. There is no reliable published history of the Irish AOH (the movement was organised separately in the USA): its early records, in any case scanty, perished in 1922. The best source for most purposes is M.T. Foy, 'The Ancient

Order of Hibernians: an Irish political-religious pressure group, 1884–1975', unpublished MA thesis, Queen's University, Belfast (1976).

14. Quoted in Boyd, *Holy War*, pp. 172–3.

15. Moss and Hume, *Shipbuilders*, pp. 52, 55.

16. Slater, 'Belfast politics', 2, p. 284.

17. Slater, 'Belfast politics', 2, pp. 291–3.

18. *Belfast Corporation Gas Act, 1874* (37 & 38 Vict., ch. cxcc); *Local Government Board (Ireland) Provisional Orders (Artizans and Labourers Dwellings) Confirmation Act, 1877* (40 & 41 Vict., ch. cxxii); *Belfast Improvement Act, 1878* (41 & 42 Vict., ch. clxxx); *Belfast Improvement Act, 1884* (47 & 48 Vict., ch. xciii); *Belfast Main Drainage Act, 1887* (50 & 51 Vict., ch. cx–xxii).

19. *Municipal Corporation of Belfast Act, 1887* (50 & 51 Vict., ch. cxviii); see Budge and O'Leary, *Belfast*, p. 117.

20. Sir R. Meyer, *City of Belfast Public Parks* (Belfast Corporation: Belfast, 1922), pp. 21–63, 98.

21. *Reports of the Inspectors of Lunatics … in Ireland, 8 July 1895* (1895 [C78041, liv, 435), p. 174.

22. K.D. Brown, 'The Belfast Fire Brigade, 1880–1914', *Irish Economic and Social History*, vol. 16 (1989), pp. 65–72.

23. Budge and O'Leary, *Belfast*, pp. 116–19.

24. Budge and O'Leary, *Belfast*, pp. 119–21.

25. Gibbon, *Origins of Ulster Unionism*, pp. 131–6; H. Patterson, *Class Conflict and Sectarianism: The Protestant Working Class and the Belfast Labour Movement, 1868–1920* (Blackstaff Press: Belfast, 1980), pp. 19–23.

26. A. Boyd, *The Rise of the Irish Trade Unions, 1729–1970* (Anvil Books: Tralee, 1972), pp. 65–7; Patterson, *Class Conflict and Sectarianism*, pp. 32–5.

27. Patterson, *Class Conflict and Sectarianism*, p. 42.

28. *Belfast News Letter*, 12 September 1899.

29. See G. Davis, *The Irish in Britain, 1815–1914* (Gill and MacMillan: Dublin, 1991) pp. 51–82, 148. It should be noted, however, that the Irish minorities in Britain, even in Glasgow and Liverpool, were comparatively small.

Notes to Chapter 10: Heyday and crisis, 1901–1914

1. For a perceptive discussion of the dual identity of Edwardian Belfast, see S. Gribbon, 'An Irish city: Belfast 1911', in D. Harkness and M. O'Dowd (eds), *The Town in Ireland, Historical Studies XIII* (Appletree Press: Belfast 1981), pp. 203–20.

2. Census reports, 1901 and 1911; S. Gribbon, *Edwardian Belfast: A Social Profile* (Appletree Press, Belfast, 1982), pp. 47 and 56, n. 90.

3. When making the family firm a limited liability company in 1865, John Mulholland took the opportunity to sell off part of his holding in order to buy more land, and he subsequently went into politics (*Dictionary of Business Biography*, 4, pp. 37–7)

4. Moss and Hume, *Shipbuilders*, p. 92; *Dictionary of Business Biography*, 4, pp. 702–8 (Pirrie); Collins, 'The Edwardian city', in Beckett and Glasscock (eds), *Belfast*, pp. 179–80.

5. Gribbon, *Edwardian Belfast*, pp. 13–14.

6. Gribbon, *Edwardian Belfast*, pp. 16–20; A.C. Hepburn, 'Work, class and religion in Belfast, 1901', *Irish Economic and Social History*, vol. 10 (1983), p. 34. I am much obliged to Desmond Fitzgerald, Armagh railway historian, for providing me with a copy of his (unpublished) account of the Adavoyle incident and for permission to make use of it.

7. A. C. Hepburn and B. Collins, 'Industrial society: the structure of Belfast, 1901;, in P. Roebuck (ed.), *Plantation to Partition* (Blackstaff Press: Belfast, 1981), p. 226.

8. Hepburn, 'Work, class and religion', *Irish Economic and Social History*, vol. 10, pp. 49–50.

9. Gribbon, *Edwardian Belfast*, p. 34; and 'An Irish city', in Harkness and O'Dowd (eds), *Town in Ireland*, p. 207.

10. Gribbon, *Edwardian Belfast*, pp. 30–1, 35–6.

11. Gribbon, *Edwardian Belfast*, p. 39; Gallagher, *At Points of Need*, pp. 52, 44.

12. Gribbon, *Edwardian Belfast*, p. 27.

13. Gribbon, *Edwardian Belfast*, p. 26; E. Malcolm, *'Ireland Sober, Ireland Free': Drink and Temperance in Nineteenth-Century Ireland* (Gill and Macmillian: Dublin, 1986), pp. 316–21; R.J. Patterson, *Catch-My-Pal: A Story of Good Samaritanship* (Hodder & Stoughton: London, 1910); Budge and O'Leary, *Belfast*, pp. 123 and 134 (n. 87).

14. Gribbon, *Edwardian City*, p. 23; Brett, *Buildings of Belfast*, pp. 67–8.

15. Budge and O'Leary, *Belfast*, p. 126; J. Gray, *City in Revolt: James Larkin and the Belfast Dock Strike of 1907* (Blackstaff Press: Belfast, 1985), p. 19; Hogg Collection, Ulster, Belfast H62/02/10.

16. T.W. Moody, 'Higher education', in T. W. Moody and J. C. Beckett (eds), *Ulster Since 1800*, second series (BBC: London, 1957), p. 202; Moody and Beckett, *Queen's*, vol. I, pp. 317–18, 342–4, 407–12.

17. Moss and Hume, *Shipbuilders*, pp. 118, 122–74.

18. Moss and Hume, *Shipbuilders*, pp. 89–90; Patterson, 'Industrial labour', in Kennedy and Ollerenshaw (eds), *Economic History of Ulster*, p. 177; Gray, *City in Revolt*, pp. 9–10. Dr McKeown made his reputation by his skill in removing metal fragments from the eyes of shipyard workers by means of magnets.

19. Sweetnam, 'Development of the port', in Beckett and Glasscock (eds), *Belfast*, pp. 68–70; Gribbon, *Edwardian Belfast*, p. 13.

20. Patterson, 'Industrial labour', in Kennedy and Ollerenshaw (eds), *Economic History of Ulster*, pp. 167–8, 178; and *Class Conflict and Sectarianism*, pp. 66–7.

21. Gray, *City in Revolt*; Patterson, *Class Conflict and Sectarianism*, pp. 66–7.

22. Quoted in Patterson, *Class Conflict and Sectarianism*, p. 90.

23. Patterson, *Class Conflict and Sectarianism*, pp. 66–7; R.F.G. Holmes, *Our Presbyterian Heritage* (Presbyterian Church in Ireland: Belfast, 1985), p. 136.

24. Budge and O'Leary, *Belfast*, pp. 121–2; Brett, *Buildings of Belfast*, pp. 65–7.

25. *The Belfast Book: Local Government in the City and County Borough of Belfast* (Belfast Corporation: Belfast, 1929), relevant chapters' Budge and O'Leary, *Belfast*, p. 135 (n. 99).

26. Budge and O'Leary, *Belfast*, pp. 111–12, 131 (nn. 37–8), 133 (n. 82).

27. Budge and O'Leary, *Belfast*, p. 127; Brett, *Housing a Divided Community*, pp. 20–1.

28. Budge and O'Leary, *Belfast*, pp. 119–21, 122–5, 125–6.

29. J.W. Boyle, 'Belfast and the origins of Northern Ireland', in Beckett and Glasscock (eds), *Belfast*, pp. 133–7; Patterson, *Class Conflict and Sectarianism*, pp. 44–6, 58–61.

30. Boyle, 'Belfast and the origins of Northern Ireland', in Beckett and Glasscock (eds), *Belfast*, pp. 137–41.

31. Gribbon, 'An Irish city', in Harkness and O'Dowd (eds), *Town in Ireland*, p. 219.

Notes to Chapter 11: The First World War and after, 1914–1939

1. Stewart, *Ulster Crisis*, pp. 241–22.

2. D.S. Johnson, 'The Northern Ireland economy', in Kennedy and Ollerenshaw (eds). *Economic History of Ulster*, p. 84.

3. Coe, *Engineering*, p. 122; Johnson, 'Northern Ireland economy', in Kennedy and Ollerenshaw (eds). *Economic*

History of Ulster, pp. 184–6.

4. Moss and Hume, *Shipbuilders*, pp. 175–207; Johnson, 'Northern Ireland economy', in Kennedy and Ollerenshaw (eds), *Economic History of Ulster*, pp. 186–8.

5. Patterson, *Class Conflict and Sectarianism*, pp. 92–110.

6. See D. Harkness, *Northern Ireland Since 1920* (Helicon Limited: Dublin, 1983), pp. 1–21, for an excellent brief account of the establishment of Northern Ireland; also P. Buckland, *A History of Northern Ireland* (Gill and Macmillian: Dublin, 1981), pp. 17–21, 31–6.

7. Budge and O'Leary, *Belfast*, pp. 140–3; Boyd, *Holy War*, pp. 181–205.

8. Budge and O'Leary, *Belfast*, pp. 136–40.

9. W. Black, 'Industrial change in the twentieth century', in Beckett and Glasscock (eds), *Belfast*, pp. 161–2, 163.

10. D.S.Johnson, 'The economic history of Ireland between the wars', *Economic and Social History*, 1 (1974), pp. 58–9; and 'Northern Ireland economy', in Kennedy and Ollerenshaw (eds), *Economic History of Ulster*, pp. 1946.

11. Johnson, 'Northern Ireland economy', in Kennedy and Ollerenshaw (eds), *Economic History of Ulster*, pp. 191–4; Geary and Johnson, 'Shipbuilding in Belfast', *Irish Economic and Social History*, vol. 16 (1989), pp. 53–4; Moss and Hume, *Shipbuilders*, chs 8–10. See also J. P. Lynch, *An Unlikely Success Story: The Belfast Shipbuilding Industry, 1880–1935* (Belfast, 2001).

12. *Dictionary of Business Biography*, 2, pp. 461–3 (Gallaher); *Ulster Year Books* (HMSO: Belfast, 1926–39); Johnson, Northern Ireland economy', in Kennedy and Ollerenshaw (eds), *Economic History of Ulster*, p. 201.

13. Northern Ireland economy', in Kennedy and Ollerenshaw (eds), *Economic History of Ulster*, p. 202.

14. M. Farrell, *The Poor Law and the Workhouse in Belfast, 1838–1948* (PRONI, Belfast (1978), pp. 87–104; R. Munck and B. Rolston, *Belfast in the Thirties: An Oral History* (Blackstaff Press: Belfast, 1987), pp. 23–7; P. Devlin, *Yes We Have No Bananas: Outdoor Relief in Belfast, 1920–39* (Blackstaff Press: Belfast, 1981), pp. 73–137.

15. See A.C. Hepburn, 'The Belfast riots of 1935', *Social History*, xv (1990), pp. 75–96 for an excellent analysis of this 'urban ethnic equivalent of a *jacquerie*'. Budge and O'Leary, *Belfast*, p. 151; Boyd, *Holy War*, pp. 205–18; J.J. Campbell, 'Between the wars', in Beckett and Glasscock (eds), *Belfast*, pp. 153–5.

16. P. Buckland, *James Craig* (Gill and Macmillian: Dublin, 1980), p. 107.

17. Budge and O'Leary, *Belfast*, pp. 145–7.

18. Budge and O'Leary, *Belfast*, pp. 147–50.

19. Brett, *Housing a Divided Community*, pp. 21–2.

20. N. McNeilly, *Exactly Fifty Years: The Belfast Education Authority and its Work (1923–73)* (Belfast Education & Library Board: Belfast, 1973), pp. 7–13.

21. D. H. Akenson, *Education and Enmity: The Control of Schooling in Northern Ireland, 1920–50* (David & Charles: Newton Abbot, 1973), pp. 72–118; McNeilly, *Exactly Fifty Years*, pp. 25–7.

22. R. Marshall, *Stranmillis College Belfast, 1922–1972* (Belfast, 1973), pp. 412; Akenson, *Education and Enmity*, pp. 119–23.

23. McNeilly, *Exactly Fifty Years*, pp. 32–5, 42–5.

24. D. H. Craig, *Belfast and its Infirmary: The Growth of a Hospital from 1838 to 1948* (Brough, Cox and Dunn: Belfast, n.d.), pp. 64, 57–60; Calwell, *A Voluntary Hospital*, pp. 79–80.

25. Johnson, 'Northern Ireland economy', in Kennedy and Ollerenshaw (eds), *Economic History of Ulster*, pp. 210–12; T. Carnwath, 'Report to the Special Committee of the Belfast Corporation on the Municipal Health Services of the City', typescript, Queen's University, Belfast, dated 23 December 1941.

26. *Belfast Book*, relevant chapters.

27. Loudan, *In Search of Water*, pp. 101–49; E. Jones, 'Land reclamation at the head of Belfast Lough', *Ulster Journal of Archaeology*, third series, vol. 21 (1958), pp. 137–40.

28. Johnson, 'Northern Ireland economy', in Kennedy and Ollerenshaw (eds), *Economic History of Ulster*, pp. 213–14; Belfast street directories, 1920–39; M. Open, *Fading Lights, Silver Screens: A History of Belfast Cinemas* (Greystone Books: Antrim, 1985), pp. 5–8.

Notes to Chapter 12: The Second World War and after, 1939–1972

1. Coe, *Engineering*, pp. 106–9, 122–3; Moss and Hume, *Shipbuilders*, pp. 323–53; J.W. Blake, *Northern Ireland in the Second World War* (HMSO: Belfast, 1956), pp. 394, 403.

2. Blake, *Northern Ireland*, pp. 383–94; E. O'Connor and T. Parkhill (eds), *A Life in Linenopolis: The Memoirs of William Topping, Belfast Damask Weaver, 1903–56* (Ulster Historical Foundation: Belfast, 1992), pp. 57–73.

3. Coe, *Engineering*, p. 179; Brian Barton, *The Blitz: Belfast in the War Years* (Blackstaff Press: Belfast, 1989), pp. 278–83.

4. Barton, *Blitz*, pp. 283–6; *Ulster Year Book, 1947* (HMSO: Belfast, 1948), p. 168, (Table 8).

5. Barton, *Blitz*, pp. 270; Buckland, *Northern Ireland*, p. 84; Harkness, *Northern Ireland*, p. 84.

6. Ibid., pp. 51–63, 47–50.

7. Ibid., pp. 65–7, 135.

8. Ibid., pp. 101–51.

9. Blake, *Northern Ireland*, p. 233.

10. Barton, *Blitz*, pp. 175–208, 136–8.

11. Barton, *Blitz*, pp. 265–72 and 280 (quoting MacRory);

P. Arthur, *Government and Politics of Northern Ireland* (Longman: Harlow, 1980), pp. 42–3 (quoting 1939 statement). The cardinal's reported reaction in 1942 to the arrival of American troops in Northern Ireland – that they were overrunning the country against the will of the nation – drew a severe rebuke from the US envoy in Dublin.

12. Barton, *Blitz*, pp. 222, 256, 166–7; Bardon, *Belfast*, p. 248.
13. Budge and O'Leary, *Belfast*, pp. 153–5.
14. Black, 'Industrial change', in Beckett and Glasscock (eds), *Belfast*, pp. 164ff.
15. Moss and Hume, *Shipbuilders*, pp. 354–99.
16. Moss and Hume, *Shipbuilders*, pp. 400–45; Geary and Johnson, 'Shipbuilding in Belfast', *Irish Economic and Social History*, vol. 16 (1989), pp. 59–62.
17. M. Donne, *Pioneers of the Skies: A History of Short Brothers plc* (Nicholson & Bass Ltd: Belfast, 1987), pp. 113–38.
18. Coe, *Engineering*, pp. 76, 121–2.
19. Black, 'Industrial change', in Beckett and Glasscock (eds), *Belfast*, p. 168.
20. *Belfast Harbour Commissioners, Reports and Accounts, 1956–70*.
21. *Ulster Year Books, 1949–70*.
22. P.E. Greer (ed.), *Road versus Rail: Documents on the history of public transport in Northern Ireland, 1921–48* (PRONI: Belfast, 1982), pp. 63–92; *City of Belfast: Official Industrial Handbook* (E.J. Burrows: Cheltenham, various issues); F.W. Boal, 'Contemporary Belfast', in Beckett and Glasscock (eds), *Belfast*, p. 180.

Notes to Chapter 13: Society and politics, 1945–1972

1. F.W. Boal, 'Contemporary Belfast', in Beckett and Glasscock (eds), *Belfast*, pp. 169–72; *Ulster Year Book, 1960–62* (HMSO: Belfast, 1962), p. 7. Belfast was ten times the size of the next largest urban area, Londonderry.
2. Ibid., pp. 172–4.
3. Ibid., *Belfast*, pp. 174–8.
4. Brett, *Housing a Divided Community*, pp. 25, 32; *City of Belfast Official Handbook*, 12th edn (1950), p. 53.
5. Brett, *Housing a Divided Community*, pp. 33–4.
6. Ibid., pp. 34–6.
7. McNeilly, *Exactly Fifty Years*, pp. 73–4, 58.
8. Ibid., pp. 76–9, 91–3.
9. Ibid., pp. 220–2, 219–20, 158–9.
10. Buckland, *Northern Ireland*, pp. 91–2; Harkness, Northern Ireland, pp. 109–10; Bardon, *Belfast*, pp. 159–61.
11. Craig, *Belfast and its Infirmary*, pp. 91–7; Budge and O'Leary, *Belfast*, pp. 159–61; Harkness, *Northern Ireland*, pp. 116–17.
12. Open, *Fading Lights*, pp. 13–15.
13. D.P. Barritt and C.E. Carter, *The Northern Ireland Problem* (OUP: Oxford, 1962), p. 21.
14. Budge and O'Leary, *Belfast*, pp. 161–2.
15. Ibid., pp 157.
16. Budge and O'Leary, *Belfast*, pp. 156, 174–8. A later opportunity to modernise the local franchise, in 1961–62, was rejected by the Unionist majority at Stormont; by then, 81,000 people in Belfast could vote in the parliamentary elections but not in municipal contests (Harkness, *Northern Ireland*, p. 136).
17. Budge and O'Leary, *Belfast*, pp. 157–8; See Harkness, *Northern Ireland*, pp. 118–23.
18. Budge and O'Leary, *Belfast*, pp. 158–9; Buckland, *Northern Ireland*, pp. 108–9, 114.
19. See Buckland, *Northern Ireland*, pp. 119–23, and Arthur, *Government and Politics of Northern Ireland*, pp. 107–10.
20. J.C. Beckett, 'Northern Ireland', in *The Ulster Debate: Report of a Study Group for the Institute for the Study of Conflict* (Bodley Head: London, 1972), p. 23.
21. Buckland, *Northern Ireland*, pp. 119–22; Harkness, *Northern Ireland*, pp. 139–54.
22. Arthur, *Government and Politics of Northern Ireland*, pp. 111–13.
23. Report of *Review Body on Local Government in Northern Ireland, 1970* (HMSO: Belfast, 1970), pp. 24–5, 36, 37.
24. J.A. Oliver, *Working at Stormont* (Institute of Public Administration: Dublin, 1978), pp. 79–80.

Notes to Chapter 14: Social change, 1973–1993

1. F.W. Boal and S. Royle, 'Belfast boom, blitz and bureaucracy', in G. Gordon (ed.), *Regional Cities in the UK, 1890–1980* (Harper & Row: London, 1986), p. 207; P. Arthur and K. Jeffrey, *Northern Ireland Since 1968* (Blackwell: Oxford, 1988), Appendix 1, p. 98.
2. R.L. Harrison, 'Population change and housing provision in Belfast', in P.A. Compton (ed.), *The Contemporary Population of Northern Ireland and Population-related Issues* (Institute of Irish Studies, Queen's University, Belfast, 1981), pp. 40–50; D.A. Singleton, 'Belfast: housing policy and trends', in Buchanan and Walker (eds), *Province, City & People*, pp. 151–2; P.A. Compton, 'Population', in Buchanan and Walker, *Province, City & People*, pp. 246–7; F.W. Boal, 'Residential segregation and mixing in a situation of ethnic and national conflict: Belfast', in Compton (ed.), *Contemporary Population*, p. 74.
3. C.W. Jefferson, 'Economy and employment', in Buchanan and Walker (eds), *Province, City & People*, pp. 206–10; see

also B. Rowthorne and N. Wayne, *Northern Ireland: The Political Economy of Conflict* (Polity Press: Cambridge, 1988), p. 98. The huge investment announced by the Secretary of State, Roy Mason, in August 1878, amounting to £56 million out of a total of £85 million to enable John de Lorean to build a new sports car was largely wasted if not indeed fraudulent.

4. Jefferson, 'Economy and employment', in Buchanan and Walker (eds), *Province, City & People*, pp. 206–7.
5. *Belfast Harbour Commissioners: Reports and Accounts,*

1970–90.

6. Brett, *Housing a Divided Community, pp. 89–90; Brick by Brick: A Short History of Northern Ireland Housing Executive, 1971–1991* (Northern Ireland Housing Executive: Belfast, 1991), pp. 57–62.
7. See F.W. Boal, 'Belfast: the physical and social dimensions', in Buchanan and Walker (eds), *Province, City & People*, p. 143.
8. Fionnuala O' Connor, *A Shared Childhood* (Belfast, 2002), pp. 17, 18.

Notes to Chapter 15: The long war: a short history

1. Bew and Gillespie, *Chronology of the Troubles*, p. 26.
2. Ibid., pp. 45–6.
3. Ibid., p. 50.
4. Ibid., pp 74–5.
5. Ibid., pp 84–5.
6. Brian Feeney, *The Troubles*, p. 48.
7. Ibid., pp 76–7.
8. Ibid., pp 76–81.
9. Ibid., p. 80.
10. Ibid., p. 88.
11. Ibid., p. 102.
12. Bew and Gillespie pp. 293–5.
13. See Feeney, *The Troubles*, pp. 107–8.

Notes to Chapter 16: Postscript: renaissance, revival, reconciliation

1. Marie-Thérèse McGivern, 'The Way Ahead', in Boal, F.W. and Royle, Stephen, A. R. (eds), *Enduring City: Belfast in the Twentieth Century* (Belfast, 2006), pp. 330–41. This article is the principal source for what follows.
2. Edna Longley, *An Irish Kulturkampf*, in D. Kennedy (ed.),

Forging an Identity (2000).

3. Gillian McIntosh, *The Force of Culture* (Cork, 2000); cited above, note 2).
4. 'A balm for 30 years of wounds from the Troubles', Peter Hain, 22 June 2007, in *The Times* Comment column.

SELECT BIBLIOGRAPHY

Arthur, Paul, *Government and Politics of Northern Ireland* (Harlow, 1980)

Bardon, Jonathan, *Belfast: An Illustrated History* (Belfast, 1982)

———, *Belfast: A Century* (Belfast, 1999)

Barton, Brian, *The Blitz: Belfast in the War Years* (Belfast, 1989)

Becket, J.C. *et al.*, *Belfast: The Making of the City, 1800–1914* (Belfast, 1983)

Becket, J.C. and Glasscock, R.E. (eds), *Belfast: The Origins and Growth of an Industrial City* (London, 1967)

Benn, George, *A History of the Town of Belfast from the Earliest Times to the Close of the Eighteenth Century* (London and Belfast, 1877)

Bew, Paul, and Gillespie, Gordon (eds), *Northern Ireland: A Chronology of the Troubles, 1968–1999* (Belfast: 2007)

Bew, Paul, *The Making and Remaking of the Good Friday Agreement* (Dublin, 2007)

Black, Eileen, *Art in Belfast 1760–1888: Art Lovers or Philistines?* (Dublin, 2006)

Blake, J.W., *Northern Ireland in the Second World War* (Belfast, 1956) Boal, F.W. and Royle, Stephen, A. (eds), *Enduring City: Belfast in the Twentieth Century* (Belfast, 2006)

Boyd, Andrew, *Holy War in Belfast*, 3rd edition (Belfast, 1987)

Brett, C.E.B., *Buildings of Belfast, 1700–1914*, revised edition (Belfast, 1985)

———, *Housing a Divided Community* (Dublin, 1986)

Buchanan R.H. and Walker, B.M., *Province, City and People: Belfast and its Region* (Antrim, 1987)

Buckland, Patrick, *A History of Northern Ireland* (Dublin, 1981)

———, *James Craig* (Dublin, 1980)

Budge, Ian and O'Leary, Cornelius, *Belfast; Approach to Crisis: A Study of Belfast Politics, 1603–1970* (London, 1973)

Chambers, George, *Faces of Change: The Belfast and Northern Ireland Chambers of Commerce and Industry, 1783–1983* (Belfast, 1983)

Coe, W.E., *The Engineering Industry of the North of Ireland* (Newton Abbot, 1969)

Devlin, Paddy, *Yes We Have No Bananas: Outdoor Relief in Belfast, 1920–39* (Belfast, 1981)

Donne, Michael, *Pioneers of the Skies: A History of Short Brothers PLC* (Belfast, 1987)

Elliott, Marianne, *The Catholics of Ulster: A History* (Harmondsworth, 2000)

Farrell, Michael, *The Poor Law and the Workhouse in Belfast, 1838–1948* (Belfast, 1978)

Fitzpatrick, David, *The Two Irelands 1912–1939* (Oxford, 1998)

Gallagher, Eric, *At Points of Need: The Story of the Belfast Central Mission, Grosvenor Hall, 1889–1989* (Belfast, 1989)

Gibbon, Peter, *The Origins of Ulster Unionism* (Manchester, 1975)

Gillespie, Raymond and Royle, Stephen A. *Belfast, part 1, to 1840*; Irish Historic Towns Atlas no. 12 (2003)

Gillespie, Raymond, *Early Belfast: The Origins and Growth of an Ulster Town to 1750* (Belfast 2007)

Gray, John, *City in Revolt: James Larkin and the Belfast Dock Strike of 1907* (Belfast, 1985)

Gribbon, Sybil, *Edwardian Belfast: A Social Profile* (Belfast, 1982)

Harkness, David, *Northern Ireland Since 1920* (Dublin, 1983)

Hirst, Catherine, *Religion, Politics and Violence in Nineteenth-century Belfast: The Pound and Sandy Row* (Dublin, 2002)

Holmes, R. Finlay, *Henry Cooke* (Belfast, 1981)

Jones, Emrys, *A Social Geography of Belfast* (Oxford, 1960)

Jordan, Alison, *Who Cared?: Charity in Victorian and Edwardian Belfast* (Belfast, 1992)

Kennedy, Liam and Ollerenshaw, Philip, *An Economic History of Ulster, 1820–1940* (Manchester, 1985)

Larmour, Paul, *Belfast: An Illustrated Architectural Guide* (Belfast, 1987)

Loudan, Jack, *In Search of Water; being a History of the Belfast Water Supply* (Belfast, 1940)

Lynch, J.P., *An Unlikely Success Story: the Belfast Shipbuilding Industry, 1880–1935* (Belfast, 2001)

Lyons, FSL and Hawkins, RAJ, eds, *Ireland under the Union - Varieties of Tension* (Oxford 1980)

Macaulay, Ambrose, *Patrick Dorrian, Bishop of Down and Connor 1865–85* (Dublin, 1987)

Magee, Jack, *Barney: Bernard Hughes of Belfast 1808–1878* (Belfast, 2001)

Maguire, W. A., *Living Like a Lord: The Second Marquis of Donegall, 1769–1844* (Belfast, 1983)

———, *Caught in Time: The Photographs of Alexander Hogg of Belfast, 1870–1939* (Belfast, 1983)

———, 'The Donegall's and their Estate, 1767–1850' in C.E.B. Brett, R. Gillespie, and W.A. Maguire (eds), Georgian Belfast, 1750–1850: Maps, Buildings and Trades (Belfast, 2001)

Mallory, J. P. and T. E. McNeill, *The Archaeology of Ulster: From Colonization to Plantation* (Belfast, 1991)

Messenger, Betty, *Picking up the Linen Threads* (Belfast, 1980)

Moody, T.W. and Beckett, J.C., *Queen's Belfast, 1845–1949*, 2 vols (London, 1959)

Moss, Michael, and Hume, John R., *Shipbuilders of the World, 125 Years of Harland and Wolff, Belfast, 1861–1983* (Belfast, 1986)

Munk, Ronnie and Rolston, Bill, *Belfast in the Thirties: An Oral History* (Belfast, 1987)

McCaughan, Michael, *Steel Ships and Iron Men: Shipbuilding in Belfast 1884–1912* (Belfast, 1989)

McCavitt, John, *Sir Arthur Chichester, Lord Deputy of Ireland 1605–16* (Belfast, 1998)

McClelland, Aiken, *William Johnston of Ballykilbeg* (Lurgan, 1990)

McNeilly, Norman, *Exactly Fifty Years: The Belfast Education Authority and its Work (1923–73)* (Belfast, 1973)

O'Hanlon, W. M., *Walks among the Poor of Belfast, and Suggestions for their Improvement* (Belfast, 1853; republished Wakefield, 1971)

Owen, D.J., *History of Belfast* (Belfast, 1921)

———, *A Short History of the Port of Belfast* (Belfast, 1917)

Patterson, Henry, *Class Conflict and Sectarianism: The Protestant Working Class and The Belfast Labout Movement, 1868–1920* (Belfast, 1980)

Patton, Marcus, *Central Belfast: A Historical Gazetteer* (Belfast, 1993)

Pollock, Vivienne and Parkhill, Trevor, *Made in Belfast* (Stroud, 2005)

Scott, Robert, *A Breath of Fresh Air: The Story of Belfast's Parks* (Belfast, 2006)

Shirlow, Peter, and Murtagh, Brendan, *Belfast: Segregation, Violence and the City* (Belfast, 2006)

Stewart, A.T.Q., *The Ulster Crisis* (London, 1967)

———, *The Narrow Ground: Aspects of Ulster, 1609–1969* (London, 1977)

INDEX

Index entries in *italic* type refer to illustrations or to information within their accompanying captions